THE
DOLLS' HOUSE D.I.Y
BOOK

THE
DOLLS' HOUSE D.I.Y
BOOK

Venus and Martin Dodge

David & Charles
Newton Abbot   London

Colour photography by Jonathon Bosley

British Library Cataloguing in Publication Data

Dodge, Venus
    The dolls' house D-I-Y book.
    1. Doll-houses—Handbooks, manuals, etc.
    I. Title   II. Dodge, Martin
    745.592'3   TT175.3

    ISBN 0-7153-8289-6

First published 1982
Second impression 1983
Third impression 1985

Photoset by Typesetters (Birmingham) Ltd,
Smethwick, Warley, West Midlands
and printed in Great Britain
by Redwood Burn Ltd., Trowbridge
for David & Charles (Publishers) Limited
Brunel House Newton Abbot Devon

Contents

PART ONE

Introduction

Through the centuries dolls' houses have been treasured playthings for both adults and children. The earliest, which were called baby houses, were usually full of beautiful and valuable miniatures and were often given pride of place in the drawing-room. Later, in a more modest form, the dolls' house moved upstairs to the nursery and became the favourite toy of the Victorian child. More recently, while remaining popular with children, dolls' houses have recaptured the interest of imaginative adults. Once again, craftsmen are producing fine miniatures for a growing number of dolls'-house owners and beautiful dolls' houses are being made for those who can afford to buy them.

Our own interest in dolls' houses began when we saw a lovely old house in an antique shop window, and determined to try to make one for ourselves.

We drew plans for a four-roomed cottage with an attic, and with some helpful advice from a carpenter friend, put our first house together. That house, albeit cumbersome, over-large and amateurish, started us on a hobby which was to become a rewarding one for both of us. Obviously we have made mistakes, and through those we have learned much about how to build and furnish dolls' houses. When we started we had no idea that there were books on the subject, or even that there were old dolls' houses in museums which could be studied. So we had to work everything out for ourselves. While this has been fun, it has often been frustrating, so we are writing this book for anyone who is where we were seven years ago — anyone who wants to make a dolls' house, and would like a little practical help on the hows, whys and wherefores.

We intend it as a guide, not as a rigid book of rules. The methods described in the book are those which we have used and found to work, but they are not the only methods. Dolls' houses are dream houses; they reflect their makers' and owners' personalities, and the imagination of the builder is the only limit to the variety of houses which can be made and the ways in which they can be furnished.

Our aim is to offer plans and methods which will enable any averagely capable person to build and furnish a dolls' house of satisfying realism. We have avoided the cardboard shoebox house and the matchbox and cotton-reel furniture: although simple, such pieces never look 'real'. On the other hand few of us are fine craftsmen, so our plans are for simple but realistic wooden and upholstered furniture, and houses which though varied are straightforward to build.

The book is divided into two parts. In Part I we cover the aspects involved in planning, building, decorating and furnishing a house to your own design, and in Part II we offer scale plans and specific step-by-step instructions for a small shop and three different houses and their furnishings. Dolls'-house families and their pets for each house are included in Part II, and a separate chapter at the end of the book deals with restoring and renovating old dolls' houses and their contents.

In Part I, Chapters 1–6, we have tried to cover everything you need to know to make your dream house a reality. Starting at the planning stage, such considerations as the scale and size of the house and the number of rooms are discussed, followed by ideas for period houses, cottages, shops and castles, with the advantages and disadvantages of each type. There are practical pointers on designing the stairs, the roof and the front openings and how they affect the design of the house, including suggestions on drawing house plans.

Part II, Chapters 7–11, starts with a simple one-roomed shop, built to display miniature furniture and accessories. Instructions are given for making the shop, using the materials and methods discussed in Part I, and suggestions are offered for extending or adapting the basic design. From this simple project, we progress to three different houses, all using the materials and techniques covered in Part I.

Chapter 11 gives instructions and patterns for making dolls'-house dolls. The dolls, made from beads and pipecleaners, can be suitably dressed, using the patterns given, to fit into the shop or any of the three houses. Instructions are given for adults, children and babies in both 1:16 and 1:12 scales. Suggestions are also offered for dolls'-house pets.

The last chapter of the book deals with all the aspects of restoring an old dolls' house. Valuable antique or just a rather battered nursery relic, this chapter offers advice on how to repair and restore your old dolls' house and its furnishings.

Most of the ideas are simple and straight-forward enough for the absolute beginner to follow. No special skills are required to build a dolls' house, just the inclination and a little time. We hope that the experienced dolls'-house person might also find our book helpful, and perhaps discover a few new ideas.

Whether you are a first time housebuilder or an old hand, we hope that you will gain as much pleasure from building a dolls' house as we do.

1 Planning

It is well worth spending some time planning, in your mind and then on paper, the kind of dolls' house you actually want. If possible, during this planning stage take advantage of the dolls' houses in museums, and the various books on dolls' houses in the library to gain inspiration.

Whether the house is for an adult or a child is usually the first consideration. Younger children generally prefer a modern house or a house with modern furnishings, with which they can identify, rather than a period house with oil lamps or a warming pan which mean far less to a child than a miniature vacuum cleaner or cooker 'just like mum's'. Adults, on the other hand, usually prefer a house in period style, full of miniature antique furniture and fittings. It is quite feasible to combine the two: perhaps an elegant Georgian exterior, furnished up to date and inhabited by a modern family. Your own taste is the only guide here.

Period houses

If you intend to make a period house or cottage, it is often helpful to consult books on architecture to see how rooms in old houses were planned. The siting of staircases and fireplaces, the height of ceilings and size of rooms varied enormously from century to century. Building materials varied from area to area — for example, Cotswold stone, Devon cob or Cornish granite — as houses were generally built of the materials which were available locally. The size, style and placement of windows and doors changed as the fashions in building changed. A Tudor cottage would have smallish windows, often irregular in size and position because they were put in where they were needed and where they would fit

between the upright timbers of the cottage. The fashion in the eighteenth century was for symmetry, with windows of equal sizes placed at regular intervals either side of a central front door. During Victorian times, as the land in towns became scarce and expensive, the tall, narrow town house with basement and attic became the general rule. Those elegant houses built in squares in the West End of London for the rich and fashionable, or the meaner versions in North or East London, were all designed to occupy the minimum area of land.

An historically accurate dolls' house can be a very satisfying project, involving research into architecture, interior decorating and furniture. It does, however, have some drawbacks. The first of these is the amount of time required for researching and tracking down exactly the right materials for the house. The purist finds that he cannot accept paper bricks and tiles, that greenish bottle glass simply does not exist in this scale, and that an inlaid marble floor is quite beyond his means! The most irritating aspect of building a completely accurate period dolls' house is probably the limitation on the things you can put in it. It is frustrating to find a perfect miniature oil lamp or warming pan, and then to realise that it is useless because such things did not exist at the time your house was built.

However, dolls' houses are dream houses and for the majority of dolls'-house builders, historical accuracy is not a major consideration. We tend to pick a period, perhaps Victorian or Georgian, and aim for the flavour of the period rather than complete accuracy, allowing ourselves licence over such things as warming pans and four-poster beds. Perhaps the best of all possible worlds would be to build

1　A few of the many styles to consider when planning your house

a period house which is now inhabited by a modern family and has been converted and modernised just as much or as little as you please. In this house the colour television could sit happily by the inglenook fireplace.

Shops

It is also worth considering at this planning stage whether a shop with living accommodation would suit you better than a house. If the building is small, with the shop on the ground floor, the living space would be limited unless you decide to have three storeys. A shop can be fun, both for the maker of the stock, who would find here an outlet for things that have no place in an ordinary house, and for the owner, perhaps a child for whom the shop doubles the play value. A Victorian draper's shop with elaborately trimmed bonnets, bolts of fabric, laces, ribbons and tiny dresses on dummies would give enormous satisfaction to the needlewoman, who could also turn her talents to the ruffled, quilted and embroidered furnishings of the appartments upstairs. A modern greengrocer's or baker's shop could be stocked with items modelled in clay or breadpaste — an ideal outlet for children's modelling talents. A miniature antique shop is another answer to the ancient versus modern dilemma, modern apartments upstairs and the shop downstairs providing the perfect setting for all the old-fashioned things which have no place in a modern house.

Castles

Consider also building a castle; the basic structure need be no more complicated than a dolls' house — a box-shaped house, given battlements, lancet windows and a Gothic door, painted or papered the appropriate grey stone colour. With most castles, the interiors are far more impressive than the exteriors, where the grim grey stone makes a marvellous background for glowing velvets, polished wood and tapestries. The imagination of the builder could run riot, devising heraldic banners, rich furnishings and miniature suits of armour. There might be a great hall with a stone fireplace, furnished with a massive table, carved chairs and tapestries. Upstairs could be a bedchamber with a four-poster bed, carved clothes chest and hooded cradle.

2   Consider a cottage or a shop

13

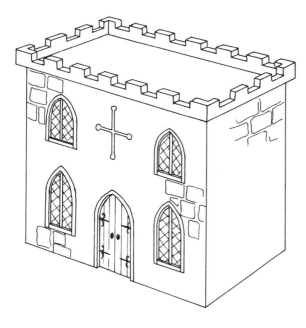

3   A simple box-shaped house can be adapted to make a castle

Cupboard houses

You may be more interested in making miniature furniture and furnishings, rather than the dolls' house itself, in which case a small cupboard will make a good home to display these small pieces. The interior of the cupboard could be decorated in the same way as the dolls'-house rooms. False doors and windows will add to the illusion and, once the furnishings are in place, the cupboard becomes a dolls' house in the old tradition of the Dutch cupboard houses of the seventeenth century. The cupboard need not be marked in any way by this conversion. A lining of cardboard can be cut to fit the walls, ceiling and floor of each shelf 'room' and held in place with small pieces of double-sided tape. The decorating scheme is then carried out on the cardboard, and can be removed completely — a good idea if you are using an antique cupboard, and it also makes changes in decor a simple matter.

Outbuildings

Think also of possible outbuildings which would add interest and scope. An old cottage might have a lean-to extension used as a scullery or outside loo. A modern house often has a flat-roofed garage built on one side. A period house might have a conservatory or stable. Porches add interest to the front of the house — a small gable porch for the front door of a modern house, a deep, enclosed porch with seats for an old house.

Scale

Having decided the style of the house, then decide on the scale. The two most commonly used scales are 1:12 — one inch to the foot, and 1:16 — three-quarters of an inch to the foot. The 1:12 scale obviously makes a larger house and is favoured by collectors — the majority of the fine craftsman-made dolls'-house pieces are in this scale. The advantages are that conversion is simple (one inch is one foot in life-size), the rooms are larger and easily accessible even to big adult hands, and if you can afford them, the 'collectors'' furniture and accessories in this scale are beautiful. The main disadvantages are that this larger-size house takes up a lot of room and, made in wood, is very heavy, so it needs to be kept permanently in one place. Also, as far as I know, none of the cheaper commercial ranges of furniture and accessories are produced in this scale in Britain, though they are readily available in America.

The 1:16 scale still provides satisfactory rooms, accessible to children and careful adults. The house is usually small enough (unless you are planning a mansion) to store and move easily. And all the cheaper commercial ranges of dolls'-house furniture and accessories, so necessary for those bits and pieces you cannot make yourself, are made in the 1:16 scale. The choice is yours!

Choice of plans

The next step is to work out some plans. These can be as detailed as you please, but simple scale drawings will suffice. The main reason for drawing plans is that dolls' houses are disproportionately tall — necessarily so, to allow access to the rooms, but annoying when designing the front of the house. You must decide how many rooms you want, how many floors, where the stairs will go, and fit all this into a basically box shape with the windows and front door in the right places.

Openings Usually a house which opens at the front is most satisfactory. A back opening allows you to make an elaborate front if you want to, but the house has to be kept in the middle of the room to allow you to get at it. The same applies to side openings; they allow for greater depth to the house, one room behind another, but access is awkward unless the house is kept in a clear space. The front-opening house can be kept with its back against a wall, and it does not have to be moved when you want to play with it. It does, however, limit you to one room depth.

Stairs Because of the extra height of the dolls'-house ceilings, you need more stairs than in a real house. As a general guide, the stairs rise at a 45° angle; therefore, to make a rise of 8 inches, you will need 8 inches depth.

Two kitchen dressers showing the relative sizes of the 1:16 and 1:12 scales, left and right respectively *(Jonathon Bosley)*

The stairs can rise in one flight to the next floor; or in a half-flight to a landing, followed by another half-flight doubling back or at right-angles. The amount of space needed for the staircase must be considered when planning the layout of the rooms and the depth and width of the house. Tape matchboxes together in various combinations and try them in different places, measuring the amount of space they occupy. If you find making a staircase beyond you, plan a house without stairs or fake them by having two or three steps which disappear behind a partition wall. If you have a staircase, remember that although some poetic licence is acceptable in a

15

dolls' house, you must allow for a reasonably realistic stairwell, otherwise not only does it look wrong but the dolls will knock themselves unconscious going upstairs!

Roofs There are two basic types of roof, a gable roof and a hipped roof, each with several variations. The hipped roof (Fig 4b) is often a good choice for a dolls' house because there is no overhang to hinder the opening of the front of the house, though it can be a little tricky to cut because the angles must be accurate to join the four pieces together. The attic space under a hipped roof is not usable as the roof must be fixed for proper support, but the whole roof can be hinged at the back to provide storage space. The gable roof (Fig 4a) can be placed either sideways or endwise-on to the house, depending on the width of the front; and the roof space can be used either as a room or for storage. The main problem with a gable roof is the overhang. If the gable is placed endwise (Fig 4d) with the attic used as a room, the front edges of the roof must end in line with the front edges of the side walls so that the front will hinge open freely. If the gable is placed sideways on (Fig 4f) there are several possibilities. The front section of the roof can be hinged at the ridge to lift before the fronts are opened, so that, propped up, it will provide an attic room. When closed, the fronts are held in place by the overhang of the roof.

Alternatively, a section of the front of the house at the top edge can be fixed permanently in place (Fig 4e), with the front cut to open below this fixed section. The roof can then be fixed in place with an overhang without hindering the front opening. With both styles it is sometimes effective to have the roof edge ending level with the top of the front wall (Fig 4c). This gives a rather 'tall' look to the house, but it dispenses with the overhang problem entirely. However, the type of roof depends on the style of the house and your own taste. There is no reason why your house cannot have a flat roof, dormer windows — or battlements.

Size The size of the house will depend on the scale, the number and size of the rooms and the style — the rooms in a cottage are smaller than the rooms in a Victorian town house. You will need enough space to put all the things you want in each room, but not so much that the rooms look bare even when fully furnished. The lack of a front wall limits the wall space for larger pieces. Generally, a cottage would be a little poky — a double bed, a washstand, a chest of drawers and the room was almost full — though a Victorian drawing room cluttered with furniture and knick-knacks still left enough space to move around in a crinoline!

Gauge the size of your rooms by the size of 'real' rooms, and if in doubt, allow more space rather than less. It is very frustrating not to have enough room for all the things you want to put in the house.

Drawing plans By this time you will either be thoroughly confused, or you will have a fairly clear idea of the kind of house you want. If the former, think about it some more: eventually it will all fall into place in your mind, and you will be ready to draw some plans (Fig 5).

A scale drawing of the front of the house is a good idea, lining up the windows with the rooms behind them and positioning the front door. Interior plans will need to show the depth, width and height of the rooms, position of stairs, stairwells, interior doorways and any windows on side walls.

As the exact measurements of rooms, ceiling heights, roof pitches, etc, are a matter of individual taste, the following sizes are offered only as a guide. In the 1:12 scale: the ground-floor ceiling is about 10in high, the first-floor ceiling about 9—10in high, and a room 14in square is fairly large. In the 1:16 scale: the ground-floor ceiling is about 8in high, the first floor about 7—8in high, and a room 9in square in this scale is a good size. Although the ceilings need to be high enough for you to see into the rooms without peering, too high a ceiling completely distorts the proportions. As an indication of size when planning doorways, stairwells and windows, the 'people' who live in a 1:12 house are about 5½—6in tall and the 'people' in a 1:16 house are 4¼—4½in tall.

A solemn warning at this stage: however meticulous your plans, dolls' houses have a way of developing personalities of their own. They never turn out exactly as designed!

4   a Gable roof; b hipped roof; c–f several possibilities for the front openings

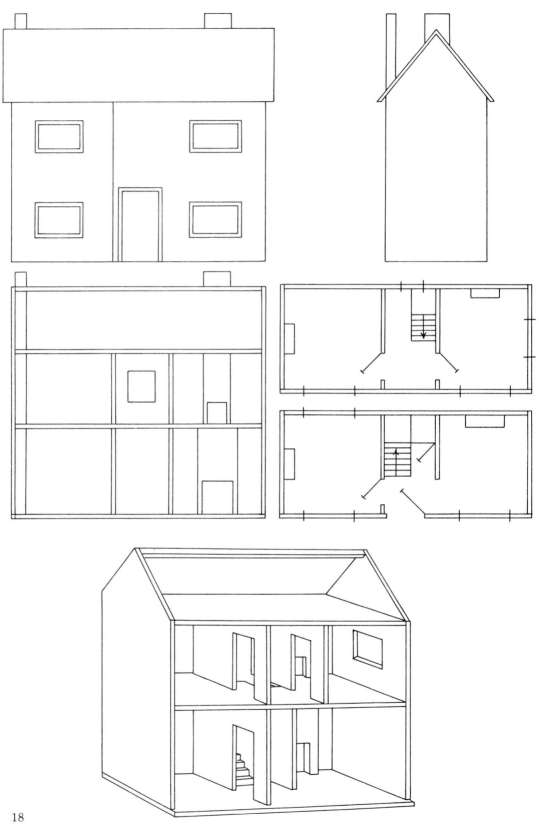

The four-roomed house built from the plans
shown in Fig 5

5 Front and side elevations and plan for a four-
roomed house with a hinged gable roof

2 Building

Materials

The first consideration is the material you will choose to build your house. The majority of modern dolls' houses are built of plywood, a satisfactory medium but by no means the only one. It is perfectly feasible to build a dolls' house in a cupboard, perhaps an old pine cupboard bought for the purpose. The front could be removed and replaced with a new house front, or the original door could be left untouched, making the dolls'-house interior a surprise. Old furniture is also a good source of real wood to re-use for your housebuilding, if it is the right thickness and warp-free (beware of wood beetle though).

If you use plywood, buy the best quality you can afford and ensure that it is warp-free. For the walls and floors use ¼in thick in 1:16 scale, ½in thick in 1:12 scale; for the roof use ⅛in thick.

We have made very successful houses of artists' Daler Board — ¼in or 6mm thick for the walls and 3mm thick for the roof. Daler Board is relatively cheap, tough enough to withstand nails, screws and serious playing, light enough for a child to carry, easy to use, and it can be cut with a Stanley knife. We only recommend Daler Board for making houses in the 1:16 scale, though, as we feel the larger size needs the extra strength of wood. Daler Board is bought in sheets from art-supply shops and is an excellent medium for either the beginner or the more advanced housebuilder.

It is possible to make dolls' houses of cardboard, or hardboard, but we do not recommend either.

Cutting

The next stage is to draw onto the chosen

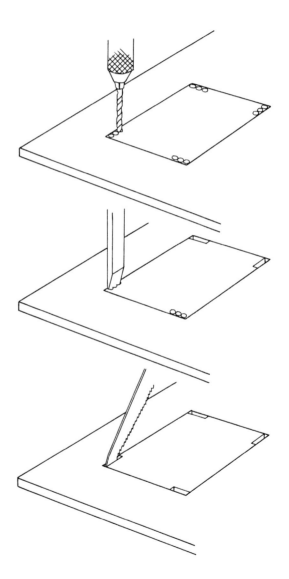

6 The method for cutting window holes with a keyhole saw

material the outlines of the house pieces. Take a great deal of care to get the lines straight, the right-angles exact and the measurements correct, as this will save a lot of time and energy later on. Mark in the doorways, the windows and the stairwell.

Wood or plywood need to be cut with a saw, but if you are using Daler Board, a Stanley knife with a new blade and a metal rule will do the job efficiently (watch out for your fingers).

To cut the doorways, windows and stairwell from wood, drill several holes side-by-side in each corner of the area to be cut out, and make a hole large enough to insert a keyhole saw by chiselling the holes together (Fig 6). Use the keyhole saw to cut along the lines you have drawn. By sawing on the lines, you then have the minimum amount of sanding to give a clean, smooth edge. These holes can usually be cut in Daler Board with a Stanley knife, but

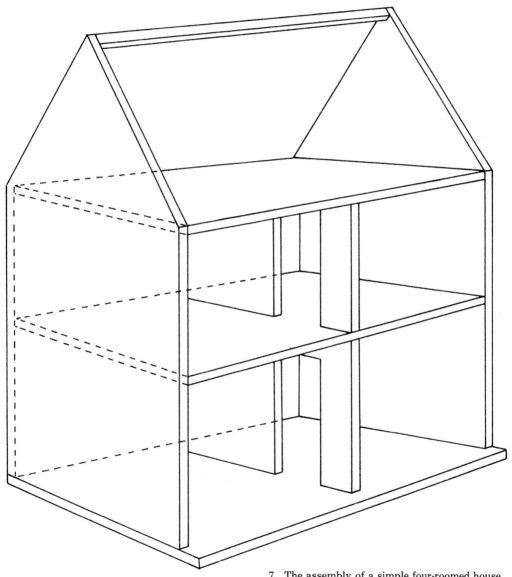

7 The assembly of a simple four-roomed house showing the floor, partition wall and ridgepole in position

any awkward corners or curves are best cut with a fretsaw inserted through a hole drilled in a corner. When cutting Daler Board, aim for a clean, accurate cut, on the marked line as it is not practicable to sand.

Assembly

When all the house pieces are cut, with doors, windows and stairwells cut out in the relevant places, try out the assembly, taping the various pieces together with masking tape. Check that floors fit closely and partition walls fit snugly together. Do not worry about small gaps, as these can be filled later. When you are satisfied that your pieces fit well together, if using plywood, sand all rough edges smooth and you are ready to assemble the house.

It is usually easiest to assemble the exterior of the house first — the back wall, side walls, base and top ceiling. We have found that glueing and pinning works well on both wood and Daler Board, using white woodworkers' glue and panel pins on wood, or a general-purpose glue such as UHU and panel pins on Daler Board. When using wood, especially in the 1:12 scale, it is a good idea to reinforce the corners with small screws. Fix the first side wall to the base, ensuring that the back edge of the wall is lined up with the back edge of the base and the wall is at a right-angle to the base. Fit the back into the right-angle made by the side wall and base, then fix the other side wall in place. Fit the top ceiling between the side and back walls.

Floors and Partition Walls

When the exterior is assembled, use a ruler and pencil to mark on the inside and outside of the three walls, ceiling and base the lines where the floors and partition walls occur. Follow these guidelines to ensure that the floors and walls are fixed accurately when you fit the interior.

Floors and partition walls can be inserted in several ways.

1 If the partition walls occur in the same place on each floor, put the partition wall in first, glueing and pinning through the top ceiling, base and back wall. A cornice made of picture-frame moulding with the back planed flat, or similar, can be glued into each room at ceiling height, mitring the corners (Fig 8a). The floors are then glued and slotted in to rest on the cornice. (This method is used in the Victorian town house, Chapter 8.)

2 Alternatively, if the partition walls occur in the same place on each floor but you do not wish to have cornices, cross-halving the floor and partition wall provides a strong method of putting both pieces in together. To cross-halve, cut a slot the same thickness as the wood to a point half-way across the partition wall at ceiling height, and half-way across the floor where it meets the partition wall. The two pieces are then interlocked (Fig 9) and put into the house together, glueing and pinning through the base, top ceiling and back, into the floor and partition. This is only successful when it is well done, and a snug fit of the two pieces is essential. (This method is used in the Tudor cottage, Chapter 9.)

3 If the partition walls occur in different places on each floor (or if there is only one room on each floor), then the floor is put in first. This can be done with or without a cornice 'shelf' to rest the floor on, but if a cornice is used, small notches must be cut out of it to allow the partition walls to slot into place. Glue and pin the floor through the sides and back walls, then slot the partition walls in place, glueing and pinning through base, top ceiling and back wall (Fig 8b).

It is easier to position the floor accurately if the ceiling height is marked carefully on the inside and outside of the house on all three walls, so that the floor lines up with the marks when it is put in place.

Roof

The roof of the house is usually fixed in place next, and again, depending on the type of roof, there are several methods.

Hipped roof (see Fig 4b) The trickiest part of a hipped roof is cutting it. The front and back pieces should be cut first, the top edges chamfered and the two pieces taped along this top edge. Tape this part in place on the top of the house while the angles of the side pieces are measured, cut and tried in place. When the

8 Methods for fixing the floors and partition walls using cornice ledges

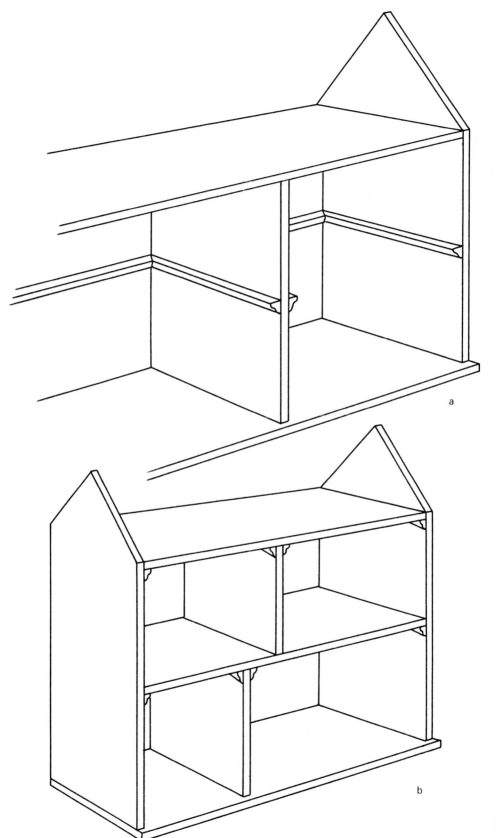

a

b

23

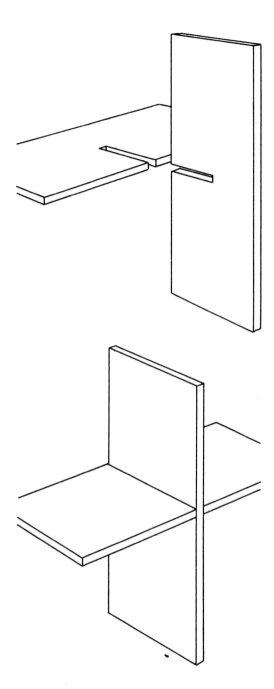

four pieces fit together properly, chamfer the edges where they join, glue and then tape over the joins. The roof is now ready to fix in place. (This method is used in the antique shop, Chapter 7.)

Gable roof (see Fig 4a)   If the gable roof is to end at the top edge of the house with no overhang, nor hinge, then it is relatively simple to fix. The two roof pieces are chamfered at the top edges where they join, and glued and taped together. If the roof is wide, then the additional support of a ridgepole may be needed (Fig 10). This is a piece of ½in square beading screwed across the top between the gable ends of the house. The roof pieces are then laid over the ridgepole, and glued and pinned to the ridgepole and the tops of the gable-end walls.

Hinged gable roof (see Fig 4f)   With this method, a ridgepole of ½in square beading is screwed between the tops of the gable ends. The back section of the roof is then glued and pinned flush to the ridgepole and the top of the gable-end walls (Fig 10). Before fitting the front, make a frame of ½ × ¼in wood-strip and fix it onto the underside of the section. The frame should be flush with the front edge, but set in about ⅜in at the sides and top edges. This frame gives rigidity to the roof section and provides a sufficient thickness to screw the hinges into (Fig 11a). To hinge the front roof in place, use either three hinges or a continuous length of piano hinge as preferred. The hinges should be rebated into both the ridgepole and the frame (Fig 11b) and the roof section fixed in place (Fig 11c). (This method is used in the Tudor cottage, Chapter 9.)

Fixed overhang roof (see Fig 4e)   When you wish to fix the roof permanently with an overhang at the front, it is necessary to open the front below this overhang. Therefore, to avoid a nasty gap at the top of the front wall, fix a piece the same depth as the overhang across the top edge of the front of the house. The roof is then attached in the same way as before, glued and pinned to the ridgepole and the top of the gable walls, and the opening front(s) of the house are cut to fit below the fixed piece. (This method is used in the modern house, Chapter 10.)

9   Cross-halving the floor and partition wall together

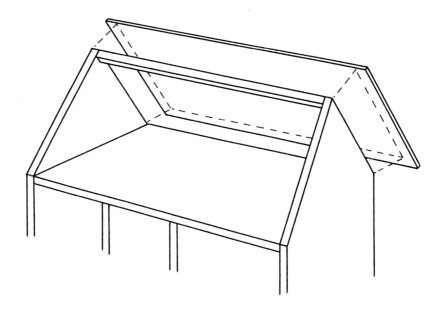

Chimney Stacks and Pots

Chimney stacks and pots on the dolls'-house roof should conform to the chimney breasts used in the house (*see* Fireplaces). Modern houses need not have fireplaces or chimneys, but most older houses have both, even though the fireplace might be bricked up.

On a flat roof, a fixed gable roof or a hipped roof, the chimney stack can be made by cutting a block of balsa wood to the size required and notching the lower edge to fit the roof angle. Obviously the chimney stack should be sited above the chimney breast. On a hinged gable roof, where this method is impracticable, it is simplest to site the chimney breast and the stack towards the back of the house, so that the chimney stack can be fixed to the back part of the roof which does not lift. The bottom of the stack is cut to the same angle as the roof and stuck in place after the roof has been decorated.

The chimney stack should be brick-papered or painted before fixing in place, and a number of chimney pots appropriate to the number of fireplaces should be stuck in place on top of the stack. Large wooden beads which come in a variety of shapes make excellent chimney pots — they should be painted with matt terracotta paint for a realistic colour. Alternatively, you might prefer to model pots in Das or clay.

10   The back roof pieces fixed to the ridgepole and the gable-end walls

Exterior chimney breasts should be made tall enough to form the stack in one with the breast, merely needing the appropriate number of pots.

Front Opening

The front of the house can be hinged on at this stage or left until the interior of the house is completed. We generally use the latter method, as access for decorating is simpler, and it is easier to fix the windows and door on the fronts before they are hinged. However, it is a matter of choice — the method for hinging the fronts is the same whether it is done now or later.

If yours is a tall, thin house, the front can open in one piece; but if the house is wider, it is better to cut the front into two hinged sections. The weight of a wide front opening can cause the hinges to sag, or even topple the house. If the front door is central, make the join to one side rather than trying to line up an exact fit through the door frame.

A wooden house needs larger hinges — usually 2in long by ½in wide, which should be recessed into the wood to give a good fit to the front. For a lighter Daler Board house, 1in hinges are usually sufficient. These can be

25

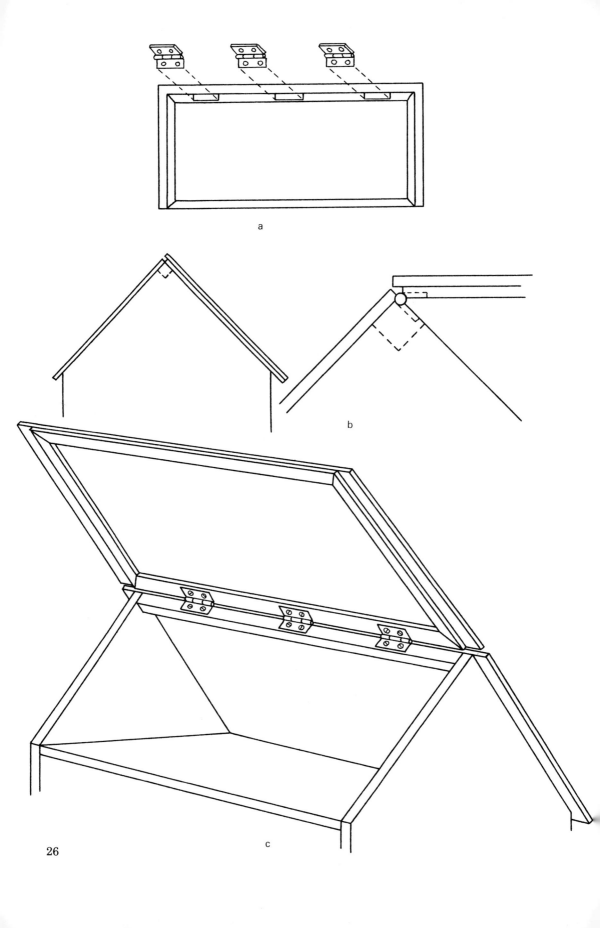

a

b

c

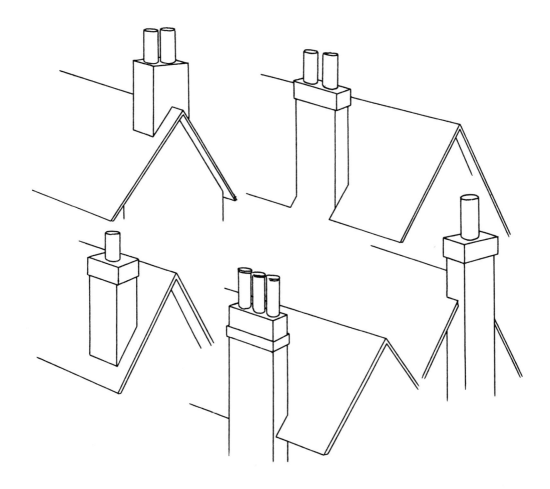

recessed by cutting the Daler Board with a Stanley knife, but it is advisable to glue both the hinge and the screws in place with superglue for extra strength, as the screws are essentially very small. Small cupboard hooks can be used to hold the fronts closed.

Lift-off fronts If you find the idea of hinging the front to the house too daunting, a lift-off front is a simple alternative. Choose a flat piece of plywood or Daler Board, and cut the front to fit in one piece. When the decoration is completed, the front is held in place by two or three cupboard hooks screwed into each side of the house.

11   The front roof section, framed with woodstrip and hinged to the ridgepole

12   A selection of chimney stacks

Stairs (*see also* Chapter 1)
There are various methods of making stairs, ranging from the craftsman's miniature with treads, risers and stringers, to amateurish matchboxes covered in brown paper. The method described here is one we have found simple but effective.

Use triangular beading (obtainable from most DIY shops), approximately ½in wide for a 1:16 scale house and ¾in wide for a 1:12 scale house, and cut into the required lengths the same width as the staircase. Take care that these lengths are accurately cut. Stick the lengths, closely butted together, on a piece of ⅛in thick obeche wood — when raised to a 45° angle they form quite realistic stairs. If a

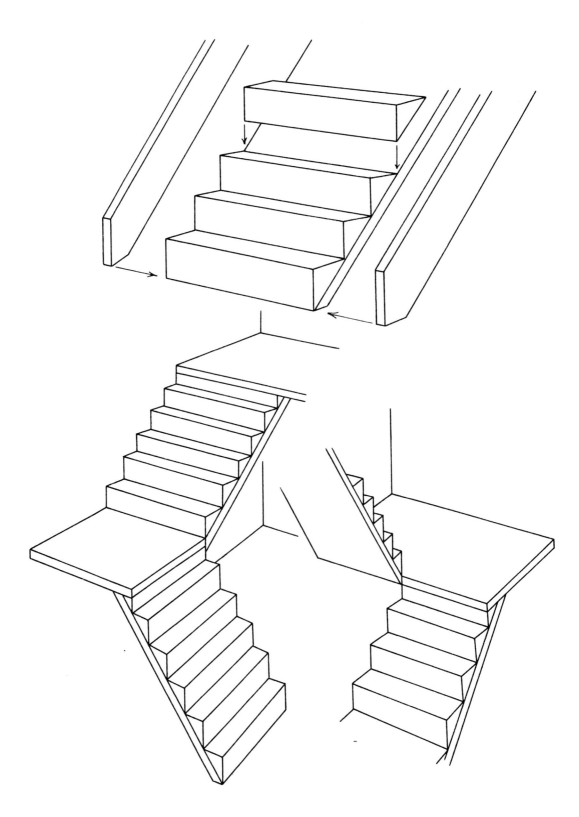

28

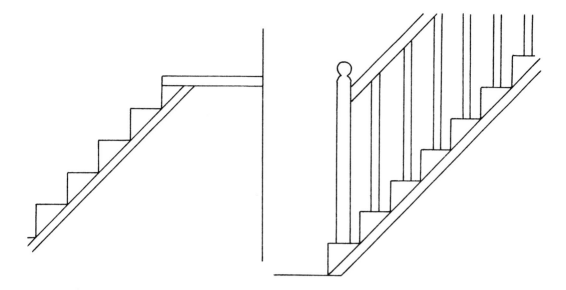

half-landing is used, this is generally the same width as the stairs. The top stair of the bottom flight and the bottom stair of the top flight, with edges chamfered flat, are stuck to the half-landing. The top edge of the top flight, chamfered flat, is glued firmly into the stair-well. If the stairs run up against a wall, they can be glued to the wall for extra stability, but if you wish to stain, varnish or polish them do it before you stick them in. It is also easier to carpet the stairs before you put them in place and to paint or paper the house before they are in, so we recommend that you make the stair-case, check that it fits well but do not stick it in place at this stage.

It is simple, though fiddly, to make banister rails and posts from fine square or round dowelling. Cut and stick a newel post in place at the top and bottom of the flight of stairs. Cut a handrail to fit snugly between the posts and glue it firmly in place. Then cut each banister rail with the top edge at a 45° angle to fit between the stair tread and the handrail. If the banisters are cut, fitted and stuck in place one at a time, this should result in a good fit and a satisfactory result.

The stairs can be left open underneath, the flat obeche-wood backing providing a smooth finish for painting or papering; or they can be boxed in with a partition wall. The boxed-in

13 Making stairs from triangular beading

14 Fixing the half-landing and banisters

area, provided with a door, forms a good under-stairs cupboard or even a loo.

A skirting board up the staircase finishes it properly. The simplest method is to cut a length of obeche wood the depth of the stair tread and stick it along the outside edge of the staircase. (This method is used in the Tudor cottage, Chapter 9. *See also* the open-plan staircase in the modern house, Chapter 10.)

Doors
Doors are made to suit the style of the house — a plain, flat door for a modern house, panelled for a Victorian house, planked for a Tudor house etc. We generally use $1/16-1/8$in obeche wood for doors, with a cloth hinge or the tiny hinges sold for dolls' houses (*see* Stockists). When making and hanging doors, remember to allow sufficient clearance to accommodate floor-coverings.

Plain door (Fig 15a) This is made of two pieces of obeche wood, $1/16-1/8$in thick as required. Cut the two pieces to the exact size of the doorway hole. If using a cloth hinge, cut a strip of cotton tape about $1\frac{1}{2}$in wide, a fraction shorter than the door. Stick the two door pieces together with the tape sandwiched between them, allowing about an inch of tape

a

b

c

to protrude along one side. When the door pieces are firmly stuck, sand the edges smooth so that the door opens and closes freely. The door is hung by sticking the protruding strip of tape firmly to the wall on the side the door will open (Fig 16a).

Planked door (Fig 15b) This is made in the same way as the plain door. When the pieces are sanded, score both sides of the door with a pointed edge such as a scissor blade to indicate the planking. The characteristic Z pieces, cut from $^1/_{16}$in obeche wood, are then stuck to the hinged side.

Panelled door (Fig 15c) This is made by sticking $^1/_{16}$in panel frames to both sides of a piece of $^1/_8$in obeche wood, sandwiching the cloth hinge between the centre wood and the panelling on one side.

Door handles can be made from beads, brass upholstery tacks, map pins or the loops of large hooks and eyes bent to 90°; alternatively, turned wood or brass handles for dolls' houses can be bought from the specialist shops.

Door frames Door-frame mouldings are best applied after wallpapering, as this gives a neater finish. Fine picture framing or thin wood-strips (from art and craft shops), mitred at the corners and fitted flush to the edge of the doorway, look very convincing (Fig 16c). Any raw edges can be painted or stained to match the door frame, or the doorway edges can be faced with fine wood-strip before the doors are cut to fit.

A mitre block is very useful for cutting mitred corners on door and window frames and cornices.

Windows

Glazing dolls'-house windows with glass is impracticable to all but the most intrepid, but thin perspex, obtainable from art and craft shops, is an excellent substitute. It is expensive, but one square foot is enough to glaze most dolls' houses. The perspex is cut most easily by first scoring the cutting line with a Stanley knife and then cutting with a

15 Making doors with cloth hinges

fine-bladed fretsaw. Cut the windows to the exact size of the window hole (a cardboard template makes this easier).

To fix the windows in place, stick a frame of fine square beading on the inside edge of the window hole, insert the 'glass' and sandwich with a similar frame of fine square beading stuck to the outside edge of the window hole (Fig 17).

Window frames, again, are better applied after the wallpaper for a neater finish and can be made of the same fine picture-frame moulding or wood-strip used for the door frames.

Glazing bars, appropriate to the house, should be stuck to both sides of the 'glass' for the best effect. Use a glue such as UHU sparingly and leave until tacky before sticking the bars in place — if they are to be painted or stained, this is best done before sticking to avoid getting paint on the windows.

Fireplaces

As in a real house, the fireplace in a dolls' house provides a focal point for the room and can give it a lot of character. Again the style of the house is one of the main considerations in deciding the kind of fireplace to install. The chimney breast could be external (Fig 18c), as in a lot of Victorian houses, or internal, which breaks up the box shape of the room. The fireplace can be sited on the back or side wall, but give the site careful thought — a chimney breast is not likely to occur in a downstairs room in the same place as a window in the room above! A corner fireplace can be an interesting feature, again breaking up the box shape of a room (Fig 18b).

An easy method of making a chimney breast is to use a block of balsa wood the width, height and depth of the required chimney breast. The fireplace opening is cut out with a Stanley knife and the chimney breast is then stuck firmly to the wall. A small piece of brick paper covering the inside and back of the opening adds to the realism. This method can also be used to make the large fireplace needed for period kitchens, where the chimney breast is wider and deeper and the opening larger to accommodate the kitchen range.

The fireplace surround again depends on the style of the house (Fig 19) — a simple beam for a medieval fireplace, or an elaborate marble

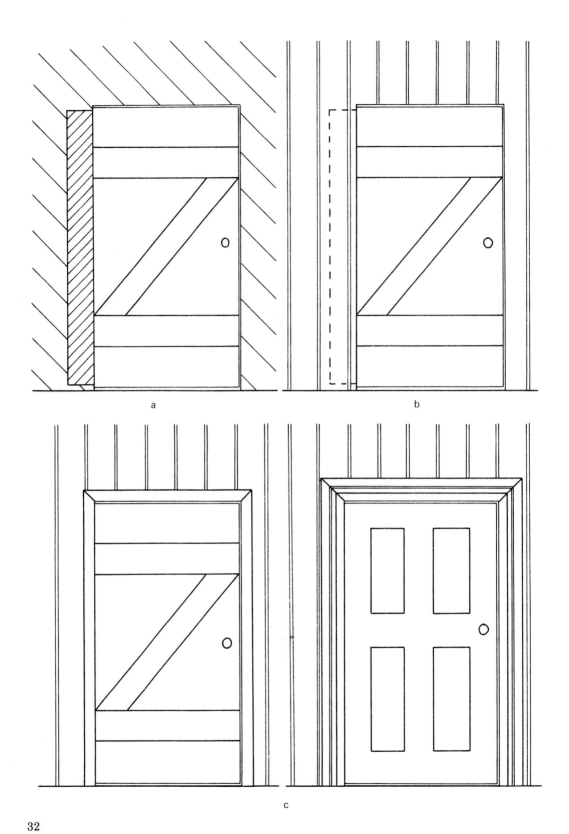

a

b

c

32

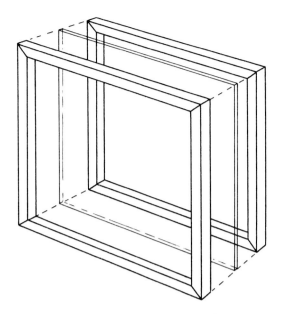

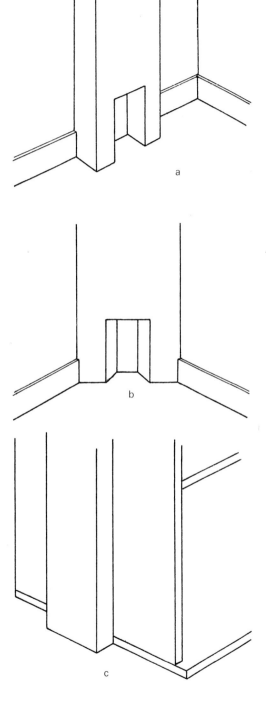

17   Making windows using mitred wood-strip frames and perspex

(right) 18   Siting the chimney breast, internally or externally

(left) 16   Fixing the cloth-hinged door in place

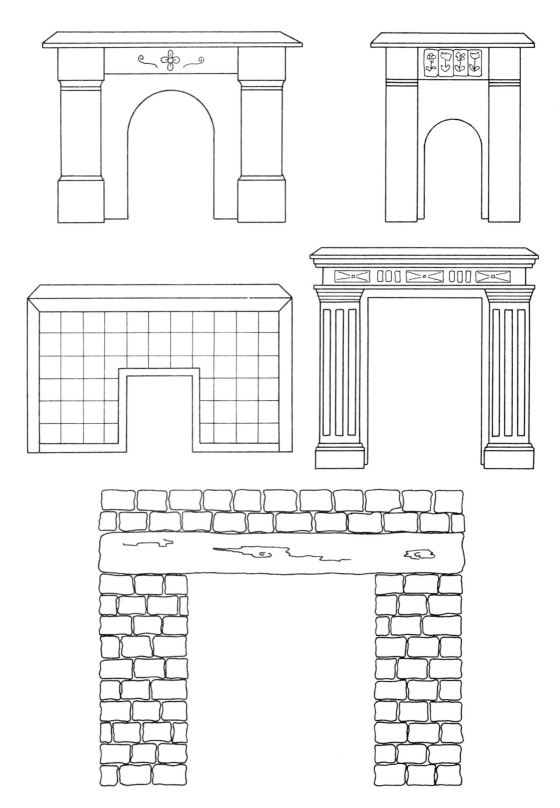

chimney piece for a Victorian house. Most kinds can be made of obeche wood, stained or painted to represent other materials if necessary, or a stone or brick surround can be modelled from Das or similar clay. A brick or tiled hearth adds realism, and can be made from paper, clay or the tiny tiles sold for dolls' houses.

It is a good idea not to finish the fireplace until the room is decorated as it is often easier to decide then on the style of fireplace which best suits the room. It is also neater to fix the fireplace surround after the chimney breast is papered.

Skirting boards

The skirting boards are cut from thin obeche wood, to the appropriate size for the house (deep in old houses, smaller in modern ones). These too are best stuck in place after the room has been papered and floored; and they should be stained or painted before being stuck in. If the back wall is skirted first, the skirting on the side walls can be butted firmly against this, dispensing with any need to mitre the corners.

Picture rails

If yours is the older style of house which requires picture rails, these can be made of fine dowelling or moulding or thin wood-strip, painted or stained before fixing and, again, stuck in place after the room is papered.

19   A selection of fireplaces

3 Decorating and Wiring

When planning a decorating scheme for your period dolls' house it is helpful to consult books on domestic architecture and interior design. Tastes and fashions have changed a great deal through the centuries, and correct details are an important part of a realistic period effect.

For example, mellow brick and oak timbers, doors and window frames are typical of a Tudor house; the Georgians favoured colour-washed stucco and white paint; and the Victorians preferred coloured brick and dark paintwork. Roofing materials ranged from thatch through red clay or stone tiles to grey slate. Of course, there were many houses which did not conform tó the fashion of their time, but the simplest way to achieve a convincing period effect is to use the architectural and decorative clichés then current. A square, red-brick house with white paintwork and a fanlight above a panelled front door is immediately recognisable as a 'Queen Anne' house. Whether it is an 'original' or the modern copy so often found on housing estates depends on how you decorate and furnish the interior! The leaflets offered by manufacturers of paints are a good source of ideas for exterior decorating schemes, showing clearly the effect of different colours on different types of house.

A modern house also benefits from planning. Fashions have changed even in the last ten years, and house magazines show up-to-the-minute trends in decorating schemes, as do the paint manufacturers' leaflets and DIY magazines. Look around your area for examples of modern houses with pleasant decorative schemes and details. A housing estate with houses of basically the same design but each decorated to its owners' taste is a catalogue of ideas — details like shutters, porches and different colours make a surprising amount of difference.

The interior decoration of the house should also be in keeping with its style and period, unless you have a period house inhabited by a modern family, in which case the decoration can be as modern as you please. Each period had its tastes in colours, fabrics, floor and wall coverings. The Victorians had a taste for heavy fabrics, dark colours and an air of opulent gloom; while pastel colours, striped papers, white paint and gilding were admired in Regency times. These are generalisations, but a little research will provide the details, and there are houses of most periods which are open to the public and might provide inspiration. The enormous variety of papers, fabrics and paints which are available make it fairly easy to find the right materials to achieve any period effect.

For modern houses, magazines and catalogues (eg Habitat) provide an excellent source of ideas — many of the fashionable wallpapers and fabrics with tiny prints are obviously ideal for dolls' houses. Miniature sample tins of paint (available from DIY shops) mean that up-to-date paint colours can be used at little expense.

As a general rule, we recommend choosing the colours and materials for the whole house before you start decorating, to ensure that they harmonise, and to prevent a disappointing result from badly matched colours and patterns. This chapter offers ideas and methods for interior and exterior decoration, plus sources of supply for the materials used, but the real deciding factor in any decorating scheme is your own taste. Fortunately, any mistakes in this scale are cheaply and easily rectified.

Exterior

Papering There is a fairly good selection of exterior papers made for dolls' houses, including old or new brick, stone, pantiles and slates. Most of them give a pleasantly realistic effect and make a straightforward job of finishing the outside of the house. They are available from most art and craft shops.

These papers are best applied with wallpaper paste. Coat the wall with paste first and allow this to dry, then paste the paper and stick it on. Take care to match the lines of bricks on both sides if the front is in two sections. A coat of matt polyurethane varnish when the paper has dried thoroughly will give protection.

Painting If the house is wood, sand it carefully and give it a coat of primer. Use two or three coats of ordinary household emulsion paint in a suitable colour.

Timbering If yours is a Tudor-style house and you want a half-timbered effect, this can be done by cutting strips of wood veneer (available from hobbies shops). Stain to the appropriate dark-oak colour and stick to the painted or brick-papered house with UHU or similar glue in a half-timbered or box-frame design. If the 'beams' are not too straight and even they look better (Fig 20).

Roof tiles Realistic roof tiles can be made simply, though it is a tiresome process. Cut strips of thin cardboard about ¾in wide, then make ½in deep cuts at ½in intervals along the lengths. Stick the strips to the roof, starting at the bottom edge and overlapping each layer by about ¼in over the one before (Fig 21). The roof is then given a coat of paint — a mixture of scarlet, yellow and brown poster paint makes a good red roof-tile colour. When the paint is dry, a few individual tiles should be given slightly different colours. This method can also be used to make a scallop-tiled roof by cutting scallops along one edge of the cardboard strips and applying them in the same fashion. The same applies to stone roof tiles, cut larger at the eaves and smaller at the ridge. A coat of matt polyurethane varnish gives protection and makes it easier to clean.

20 Timbered effect for a Tudor house using veneer strips

Thatching A thatched roof is extremely difficult, but it can be done by sticking layers of natural raffia or bleached coir to the roof until a sufficient depth has been built up. Thatching is not recommended for a hinged roof — it is really only suitable on a house with a fixed roof and a fixed front top edge.

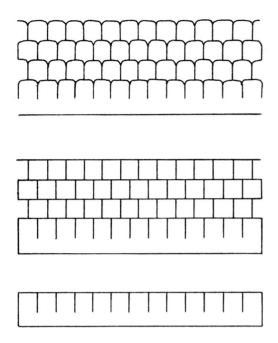

green. Fill the boxes with an arrangement of small plastic or dried flowers pushed and glued into Styrofoam or similar flower-arranger's material, or plasticene, in the bottom of the box.

The small artificial Christmas trees for decorating cakes make excellent shrubs on either side of the front door. Fix them into tubs, suitable plastic lids painted the required colour, with clay or plasticene. A length of small trailing plastic plant, glued carefully around the front porch will make a climber, with tiny pink or yellow artificial flowers stuck on for roses.

21 Cutting and fixing cardboard roof tiles

Bargeboarding Bargeboarding makes a nice finish on gable-end walls. Plain bargeboards can be made from picture-frame moulding, or more elaborate boards cut from obeche wood with a fretsaw. The boards are stuck in place, after painting or staining, under the roof edges (Fig 22).

Plaques A small plaque of engraved metal, carved wood or clay, with the housebuilders' initials and the date, fixed to the front of the house adds a nice finishing touch.

Garden effects If your dolls' house is a country cottage, you might want to have flowers round the door. A town house could have window boxes, or shrubs in tubs. A visit to a good florist who stocks a selection of arti-ficial flowers as well as real ones should provide inspiration as well as materials for garden effects. Delicate plastic plants or dried flowers are usually best, although dried flowers will deteriorate with age.

Window boxes made from thin obeche wood should be stuck to the wall just below the window. They can be painted to match the exterior decor of the house or traditional

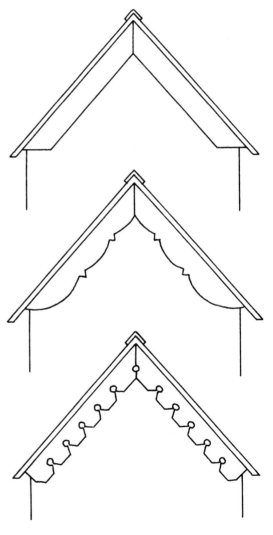

22 Bargeboarding for gable-end walls

A pretty flower border can be made by applying a selection of flower transfers (available from art and craft shops) to the lower front of the house. Alternatively, those with artistic talent might prefer to paint flowers in oil or poster colour. Many toy shops sell a selection of small plants and flowers in pots made for dolls' houses. The more realistic of these look well grouped together on a dolls'-house patio, and also make useful house plants.

Interior

Interior decorating in a dolls' house is as much a matter of taste as in a real house, but there are a few differences which are covered in this section. The most obvious difference is that an open dolls' house is viewed as a whole, and the effect is therefore usually more pleasing if the colours and patterns used in the individual rooms harmonise with each other.

Painting Before you begin decorating, especially if you intend to paint the walls, fill any gaps with a filler such as Polyfilla. Papering the walls with lining paper provides a really good surface to paint on, and hides any minor defects in construction. We have found that ordinary household emulsion paint with a matt finish works very well, using one or two coats as required. Unless the house is modern in style, avoid brilliant white as it looks quite wrong in any period house. Magnolia or ivory give a much softer 'white'. This also applies to ceilings: the quality of light reflected by brilliant white is too harsh and garish for any old-fashioned house. A similar rule applies to the gloss paintwork for an old house. We generally use the small tins of Humbrol enamels, mixing white with cream or ivory gloss to get the right colour. Alternatively, the woodwork could be stained.

Wallpapering Wallpapering is simplest if you cover each wall in one piece. Make a paper template for each wall, marking around doorways, windows, and fireplaces. This will enable you to fit the wallpaper exactly and match any pattern, if necessary, with the minimum of fiddling. Start with the back wall, lining up the paper neatly at the ceiling, or where the picture rail occurs if you intend to

put one in. Overlap the paper about ½in onto the side walls and floor and press it firmly into the corners. Then paper the side walls, again ensuring a neat edge along the top, papering just into the back corners, and overlapping the floor by about ½in.

This overlap onto the floor gives a clean edge when the floor-covering is in place, which is particularly important if there are no skirting boards to cover little deficiencies in this area. If, however, you intend not to use a floor-covering, but rather to score and stain a wooden floor to represent floorboards, then obviously you will need to cut the wallpaper to end at the bottom of the wall.

Use a household wallpaper paste to stick the wallpaper, as glues and gums are not efficient. Apply a coat of paste to the walls and allow it to dry out. Then paste and apply the paper. If you find once it is in place that you dislike it, it is relatively simple to peel it off before it dries and start again.

There are wallpapers specially made for dolls' houses, available from art shops or dolls'-house stockists. Many gift-wrapping papers have suitable small prints, or you could print or paint your own. One simple way to find dolls'-house wallpapers is to look around the local wallpaper shops and if you find something suitable, beg or ask to buy a sample piece. Some wallpaper makers have a range of tiny prints, for example Laura Ashley or Petites Fleurs — the design must be tiny as a large pattern will completely overpower a room.

Floor-coverings Unless you have a wooden floor which you intend to score and stain as floorboards, you will need some kind of floor-covering, even if it is later mostly concealed by rugs. One of the simplest and most effective finishes is plain brown wrapping paper. In an old house, with lots of rugs rather than fitted carpets, it looks very realistic.

Several of the Fablon or Contact designs make good tiles for a kitchen or bathroom. If the design is right but the colour is too bright, try toning it down with a coat of brown shoe polish. Some of these designs make convincing lino floors. Cork floor tiles can be cut to fit a modern house — they are rather thick, but if used all over the house this is not noticeable.

There are floor papers made for dolls' houses, rather limited in design, available from art and craft shops. They include a herringbone parquet and stone flags.

You could make your own floor-coverings, using thin card or paper with the design drawn in ink or paint. A good but rather expensive wooden planked floor can be made with the sticky-backed-veneer tape sold in do-it-yourself shops. This tape looks effective, can be stained and is easy to use, but make sure it is well stuck down. We made one impressive floor with the illustrations cut from the front of packets of woodblock flooring panels — they were just the right scale for the miniature woodblock floor. There are similar pictures of tiles or floorings in the leaflets advertising these products.

Carpets Fitted carpets can be made from various materials. Felt is simple, but beware of over-bright colours. Fine needlecord, printed or plain, looks good. Lightweight wool, denim or heavy printed cotton are all suitable. For a really plush effect, velveteen is excellent. Take care to use a fabric which is not too thick — it will look clumsy and you will have trouble opening doors.

To make the fabric easier to manage, back it with lightweight iron-on Vilene, which will prevent the edges fraying and make it easier to cut and stick. Where possible, cut the carpet with a selvedge at the front edge. Use wallpaper paste applied all over the back, or UHU applied around all edges, to stick the carpet to the floor. Stair carpet can be made of any of the previously mentioned fabrics but felt is particularly good as it does not fray and tucks firmly into the angle of each stair. Also worth considering for stair carpet are woven braids and ribbons; if these are the right width and have a suitable pattern they look convincing. Simple stair-rods can be made by inserting black or brass-coloured hair grips, straight edge uppermost, after the carpet is stuck to the stairs.

Curtains When choosing materials for dolls'-house curtains, look out for fabrics which are fine but quite heavy. Natural fabrics like cotton or silk are usually better than crease-resistant man-made fabrics such as crimplene

and polyesters; well-washed cotton is usually very good. It is difficult to get such small curtains to hang convincingly, but given patience it can be done and is well worth the effort.

It is realistic if the curtains open and close, so cut them large enough to cover the window when drawn, but not so large that they make big bunches either side of the window when open. The following method is the one we use for making and hanging curtains.

Hem the sides with as fine a hem as possible, and along the bottom edge with a slightly deeper hem. Turn the top edge over to form a casing and sew it down. Use a piece of fine dowelling or thin wood-strip as a curtain pole or track and thread it through the casing (Fig 23a). The curtain pole or track should be wider than the window so that, when open, the curtains hang clear of the window rather than obscuring it. Gather the curtains to each side of the pole and steam them over a kettle to set the folds. To fix the pole to the wall, glue tiny blocks of wood or square wooden beads to the wall, above and to either side of the window, then glue the ends of the curtain pole to these wooden blocks (Fig 23b). Alternatively, the pole can be suspended from small eye-hooks screwed into the wall instead of the blocks. If steaming is not sufficient to make the curtains hang properly, a few pins or a little double-sided sellotape will hold them in place and can be removed when they have given up the fight.

As an alternative to this method, the curtains could be hung from gilt jewellery jump rings as curtain rings, from a fine dowelling curtain pole with small beads at each end for finials.

Café-style curtains hung in tiers can look good; or the curtains can be looped back to each side of the window with narrow ribbon. Lace curtains can be made and hung in the same ways as the heavier curtains, either on their own for a light, airy effect or under heavier curtains as in Victorian houses. Wide petticoat-edging lace, left ungathered, also looks well as lace curtains. Lace curtains give the dolls' house a homely air, especially from the outside.

Curtain frills and pelmets can also be added where appropriate. A box pelmet can be cut

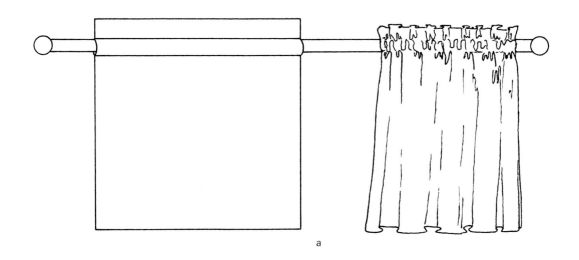

a

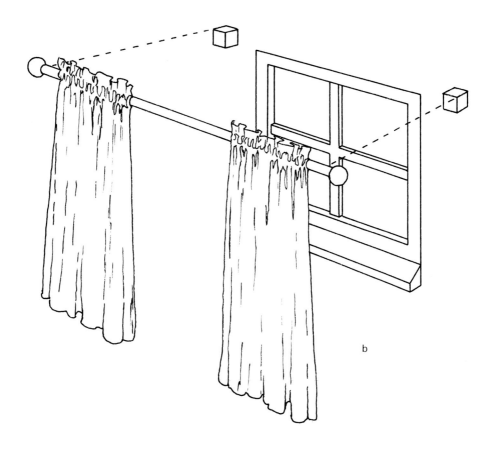

b

23 Hanging curtains

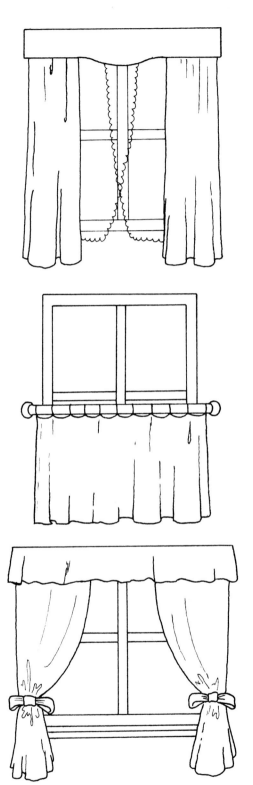

(left) 24   The style of the curtains should be chosen to suit the house

from obeche wood and stained or painted and stuck to the wall; a frill to match the curtains can be stuck to a small block of wood fixed on the wall above the curtains (Fig 24.)

When planning the curtains, make sure that the chosen fabric harmonizes with the wallpaper, and consider using the same fabric somewhere else in the room, perhaps as a bedspread or cushion — this co-ordinated effect enhances the look of the room enormously.

Roller blinds

Roller blinds are an appropriate alternative to curtains, not only for a modern house, but also for Victorian and Edwardian houses.

To make the roller, cut a length of dowelling approximately ⅛in thick the same width as the window, and push a small gimp pin into each end. The blind is best made from a firmly woven cotton fabric; dark blue, green or cream for the period effect, virtually anything you please for a modern house. Cut a rectangle of fabric to fit the window, soak it in wallpaper paste and allow it to dry flat. When the fabric is stiff and dry, stick the top edge to the roller with UHU or similar glue, then roll the blind tightly around the roller. The blind is hung by

24b   Simple roller blind, made of fabric, hung from a dowelling roller on small hooks

putting the two gimp pins in the roller through small eye-hooks screwed one each side of the window. Made by this method, the blind will pull down, but it will, of course, have to be re-rolled by hand.

If you are making a blind for a wide window, it may need the extra weight of a small strip of wood pushed through a narrow casing at the bottom edge. Old-fashioned blinds look good with a narrow cream-lace edging at the hem. A small cord made from cotton thread with a tiny bead on the end makes an effective pull.

Fronts When decorating the interior of the house, do not forget the inside of the fronts. These are usually dealt with in one of two ways. Either the fronts are divided into sections to match the rooms behind them, and each section is decorated to match the corresponding room; or the entire inside front is painted or papered as one piece, taking one of the colours or papers used in the house or a different but harmonising colour or paper. The first method looks well on a tall narrow house with one room on each floor, but it can look rather 'bitty' on a larger house, where the second method is usually better.

Front edges The front edges of walls and floors can be painted or stained, or papered with brick paper.

When the house is decorated outside and inside, the fronts can be hinged in place and the house is ready to furnish.

Wiring

Unless you are a competent electrician, much the simplest way to wire a dolls' house for electricity is to use the wiring kits made by the commercial dolls'-house manufacturers. These kits are available at toyshops which sell dolls' houses and furniture manufactured by Lundby and Caroline's Home, and the products of both manufacturers are interchangeable. Fully detailed instructions on installing the systems are included in the kits.

The range of light fittings is fairly comprehensive, including ceiling, wall and table lamps in many different styles. They are made mainly in plastic, but a few are brass with fabric shades, and the designs generally are good. Careful selection should provide lights suitable for most dolls' houses, as the ranges include oil lamps and chandeliers.

To wire the ceiling lights, you will need the light fittings required for each room, each with a bulb inside the shade and a small plug on the end of a wire. The light fittings stick to the ceiling by means of a sticky pad and the fine wire can be taped almost invisibly across the ceiling to emerge through the back wall of the house. The small plug can be removed so that only a tiny hole needs to be drilled through the wall to feed the wire through. The plug is then replaced when the wire emerges at the back of the house. These plugs are connected to multiple sockets on the back of the house which in turn are connected to the transformer which plugs into the mains electricity supply. There are also tiny single sockets which stick to an inside wall with wires passing through the wall beside them, for plugging in table or standard lamps.

This system, using commercial light fittings, sockets and transformer, makes wiring a simple process and produces a good soft lighting effect, the brightness of the light perfectly scaled to the size of the rooms. Although the individual light fittings are relatively inexpensive, buying sufficient does add up and the transformer is a fairly expensive item. However, the effect of a dolls' house with lights is quite magical and the result more than justifies the expense.

Suggested Building and Decorating Guide
1 Draw all pieces on the building material and cut out, including door, window and stairwell holes.
2 Tape pieces together to try assembly, making any necessary adjustments to ensure a good fit.
3 Assemble exterior, base, side walls, back wall and top ceiling.
4 Assemble interior floors and partition walls and fix in place.
5 Assemble the ridgepole and roof sections and fix in place.
6 Paper or paint exterior walls and front edges.
7 Paper, paint or tile the roof.
8 Hang doors and fit windows.
9 Cut and fix the chimney breasts in place.
10 Fill any gaps.

11 Line and paint the ceilings and painted rooms.
12 Wallpaper the rooms.
13 Fit floor-coverings.
14 Assemble, paint or stain and carpet the staircase and fix in place.
15 Stain or paint skirting boards, picture rails, door and window frames, decorative cornices and ceiling beams and fix in place.
16 Assemble, paint or stain and fix fireplace surrounds.
17 Paint or paper inside fronts.
18 Hinge fronts onto house and fix cupboard hook if required.

4 Fixtures and Fittings

If yours is a modern house, such items as the kitchen stove and sink and the bathroom fittings are often best bought from the commercial ranges of dolls'-house furniture available from most toy shops. It is difficult to make them more realistically than the commercial items, and as the prices are so reasonable it is hardly worth the effort. Old-fashioned fixtures, however, are a different matter. These are difficult to find, but quite easy to make.

Fireplaces

An empty fireplace, however elegant the surround, looks very bare. If you don't wish to have a grate, fill the fireplace with a vase of dried flowers, a paper fan or a firescreen. If, however, you prefer a grate, this should fit in style with the period of the house; for instance, the large open hearth in a Tudor house would have burned logs supported on firedogs.

Firedogs (Fig 25a) Simple firedogs can be made from soldering wire, or plastic-covered garden wire with beads stuck to the top for finials. Painted with matt-black enamel paint, these andirons look quite convincing supporting several logs in the hearth.

Basket grate (Fig 25b) A basket grate can be made from fine wood-strip. Only the front of the basket need be made as, when it is fixed in place and filled with logs, only the front is visible. Cut the cross-bar to fit the width of the grate and the upright bars high enough to hold the fire in place. Stick the uprights to the cross-bar and paint the grate front with matt-black enamel paint. Cut a small block of wood approximately ⅛in thick to fit into the

fireplace and paint this block matt black to match the grate. The basket front is then glued to the block and pushed into the fireplace.

Fireback (Fig 25b) A finishing touch for a basket grate is a fireback. This can be cut in thick cardboard or thin obeche wood and painted matt black. It can be stuck to the back wall of the fireplace or to the back of the wooden block.

Metal grates (Fig 25c) Soft lead strip, of the type sold for stained-glass window kits, or other soft metals, perhaps cut from tin cans, can be used to make a variety of grates in different styles. A small support block of wood cut to fit the fireplace opening, with a straight or curved front edge as required, will shape the grate and support it. Cut the metal strip to fit around the wooden block, ensuring that it is deep enough to contain the fire, and stick it in place. The grate can be left in its natural colour or painted with black-gloss enamel paint to represent black leading. A small knob, perhaps a glass-headed pin, pushed into the front looks effective.

Fenders (Fig 26) This soft metal can also be used to make fenders. Cut a piece of soft lead strip or soft metal long enough to enclose the front of the fireplace. The top edge can be cut into a curved shape and the fender painted with brass-coloured enamel paint. Alternatively, the gilt metallic braid for trimming lampshades makes a rather grand fender stuck to the soft metal. Square wooden beading can be used instead of metal strip — use it either as support for a braid fender or painted or stained to make a simple wooden fender.

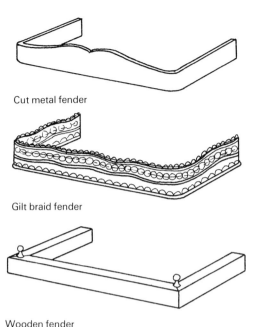

Cut metal fender

Gilt braid fender

Wooden fender

26 Fenders

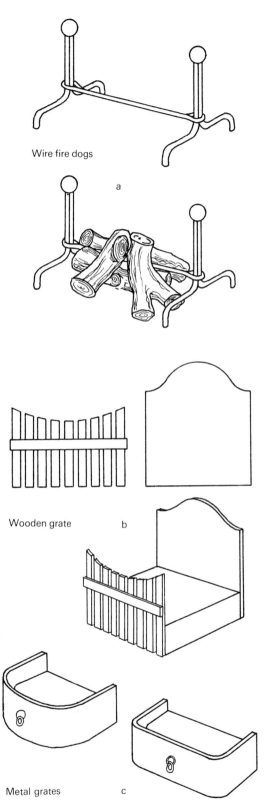

Wire fire dogs

a

Wooden grate   b

Metal grates   c

Hearths Fenders generally enclose a tiled hearth. Tiles can be cut from magazine illustrations, hand painted or modelled in clay. If you use paper tiles, a coat of varnish (colourless nail varnish works very well) will make them look more realistic. A few of the same tiles might be used to decorate the fireplace surround.

Fires The finishing touch to the fireplace is, of course, the fire. It is simple to cut some small twigs into short lengths for a log fire. Arrange them in the grate, and glue them lightly in place. A few more logs in a log basket or piled beside the fire look good.

A coal fire is a little more fiddly as, to look convincing, it should be laid like a real fire, but with the component parts glued in place. Stick a small scrap of crumpled newspaper to the wooden firegrate base, then glue slivers of wood (matchsticks split in half) to the newspaper for kindling. You could use tiny pieces of real coal or imitations like crushed black sweets (black fruit gums, left in the fridge for

25 A selection of furniture for the fireplace

46

a while, will crush well) or black glass beads. Stick each piece of coal in place, almost covering the sticks and paper. The finished result should be realistic enough to need only a match set to it to burn!

Flames Realistic flame effects are difficult to achieve, so we generally lay a coal or log fire as if ready for lighting. If you want a burning fire though, the simplest method is probably to stick a picture of a burning fire from a magazine to the back of the fireplace opening; then lay the fire in front of the flame picture, using blackened logs and red-tinfoil sweet papers, or coal and red tinfoil, to give the impression of a burning fire. An ingenious electrician might be able to contrive a red light bulb in the fireplace, discreetly hidden by logs or coal, which would look effective.

Lighting

The light fittings in this section are designed for effect, rather than practical use. It might be possible to wire some of these ideas to an electric transformer, as was described in the previous chapter on electric lighting for a modern house, but this section concentrates on old-fashioned methods, such as candles, oil lamps and gas lights.

Candles (Fig 27a)   Candles, one of the earliest forms of lighting, are appropriate to any period house. The small candles sold for birthday cakes are the simplest, but they are rather thick — this looks well in a castle where thick candles are appropriate, but in a house they look like birthday-cake candles! The best solution is to dip your own candles, by repeatedly dipping a fine wick into melted candle wax until the required thickness is built up. If this is rather more effort than you wish to make, cocktail sticks cut to the right length and painted ivory look quite effective glued into candlesticks.

The candlesticks might be brass or china ones bought from dolls'-house shops, or home-made ones, using tubular-shaped beads, fine brass tubing, or dowelling and buttons. Long tubular beads, stuck to small buttons and painted to represent china will make a fine

27 Candlesticks, oil lamps and gas brackets

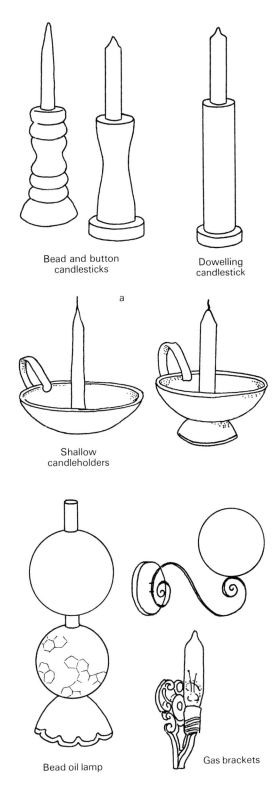

Bead and button candlesticks

Dowelling candlestick

a

Shallow candleholders

Bead oil lamp

Gas brackets

b

c

pair of candlesticks with convenient holes for the candles. Dish-shaped buttons, painted to represent pewter or brass, make good shallow candleholders, preferably with a wire-loop handle stuck to one side. Lengths of dowelling stuck to buttons and painted to imitate brass or china make simple but effective candlesticks; the candle must be stuck firmly to the top of the dowelling.

Oil lamps (Fig 27b) The designs of oil lamps vary, but the basic parts are a base which holds the oil, a chimney and a globe or shade.

Simple but pretty oil lamps can be made from beads, buttons and jewellery. Choose crystal or opaque beads of the appropriate size for the base and globe of the lamp, plus a prettily shaped button for it to stand on, and cut a short length of empty biro refill for the chimney. Super-glue the pieces together, taking care that they are straight — start at the bottom of the lamp and build upwards. Glue the base bead to the upturned button; stick on a short piece of biro refill, followed by the globe of the lamp, and a longer length of biro on top. The base bead and button could be painted with white-gloss enamel paint to represent china and decorated with painted flowers or transfers, or the base could be enamel-painted to imitate brass. Coloured glass or opaque white glass beads look pretty, and typically Victorian, as both bases and globes.

28 Kitchen stove made of a mustard tin and fitted into a deep fireplace

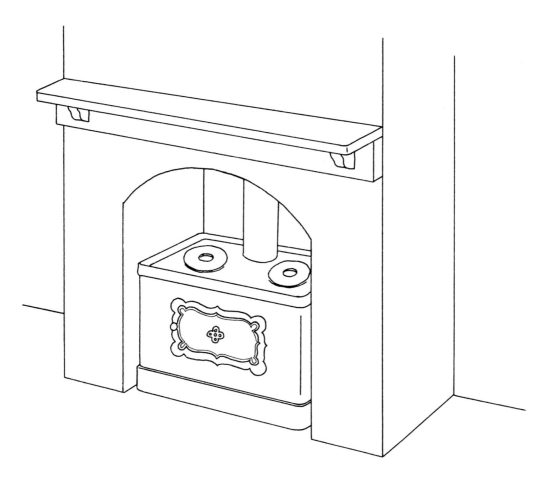

Gas lights (Fig 27c) Gas lighting became general in town houses by the 1850s, though country people still had only oil lamps and candles. Gas brackets, which were usually placed on either side of the chimney breast, can be made from fancy picture hooks (sold in art and craft shops) glued to the wall, or plastic-covered wire bent into a scroll. The wire should be painted a brass colour and attached to a button (using its holes) with fuse wire. The button is then stuck to the wall. The gas lights can be made from fairy-light bulbs or faceted glass beads glued or wired to the bracket.

Commercial lights It is worth considering the commercial dolls'-house light fittings, even if your house is not wired for electricity. It is simple to remove the wires from the lights, and many of them are designed to fit into period houses. The oil lamps and chandeliers are particularly effective, even when they do not light.

Kitchen range
A simple, but effective, kitchen range can be made from a tin — the smallest size of 'Colmans' mustard is the perfect size; another possibility is a Spam tin.

Clean the tin. If it has a lid, this can provide a base to stand the stove on. If the tin is too tall, cut a piece off the open end with scissors. Turn the tin upside-down and paint it all over with black-gloss enamel paint, except for the raised rim around the now top edge which is left unpainted.

The metal label from an aftershave lotion such as Brut (or a similar fancy metal label, perhaps a buckle) with the centre painted in black enamel, leaving the raised pattern around the edge unpainted, is then stuck to the front of the stove to represent the oven door. A black map pin can be pushed through to represent the door handle. The stove pipe is made from a felt-pen casing or a piece of dowelling, black enamel painted. This is glued to the centre back of the top of the stove, and the end of the pipe disappears up the chimney. Hot plates are made of silver-coloured washers, stuck one either side of the stove.

Although the oven door does not open, this stove is convincing and suitable for a variety of old-fashioned kitchens. It could be sited in a large fireplace opening or used as a free-standing range against an outside wall, in which case the chimney pipe should seem to disappear through the wall.

Kitchen sinks
Kitchen sinks can be made of metal or plastic lids, wood or clay, all of which, painted in the appropriate colour, are quite effective. The simplest kind is made from a shallow rectangular metal lid, for example, the lid of a Vaseline jar, which is the right size and shape for an old-fashioned pottery sink. Paint the lid with several coats of Humbrol enamel in a matt yellow-brown colour to represent pottery, or a creamy-white gloss for the fire-clay found in Victorian kitchens (Fig 29).

If you have no suitably shaped lid, or if you wish to make the deeper sink which came into general use during the 1920s, a box of obeche wood will make a good sink. Use the directions given in the section on furniture-making for a dower chest or blanket box to construct a small box of the shape and size you require. Sand the top edges and all the corners smooth and rounded and give the sink several coats of paint (Fig 30).

The most realistic sinks are modelled in clay. You can use ordinary clay which will need firing, or — more practically — Das or a similar material which dries hard without firing. Clay is easiest to work when it is 'leather dry' — so work it to make it malleable, then leave it to dry a little before beginning your modelling. The sink can be modelled using the finger-pot method, but, unless you are experienced in working with clay, it is simpler to roll it out like pastry and cut a bottom and four sides with a knife. Use the clay or Das fairly thick as this will give substance to the sink and make the pieces easier to handle. Assemble the four sides and the bottom and join them by damping the edges liberally with water, using a small paintbrush. When the clay is almost dry, use the paintbrush and water to smooth the surfaces and round the top and sides of the sink. When it is completely dry (with Das this usually takes about twelve hours), paint the sink as described for the tin lid.

Mount the sink on a frame made of fine

29 Shallow sink mounted on brick piers

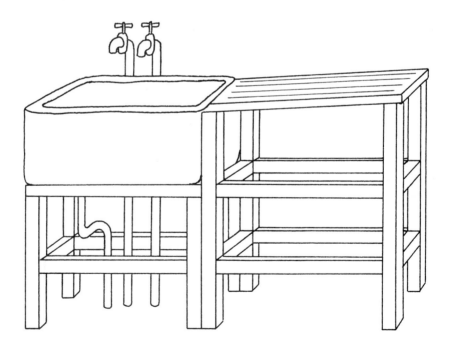

30 Deep sink and draining board mounted on a
wooden frame

square beading (Fig 30), or on brick piers made of suitable small blocks of wood painted to represent bricks or covered in brick paper (Fig 29).

Draining boards should be appropriate to the sink; for example, the oldest kind of shallow pottery sink would have a slate or stone slab as a draining board. A roofing slate will split easily, and a piece the required size can be cut with a hacksaw. Alternatively, a piece of obeche wood, preferably with grooves cut with the point of the scissors, would be suitable for the deeper fireclay sink. The draining board can be supported on small wooden brackets stuck to the wall, or mounted on a wooden framework like the sink.

Taps and pipes Taps and pipes add the necessary finish to the kitchen sink. The

In this house the space under the stairs has been put to good use — the loo is modelled in Das, the cistern is made from a small plastic box. In the kitchen, the sink (also modelled in Das) has a slate draining board supported on brick piers *(Jonathon Bosley)*

plumbing in old houses was usually obvious, so a waste-pipe and at least one tap are required. The pipes can be made of fine dowelling painted lead-grey and stuck to the wall behind the sink. This will serve for a simple straight pipe, but to get some interesting bends in the pipes, it is best to use either lead strip, which is easy to work and already the right colour, or plastic-covered garden wire which can be bent to the required shape with pliers and will need a coat of matt lead-grey paint.

Taps are rather more tricky and we have not

51

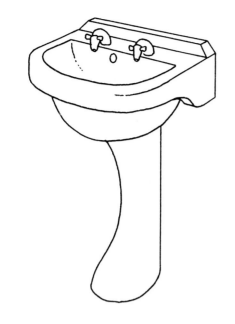

yet discovered a simple method. There are, however, several possibilities, depending on the materials at hand. A tap from a piece of miniature, modern, bathroom furniture might be utilised if given a coat of brass-coloured paint. Various plastic oddments can be used for taps, for example, those left in plastic model kits when the components have all been broken away from the supports make credible tap shapes when painted and glued in place. Gilt jewellery findings, or even broken scraps of gilt jewellery, can be glued with super glue into a tap shape; for example, the wing-shaped piece from the back of an ear-ring stuck above a barrel-shaped necklace catch. If all else fails, taps in lead or brass are available from the specialist shops.

Bathroom fittings
Bathroom fittings are only appropriate to a house of the late nineteenth or the twentieth century, as until then bathrooms did not exist. Modest households managed with a tin bath used in front of the kitchen fire and hung on the wall when not in use. An oval-shaped lozenge tin with a wire-loop handle and the top edges gently splayed outwards will make a reasonable tin bath. Grander households had hip baths (try a china soap dish or Das model), usually decorated with flowers. Curious slipper baths, shaped like large shallow bowls, were also used in the bedroom — these could again be modelled in Das or, possibly, the sugar bowl from a dolls' tea-set would serve.

The early bathroom fittings were elaborately made of cast iron or porcelain. It is possible to adapt a modern plastic bathroom set with two coats of creamy-white, gloss enamel paint, to make it look like porcelain, and boxing of mahogany-stained obeche wood (Fig 31). The bath and basin look quite acceptable when the taps are painted with brass paint, and perhaps a flower decoration applied (paint or transfers). The loo needs more effort: firstly, the low-level cistern must be cut away with a craft knife, then the seat must be painted brown to represent wood and the painted flower decoration applied. If the cistern is the appropriate size, it can be painted matt grey and mounted on the wall on wooden brackets above the loo. If, however, the original cistern is unusable, a replacement

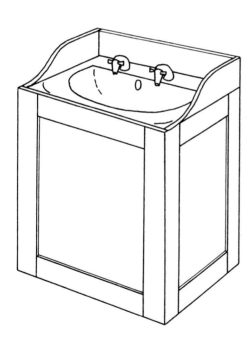

31 Modern commercial washbasin, boxed-in for a Victorian effect

can be made from a plastic box, such as a cut-down Tic Tac sweet container, painted and mounted as above. A pull made from a short length of jewellery chain with a bead for a handle is stuck to the side of the cistern.

The intrepid or experienced clay modeller might try making an old-fashioned bath, loo and basin in Das, using the finger-pot technique and 'leather dry' clay. The ingenious might try using various containers such as the plastic pots which contain individual portions of jam, painted with several coats of enamel paint.

A geyser (Fig 32) To complete the bathroom fittings, mount a geyser on a corner shelf over the bath. A piece sawn from thick dowelling or the top of a broom handle (shorter and fatter for the Victorian bathroom, longer and thinner for the Edwardian effect), will make the cylinder of the geyser. Paint this with copper enamel. Pipes can be made of lead strip or plastic-covered garden wire, pushed and glued into small holes drilled in the cylinder. Here, as in the kitchen, the plumbing should be obvious and should be seen to connect the geyser to a gas pipe. A small spout, a piece of wire or lead strip glued into a hole in the cylinder, should be positioned so that hot water can pour into the bath.

Furnish the bathroom with bath mat, towels, sponge, loofah, soap and toilet roll, made from pieces of the life-size items, and the realism is complete.

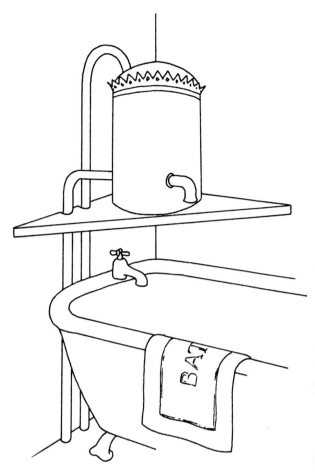

32 Geyser mounted on a corner shelf above the bath

5 Furniture

The pieces of furniture you choose to make for your dolls' house will depend on the period of the house, the space available in the rooms, your own taste and ability. Some research into period furniture, in reference books, stately homes or antique shops, can be very helpful, both for finding designs typical of the period and for choosing pieces for each room.

As with building and decorating, tastes in furniture have changed considerably through the centuries as a result of fashion, need, and increasing prosperity. Medieval trestles, benches and straw-mattressed box beds gave way to Tudor chairs, tables and buffets with carved bulbous legs, and massive curtained four-poster beds. The great houses of the eighteenth century required suitably elegant furniture to grace them; the nineteenth century brought its classical revival; and Victorian taste found expression in solid carved mahogany and over-stuffed horsehair.

Each generation, as far as means allowed, refurnished in the latest style, and each period had its typical pieces, like the Tudor chest, indispensable in its time for both storage and seating but rarely found in later houses. Regency is typified by the Grecian sofa, upholstered in striped fabric with bolster cushions; the Victorian parlour is immediately evoked by a round pedestal table or mahogany chiffonier. Modern houses too are subject to changing tastes: the chrome and glass popular in the sixties and the stripped pine of the seventies are still to be found in most modern houses. Furniture catalogues (Habitat for example) and homes magazines are the best sources of reference.

However, few people have the resources or the inclination to redecorate and refurnish as often as fashion changes, so most homes are a mixture of old and new, and doubtless always have been. A Georgian house might contain a Tudor chest, though it may be relegated to the nursery; a Victorian house might have a Regency workbox, just as a modern house might have — and be proud of — an Edwardian kitchen dresser.

When choosing furniture for your house, consider the space each piece will occupy in the various rooms. It is frustrating to make a piece of furniture and then find that you cannot arrange the room to fit it in — careful planning will avoid this problem. For example, in a bedroom the bed is the largest piece of furniture, and occupies the most space, so if the bed is placed first, the smaller pieces can be planned to fit around it. If you have the bed against one wall, a window in another wall and a chimney breast on the third wall, there is probably nowhere to put a wardrobe! As in a real house, doors need enough space to open without obstruction, and cupboard doors and drawers should be accessible. By placing the largest pieces first, and planning other pieces to fit into specific spaces, eg a chest of drawers or a bookcase in an alcove, a pleasing arrangement of furniture can be built up.

Some pieces show to better advantage in one position than another; for example, a kitchen dresser filled with plates, cups and saucers, looks best viewed from the front where the details can be seen most clearly — this aspect must also be considered when planning the room layout. Dolls'-house rooms are, in some ways, more like stage sets than rooms — they are three-sided boxes, designed to be looked at from the front — so the furniture has to be arranged for the most pleasing effect

33 The basic tools for making wooden furniture

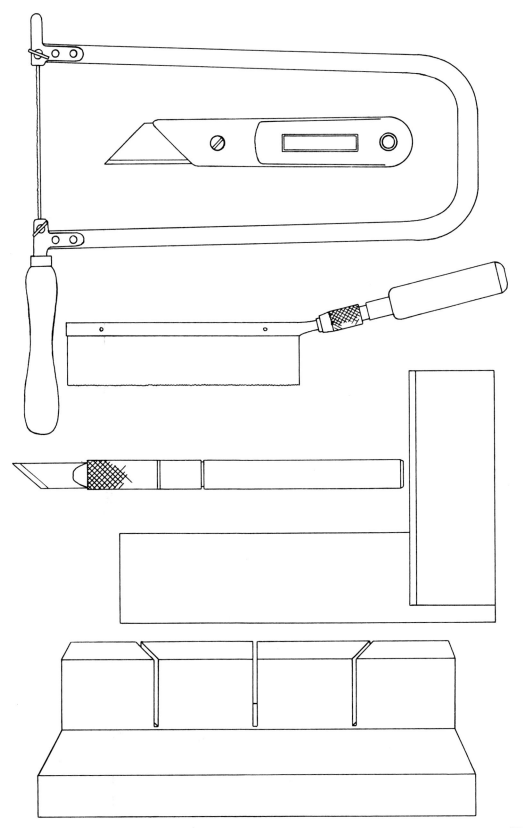

55

rather than the most practical arrangement.

This chapter covers the basic tools, materials and methods we use to make furniture. Patterns may be taken from the project chapters in Part II, which include scale patterns for all the pieces in the houses. These patterns can be adapted, if required, to a variety of period styles — by using a thicker wood, adding a pediment, staining or painting to a different finish, and other such minor alterations. The projects cover a wide range of furniture pieces, which are simple to cut and assemble using the methods described here. Alternatively, you might prefer to draw your own furniture patterns.

The various pieces of furniture fall into categories, eg hinged cupboards, tables, upholstered furniture, etc, which are dealt with individually after the basic method. The notes on tools and materials apply to all the wooden furniture in this chapter.

Tools and materials

Tools The tools we recommend for making wooden furniture are: a razor-toothed saw (small saw with a fine-toothed blade which will cut cleanly through wood); a fretsaw with a fine blade, for cutting curved pieces; a craft knife with a supply of new blades; a try-square for marking accurate angles; a mitre block for cutting angles; a white wood-glue and a fine-grade abrasive paper such as flour paper (Fig 33).

Materials You can, of course, make dolls'-house furniture of almost any wood if it can be planed to a suitable thickness and the grain is reasonably small. Obeche wood, which can be bought in sheets in a variety of thicknesses from art and craft shops, is excellent. It is light, although it is a hardwood, and is easily cut with a craft knife or a fine-bladed saw. Obeche can be painted, or stained to imitate almost any wood, using the appropriate wood stain. We do not recommend balsa wood for dolls'-house furniture, it is flimsy and crumbly and the result is unrealistic.

A good selection of wood stains is available from DIY shops, together with matt and gloss polyurethane varnishes. If you intend to varnish your furniture, avoid a too-glossy finish by diluting the varnish with a little white spirit. For painting furniture, try the small tins of Humbrol enamel paints, using a coat of gloss over an undercoat of matt. The undercoat should be allowed to dry thoroughly and sanded before the top coat is applied. Alternatively, poster paint or gouache can be used, but will need a coat of varnish for protection. We do not recommend household gloss paints, as these are too dense for painting such small pieces. We prefer the subtle effect of polished wood, so we generally finish wooden furniture with a coat of amateur French polish and several coats of a good wax polish.

Recommended products The following list of tools and products are those which we use and recommend. The first-time housebuilder might find it helpful to know which products to buy when faced with a variety of similar brands in the DIY or art and craft shop.

Xacto razor saw
Eclipse fretsaw (12in)
Xacto craft knife and blades
Swan Morton craft knife and blades

Evostik woodworking adhesive
UHU all-purpose clear adhesive
Blackfriars French polish
Blackfriars button polish
Blackfriars wood stains
Goddards cabinet makers' wax polish

Method
The following directions apply to all the pieces of wooden furniture described in this section.

Firstly, draw the furniture plans onto the wood, using a sharp pencil and ensuring that the grain of the wood lies in the correct direction on each piece. Use a set square to mark the right-angles. Cut the pieces out, using a razor-toothed saw for straight lines and a fretsaw for curves. When cutting across the grain of the wood, scoring the cutting line first with a craft knife will provide a clear groove to guide the saw. Sand each piece carefully, using abrasive paper wrapped around a small block of wood to avoid rounding the edges of the pieces. Check that the pieces fit well together, and then stain them before assembly, as wood stain will not 'take' over glue. Applying the wood stain with a soft cloth gives a better finish than brushing it on. When the stain is thoroughly dry, glue the pieces together, supporting them if necessary until the glue is dry. Varnish, paint or polish are applied when the piece is assembled. For the best results with polish, carefully apply one coat of amateur French polish to the well-sanded piece with a small paintbrush or soft cloth. When this is dry, sand carefully again and then apply several coats of wax polish, well-buffed between each coat.

If care is taken at each stage in the assembly, especially with the finishing, the result should be a realistic piece of miniature furniture.

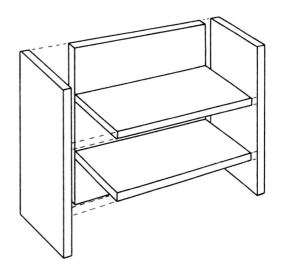

34 Assembling a basic shelf unit

Shelf units (Fig 34) This method for making a shelf unit can be used for making wall shelves, the top part of a kitchen dresser or a free-standing wall unit or bookcase — only the sizes vary.

First, cut the back of the shelf unit to the required height and width. This is generally cut in the thinnest wood available, and the piece can be scored lengthwise with a scissor blade to represent planking. Next, cut the side pieces the same height as the back piece and the full depth — the back will fit inside the side pieces. The top and bottom are cut to fit, or, as for the kitchen dresser, to overhang at the top edge. The shelves are then cut to the required width and depth.

The plain shelf unit is suitable for a bookcase or a simple kitchen dresser, but if the sides are cut with a fretsaw into a curved shape and a similar curved piece is fixed under the top front edge, it becomes a more elaborate dresser top. A curved pediment can be added for a Chippendale effect.

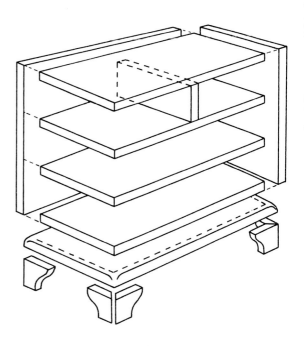

Drawer units (Figs 35 and 36) The shell of the drawer unit is the same as the shelf unit, except that it is generally deeper. Whether the drawer unit is to have one or six drawers (or any other number!) the shell is made, assembled and stained before the drawers are made.

To make the drawers, cut the drawer fronts first — to fit as snugly as possible into the drawer spaces. The base of the drawer, cut to the same width as the drawer front and

35 Assembling the chest-of-drawers carcase

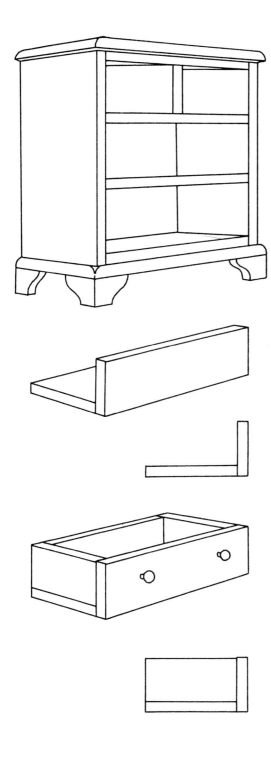

trimmed to fit into the drawer space, is glued to the drawer front. The side and back pieces are then cut to fit onto the base to complete the 'box'. Made this way, the drawer should fit well, but glide easily in and out of the drawer space. Drawer handles can be made from map pins, beads, the loops of hook and loop fastenings (these need to be pulled apart slightly with pliers), pieces of dowelling or fine square beading. Tiny, brass, turned or drop handles for dolls'-house furniture are also sold by the specialist shops.

A set of four, five or six drawers, one above another, makes a chest of drawers. Two drawers, side-by-side, can be incorporated into a kitchen dresser. One small drawer can be used in a kitchen table or dressing table.

Cupboard units (Fig 37) Cupboard units are all basically boxes with hinged doors. There are tiny brass hinges available from the specialist shops, but the following method successfully uses dressmakers' pins for hinging.

The back, sides and base of the cupboard are made the same way as shelf and drawer units, but the top is not fixed on at this stage. If shelves are required inside the cupboard, they must be cut to allow space for the doors to close in front of them. The door or doors are cut to fit as snugly as possible into the front. A fine hole is bored with a dressmaker's pin in the top and bottom corners of the door, as close to the edge as possible, taking care to work gently so as not to split the wood. The pins are then pushed into the holes and snipped off with about ⅛in protruding. The doors are positioned on the front of the cupboard and small holes bored in the base to receive the pins. The top of the cupboard is then fitted, and small holes made to receive the pins. When these are correctly positioned, the top can be fixed in place. It may be necessary to sand the hinged edges of the doors slightly rounded to ensure that the doors swing open freely — check this before the top is glued in place. For handles, see suggestions for drawer handles.

Cupboards with one door will make broom or bedside cupboards, depending on size. With two doors, they can be used as base units for kitchen dressers, wardrobes or sideboards,

36 Assembling the drawers

etc. Combinations of shelf, drawer and cupboard units can make kitchen dressers, sideboards or modern wall units. They can also be used to make built-in furniture for a modern house.

Tables (Fig 38) The basic design and method for a table with four legs can be adapted to a round, square, rectangular or oval top as required, or, with the legs shortened, a coffee table or stool.

Cut the table top from wood of a suitable thickness, appropriate to the style of the intended table. The legs are cut from square beading or dowelling, and can be 'turned' by whittling with a craft knife, but it is important that they are all exactly the same length! A frieze of wood (thinner wood than that used for the table top) is cut in four pieces to fit the underside of the table a little way in from the edge. The amount of the overhang will depend on the style of the table. The frieze is stuck in place to form a rectangle: either 'closed', so that the table legs are stuck inside the corners; or 'open', so that the table legs fitted into each corner complete the rectangle. After the pieces have been sanded and stained, assemble the table, supporting the legs straight while the glue dries. The frieze will help to hold them in place, but additional support may be needed. On certain styles of table, stretchers cut from the same beading or dowelling look well. These are cut to fit between the legs when the table is completed, stained and glued into place.

The basic table can be varied enormously by the way it is finished. The traditional dining table, whether square, rectangular, round or oval, usually has a highly polished wooden top. The traditional kitchen table, usually rectangular with heavy legs has a well-scrubbed wooden top. The modern dining table could be the round-topped, white-painted kind, and the modern kitchen table might have a formica or Fablon top. Glass-topped coffee tables can be made from a piece of perspex with well-sanded edges.

This method can also be used to make stools by cutting a smaller top and short legs. If the seat is to be upholstered, cut a small piece of foam or wadding to fit the seat, cover it in fabric and glue it in place.

37 Assembling a basic cupboard with pin hinges

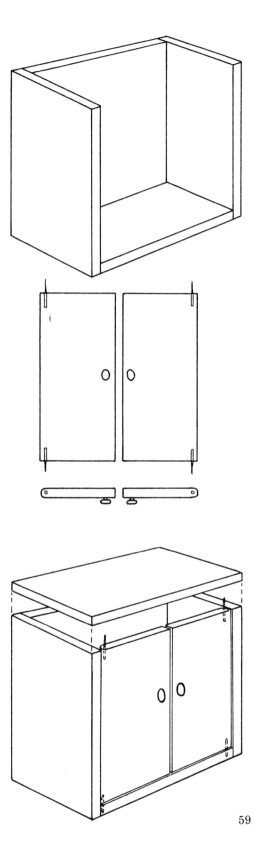

Shelf and drawer units assembled to make a basic kitchen dresser. The kitchen table and ladderback chair are shown here in their simplest forms

Refectory tables and benches (Fig 39) The top of an old refectory table is of thick wood, thinner if it is one of the modern pine type. Cut the narrow, rectangular top piece and the two legs from the same thickness of wood. The top of the table can be scored with a scissor blade to represent planking. The legs can be plain rectangular pieces, or cut with a fretsaw to a curved shape; they are fixed in place at each end of the table, in from the edge. A stretcher is cut to fit between the legs and glued in place.

Benches are made in the same way, but the stretcher is fixed immediately under the seat.

Chairs There are many methods for making wooden chairs; here we describe three of them.

The first chair (Fig 40) is made of thickish wood, in three pieces; the back (including back legs), the front, and the seat, which is glued between the back and front. The style of the chair can be varied by the choice of stain or paint, the shape of the back and the use of upholstery, made by cutting small foam or wadding pads to fit the seat and back, covering these in fabric and sticking them in place. Stretchers, if appropriate, can be cut to fit and glued in place between the legs.

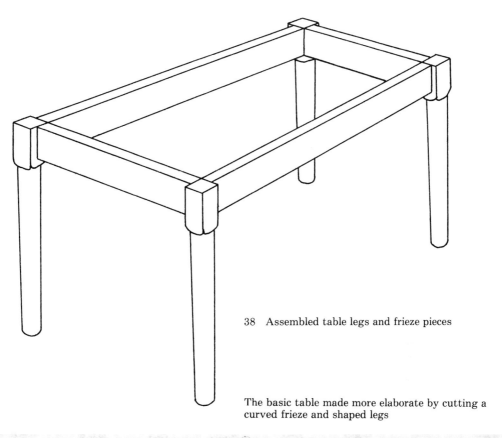

38   Assembled table legs and frieze pieces

The basic table made more elaborate by cutting a
curved frieze and shaped legs

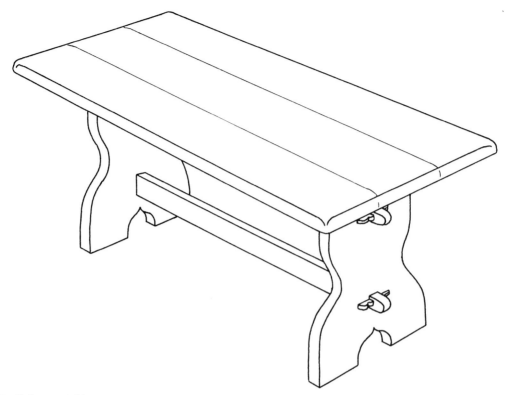

39   Refectory table

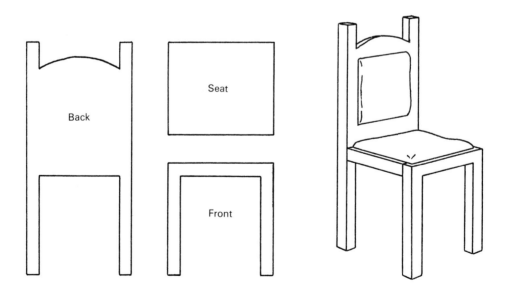

Back

Seat

Front

40   Scale pattern for a simple chair

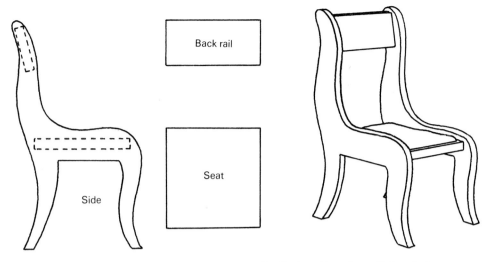

Back rail

Side

Seat

41 Scale pattern for a dining chair

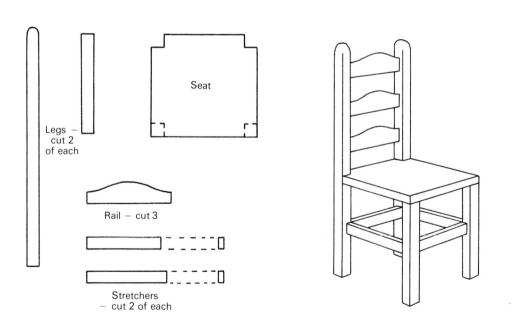

Seat

Legs –
cut 2
of each

Rail – cut 3

Stretchers
– cut 2 of each

42 Scale pattern for a ladderback chair

The second chair (Fig 41) is made in four pieces, two sides, with the seat and back rail sandwiched between them. The sides can be cut with straight edges, or with curved back and legs, but the wood used should be reasonably thick to give substance to the sides of the chair. This chair also can be upholstered with fabric-covered pads, glued in place and can have stretchers fitted between the legs.

The third method is a little more complicated than the previous two, but can be used to make a variety of chairs in the ladderback style (Fig 42). The legs can be cut from fine square beading or dowelling; the rails from dowelling, beading or wood-strip, either used flat or steamed over a kettle and bent to a curved shape (while it dries, tape it around an object which has the correct curve eg a jam jar). The seat can be either a solid wooden one, or dowelling rails infilled with woven raffia to imitate a rush seat.

Cut the back legs to the length of the finished height of the chair, and the front legs to the height of the seat. If the seat is to be a wooden one, cut a square piece of wood and from the back corners cut out square notches the size of the back legs. Glue the front legs under the front edge of the seat and the back legs into the notches cut in the seat. Ensure that the legs are straight as the glue dries, and that the chair stands firm without wobbling. The back rails and the stretchers are then cut to fit and glued in place between the legs. If the seat is to be a rush one, the front and back legs are cut as before and stretchers of dowelling or beading are cut to fit between the legs, back, front and two sides. These are glued in place, making a frame. Raffia is then woven over and under the frame to make the rush seat. The leg stretchers and back rails are then glued in place. If the chair is made of round dowelling, cocktail sticks or toothpicks can be used for the stretchers, drilling small holes in the legs to take the ends.

Dower chest or blanket box (Fig 43) The dower chest is made of a medium-thin wood, the lid slightly thicker. Cut the base, front and back the same length. Cut the two ends the width of the base plus the thickness of the back and front. Stick these together to form a box, with the base inside. The lid is cut

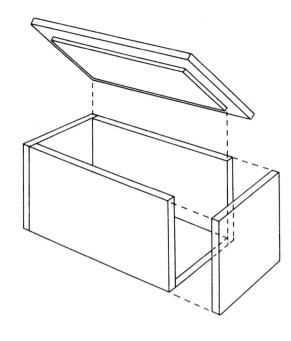

43   Assembling a simple blanket or toy box

slightly larger than the box so that it overhangs. Cut a second piece of wood to fit snugly into the open top of the box and glue it to the underside of the lid — or the lid could be hinged in place with tiny hinges.

The front and sides of the chest can be panelled with a fine wood-strip mitred at the corners, or a stencilled design could be painted on the front and lid. Given a coat of brightly coloured paint, the chest would make a good toy box for the nursery. Used without the lid, with bead feet or rockers, it would make an old-fashioned cradle.

Beds

The bed in its simplest form is a divan, but even in a modern house it is made more interesting by the addition of a headboard and footboard.

As a rough guide for size, in the 1:12 scale house the bed will be about 6¼ × 3in for a

The Victorian town house (Chapter 8) is small and easy to build. The front, with its sash windows and window boxes, hinges open to show these three elegantly proportioned Victorian rooms

single bed, or 6¼ × 4½in for a double bed. In the 1:16 scale house a single bed is about 5 × 2½in and a double bed 5 × 3½in. These measurements can, of course, be altered slightly to suit individual taste or to fit a bed into a specific space in the dolls' house. As a general rule, modern beds are lower than old-fashioned ones but this is also a matter of taste. The example shown here is made in obeche wood, but it could be adapted with a padded headboard, or abandoned in favour of a brass bedstead made from brass tubing soldered together. (Brass tubing can be bought from hobby shops — or use metal knitting needles or even dowelling painted with Humbrol enamel paint.)

(above left) The main feature of the Victorian attic bedroom is the half-tester bed with its rose-pink silk hangings and bedspread

(below left) These whitewashed walls, built-in dresser and tiled floor make a pleasant, airy kitchen for the Victorian cook

A bed with curved head and footboards; and a washstand, a small table with curved back and side pieces

Basic bed (Fig 44)   Cut a base of the appropriate size from wood. The headboard and footboard are cut to the same width as the base, and two side rails about ½in deep are cut the same length as the base. The pieces are sanded, stained and assembled with wood glue: the side rails are stuck to either side of the base, the head and footboards are then stuck at each end. The bed-posts, cut from 4mm wooden beading, are then fitted into the notches left between the side rails and head and footboards. Ensure that all four bedposts are properly aligned.

Half-tester   A half-tester bed is made in the same way except that, instead of a headboard, a rectangle of wood the same width as the bed and approximately the same length is glued upright to the head end of the bed. The roof of

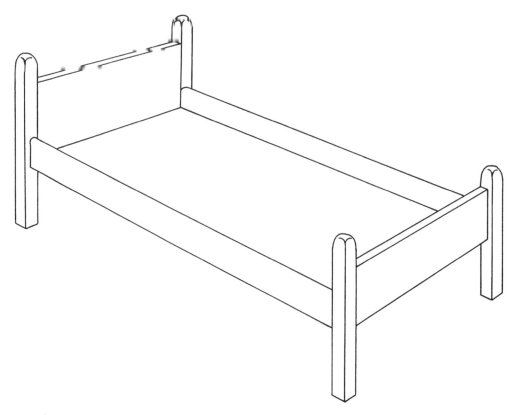

44 Basic bed with head and footboards

the half-tester is approximately one-quarter of the length of the bed, and is glued to the back piece to form a right-angle. The back piece can be stained, painted or covered in fabric to match the bed curtains.

Four-poster (Fig 45)   A four-poster bed can be made using dowelling, fine square beading or paintbrush handles for the posts with a frame of fine square beading to support the canopy. It can have a backpiece, as for the half-tester, or a headboard.

Curtains and frills for the half-tester or the four-poster are made using the same method and fabrics as for window curtains. The curtains are cut and narrowly hemmed to the required length and width, then gathered at the top edge and stuck in place on the side of the tester roof or the top frame of the four-poster. They look best if they are looped back to the head of the bed with narrow ribbon or a strip of matching fabric. If you wish to roof over the four-poster bed, this can be done with

wood or fabric. Cut the wood to exactly the size of the canopy frame, stain it or cover the underside with fabric and glue in place to the canopy frame. Alternatively, cut a rectangle of fabric slightly larger than the frame, turn a narrow hem all-round and glue the fabric to the frame, stretching it taut. A frill, although not essential, finishes the bed properly. Cut a long, narrow strip of fabric, hem the bottom edge, turn in and gather the top edge and stick in place over the curtains, around the sides and front of the half-tester, or the canopy frame of the four-poster.

Bedclothes A mattress can be made by stuffing a cotton bag with wadding or cotton-wool, but has a better shape if the side edges are boxed with a narrow edge of stitching. If you wish, the mattress can be 'buttoned' with French knots. If the mattress is made slightly smaller than the base, this will allow space for the bedcovers to be tucked in, and the side rails will hold everything firmly in place.

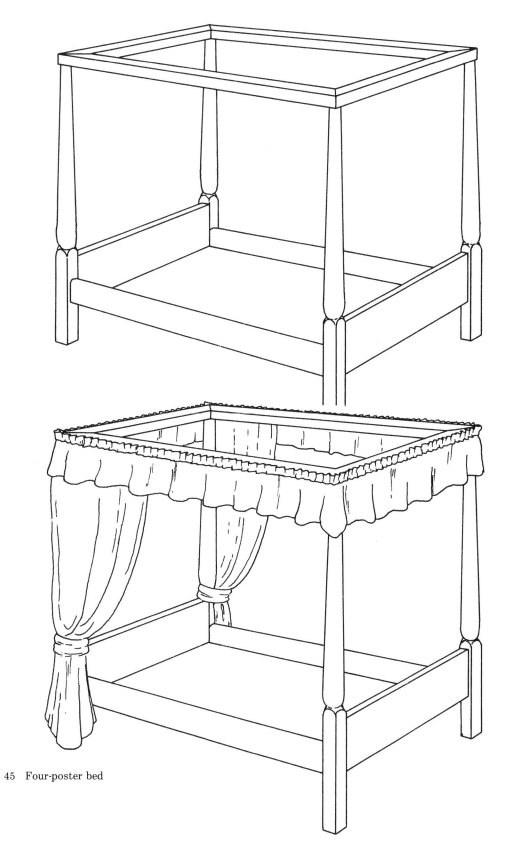

45   Four-poster bed

Sheets and pillowcases can be made of fine cotton; old handkerchiefs are perfect — white or cream for old houses, but almost anything goes in a modern house. Double beds look better with two small pillows rather than one large one. Blankets, perhaps cut from an old vest with edges ribbon bound or blanket stitched, are suitably lightweight. Alternatively, Viyella, flannel or winceyette all make good blankets. An eiderdown or bedspread adds the finishing touch: an eiderdown should be of lightly padded, fine fabric; a bedspread matching the bed or window curtains looks good. A miniature patchwork quilt can be quite a challenge, but well worth the effort — choose firmly woven, cotton fabrics, but if your sewing skill is not up to the real thing, a fake can be made by drawing small squares onto a plain-coloured cotton and filling them in with various coloured felt pens.

Upholstered furniture

For the upholstered furniture described in this section, use a cardboard base, thin foam or wadding for padding, and fabric covers. The finished results, if the pieces are carefully made, are very realistic, but it is important to use the correct materials. The cardboard should be good-quality art cardboard (available from art shops) — cereal packets or cardboard boxes are not suitable. The foam should be about ⅛in thick, and is preferable to wadding. The choice of fabric for the covers is important — avoid anything thick, heavy or with a large pattern. It is worthwhile finding colours and patterns in the right scale and style for the house. Felt is a useful fabric to work with as it does not fray and stretches easily; very fine velveteen, cotton, and fine wool or silk are all suitable, but man-made fabrics such as crimplene are not, as they stretch too much. The choice of shape and fabric will make the piece suitable for the type of house you are furnishing.

Cut a cardboard base from the pattern; then cut a piece of foam or wadding the same shape but about ½in larger all-round. Cut two fabric covers, one on the straight grain of the fabric, one on the bias grain, also about ½in larger all-round than the pattern. The outline of the pattern is used as the sewing line on the fabric covers.

Score the two vertical dotted lines on the pattern onto the cardboard base, using a

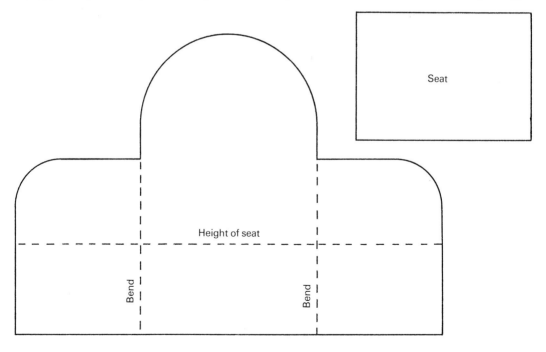

46   Scale pattern for an upholstered armchair

scissor blade — this allows the arms of the chair to bend forward. Glue the padding to the inside of the chair, rolling the ½in overlap over the edges and glueing it to the back all the way round. This will give a padded inside and padded edges to the chair (Fig 48a).

Sew together the two fabric covers, right sides inside, using small tight stitches to make a strong seam. Clip the curves slightly and turn the cover right sides out. With the bias-cut side of the cover to the inside of the chair and the straight grain to the outside, gently stretch the cover over the padded cardboard. The raw edges at the bottom are turned in and slipstitched closed. The more tightly the cover fits, the better the chair will look, so use the exact pattern line (the outline of the cardboard base) as your sewing line and pull the cover down as tightly as possible when slipstitching the edges (Fig 48b).

The seat of the chair is made by cutting a block of balsa wood to fit inside the back and arms, to the height required. The block is

The upholstered armchair, made on a cardboard base, is shown here with a pin-hinged wardrobe and a chest of drawers

padded and covered in fabric like a parcel, with the ends glued firmly in place; the back and sides of the block are glued and put in place inside the chair. Pins pushed through from the outside will hold everything in place until the glue is dry (Fig 48c).

If you want a frilled skirt on the chair, cut a strip of matching fabric long enough to go around the chair one-and-a-half times and a little deeper than the finished frill is to be. Seam the short edges together and turn a small hem on one long edge. Turn the other long edge in and crease the fold, then run a row of small gathering stitches as close to the fold as possible. Place the frill on the chair and pull up the gathers to fit. Distribute the gathers evenly and slip stitch the top edge of the frill in place.

Obviously, the neater the work, the better

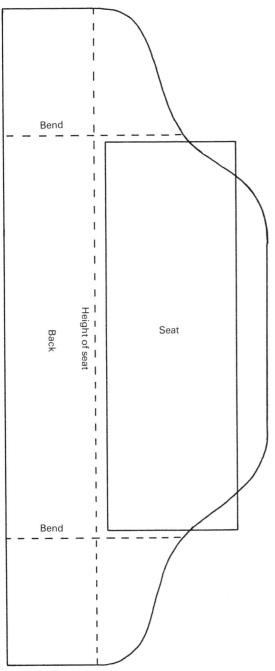

Bend

Back

Height of seat

Seat

Bend

the finished result will be — care taken with the cutting, sticking and stitching is well rewarded. To neaten the underside of chairs, sofas or stools, a small piece of felt can be stuck on to cover any raw edges, and small blocks of wood or wooden beads can be stuck under each corner for feet. As trimming, narrow lampshade braid or russian braid piping can be sewn in place. Cushions in a matching or harmonizing fabric, or scatter cushions, made of small pieces of fabric or ribbon, can be arranged along the back of the sofa, or tucked invitingly into the corner of an armchair.

47 Scale pattern for an upholstered sofa

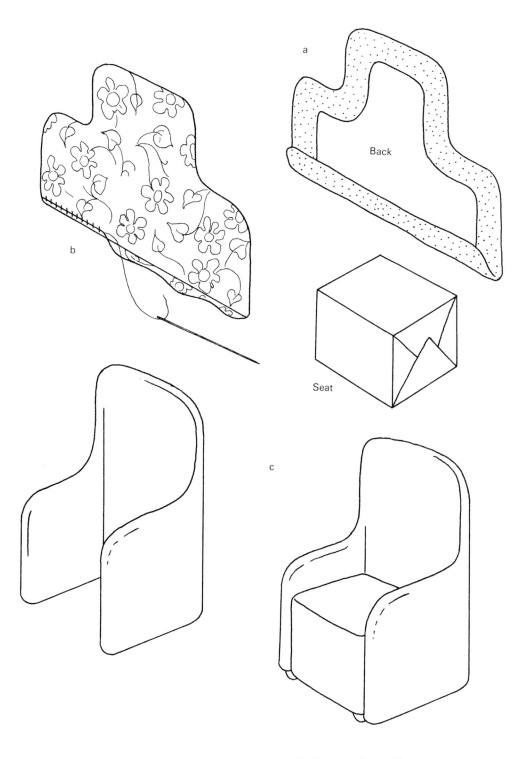

a

Back

Seat

b

c

48 Making upholstered furniture

An upholstered sofa, made by the same method
as the chair, looks realistic with cushions and
antimacassar. The lamp is made of glass beads
and a button

6 Accessories

The dozens of tiny items which complement a dolls' house and give it character and charm are the easiest things to make and find, and often one of the most pleasurable aspects of dolls'-house making. Many of these items can be bought from the toy shops which sell commercial dolls'-house ranges, but they seem to be generally made in plastic, which may be acceptable in a modern house, but is most unrealistic in an old one. However, for items like tea-sets and saucepans which are very difficult to make, it is worth buying the plastic items and re-vamping them. Bright red or yellow plastic saucepans or kettles look quite different when given a coat of copper or brass enamel paint. Pink, plastic tea-sets look like china when given a coat of white gloss enamel and perhaps a tiny painted design or minute flower transfers. These little items are easier to paint if you spear them on the point of a needle, pushing the other end of the needle into some cork or balsa wood while the pieces dry.

However, the majority of dolls'-house accessories can be made more realistically than their plastic counterparts. With a little skill and ingenuity the most unlikely everyday objects can be turned into dolls'-house items. The golden rule is to disguise the origin of the oddment you are using — for example, a toothpaste cap will make a good flowerpot given a coat of matt terracotta paint, but if you use it just as it is, it still looks like a toothpaste cap.

This chapter gives suggestions for making many dolls'-house items, but if you look around, you will probably find many more.

Rugs

Rugs can be made in a variety of ways, ranging from a simple rectangle of cloth to beautifully worked petit-point. Suitable pieces of wool, weaving or velvet, etc can be cut to the appropriate size, the shorter edges fringed and a piece of heavyweight iron-on Vilene or carpet tape placed on the back to prevent fraying and give the rug weight, so that it lies flat. A piece of short-pile fur fabric or a wide braid with suitable pattern, similarly backed, looks effective. If you plan to work a petit-point rug, choose the finest available canvas and use fine embroidery wool or silk. Designs for rugs can be copied from pictures in magazines, or you could design your own, drawing it on to the canvas with felt pens.

One of the most effective and simple methods for making rugs, is to draw with felt pen on felt. Use good-quality felt in a light colour, cut to the required size and backed with carpet tape. Draw on the design with pencil or a light-coloured felt pen. Choosing felt pens which are not too bright or garish, in colours which harmonise, fill in the design. Work the colour well into the felt all-round the edges, to give the effect of pile. A large rug with a complex pattern can be quite time consuming, but if the design and colours are well-chosen the end result will justify the effort involved. A suitable rug or carpet for any period or style of house can be made by this method.

Braided rugs Braided rugs are made by plaiting three strands of wool (tapestry wool is the right thickness and the colour range is extensive) and coiling the plait into a spiral, starting from the centre and working outwards, stitching each round to the previous one with tiny stitches. Plait as long a length of wool as you can comfortably work with to cut down the number of joins, and keep all joins to

the underside of the work. The rug will be circular or oval depending on whether it is started by coiling the first few rounds into a circle or sewing them straight up and down. When the rug has reached the required size, finish it by tucking the end to the underside and stitching it in place. A backing of carpet tape or iron-on Vilene will prevent any curling up at the edges.

Pictures, clocks and mirrors
Magazines are an excellent source of miniature pictures, especially advertisements for prints, which are often found in the colour supplements. Other sources include postage stamps, cigarette or tea cards or your own miniature originals. Try to find pictures which are appropriate to the style of the house — Picasso looks very strange in a Victorian house! Look out for pictures of clock faces of a suitable size.

Pictures can be framed by sticking them onto thin card and using fine wood-strip, mitred at the corners, stuck around them. The surplus cardboard is then cut away and the frame can be painted or stained. Flat buttons with a raised rim make good picture frames and are suitable for wall clocks. Brooch mounts make elaborate frames for a more opulent house. Small standing picture frames can be made in any of these ways, with a block of wood stuck behind the picture to hold it upright.

Pictures can be glazed by using the thin acetate sheet used for packaging, cut to size and held by a fine smear of glue at the edges; but the majority of pictures look better unglazed, as light tends to reflect from the acetate, obscuring the picture.

Any of these framing methods can also be used for mirrors. We generally have mirrors cut to the required size at a glass merchant's. Most glass merchants will do this, it is not expensive, and you end up with a suitably thin mirror with bevelled edges and exactly the right size. Handbag mirrors or mirror tiles are too thick and tin-foil is unrealistic.

(left) 49 and 50 Patterns for rugs made of printed felt or needlepoint embroidery

(right) 51 Picture frames, clocks, mirrors and basketware

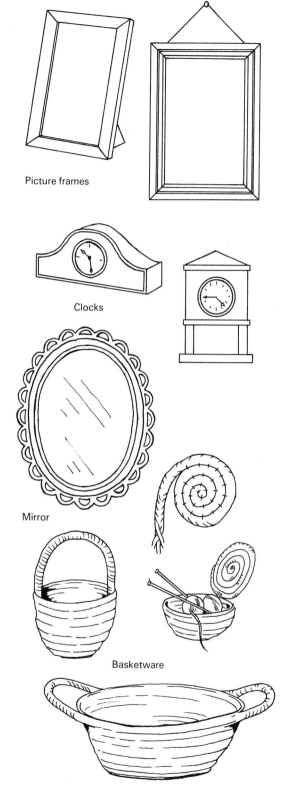

Picture frames

Clocks

Mirror

Basketware

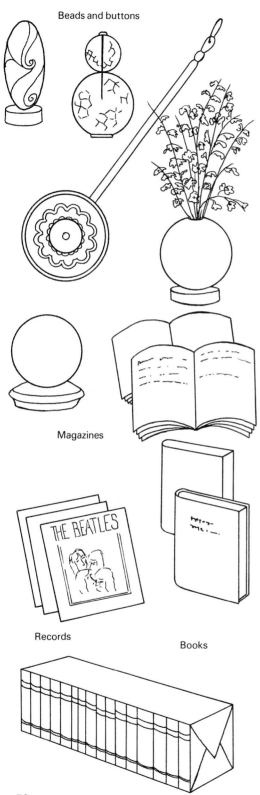

Beads and buttons

Magazines

Records

Books

Mantel clocks can be made from a block of wood, with a clock-face picture stuck to the front, perhaps framed by a brass curtain ring. Old watches can be used to make dolls'-house clocks, but they are usually too large for anything but a grandfather clock.

Pictures, wall clocks and mirrors all look best stuck onto the wall, rather than attempting to hang them. Use double-sided Sellotape or a small piece of Blu-Tac.

Books, magazines and records

For making miniature books, magazines and record covers, pictures in magazines are again an invaluable source of materials. If you need a set of books to fill a shelf, cut a block of wood to fit the shelf space and cover it neatly with a magazine picture of a set of books. Advertisements for encyclopaedias show sets of books in about the right size. Alternatively, the wooden block can be covered with plain-coloured paper and the spines of the books drawn in with felt pen.

Individual books can be made by covering blocks of wood in a similar way, or, more realistically, by cutting pages and a cover from thin paper, folding them in half and stitching the spine. If the books are pressed under a heavy weight for a couple of days they will flatten to the proper shape. Magazines can be made by the same method, perhaps using a miniature picture of a magazine from an advertisement for the cover. Given a lot of practice, a magnifying glass and a fine-nibbed pen, you can write your own text and illustrations in the books and magazines!

Record clubs often advertise themselves in magazines by showing a whole page of record covers. These could have been designed especially for a dolls' house as they are exactly the right size, printed clearly and in colour. Cut the page out and stick it to a sheet of firm cardboard. Choose your record collection, and simply cut out the ones you want!

Basketware

The methods described here can be used to make virtually any kind of basket, from a tiny workbasket to a large log basket, using the

52 Bead and button items, books, magazines and record covers

appropriate thickness of raffia strands (Fig 51). Use natural garden raffia, or the artificial kind sold in art shops.

Cut three strands of a suitable thickness for the item you are making — fine for a small workbasket, thicker for a laundry or log basket. Use the raffia strands as long as you can comfortably work with, as this will reduce the number of joins needed. Knot the three strands together at one end, then plait them together, knotting the other end to finish.

Starting at the centre base of the item you are making and working outwards and upwards, coil the plaited raffia around and around, oversewing each coil to the one before with a strand of fine raffia. Join in new lengths if necessary, keeping all the knots to the inside. When the basket is finished, oversew all-round the top edge to neaten it and make it

Selection of kitchen accessories suitable for an old-fashioned house

firm. Handles can be made by sewing plaited raffia loops at the appropriate place.

A workbasket can be filled with a few tiny balls of wool and a piece of knitting worked on dressmaker's pins (sand the points off the pins before you begin), or a piece of miniature embroidery and some cottons wound around tiny lengths of fine dowelling. A pair of scissors from a charm bracelet adds the finishing touch. The log basket can be filled with twigs of the right thickness sawn into roughly ½in lengths. The laundry basket could have neatly folded washing; the wastepaper basket, miniature rubbish; the shopping basket, tiny groceries.

Thick strands of plaited raffia can be used to

A dolls'-house dolls' house, with patchwork quilt and other small accessories

make rush mats, either round or oval — a piece of carpet tape stuck to the underside will prevent any tendency to curl up. It can also be used to make a baby's moses basket or rush cradle, a dog or cat basket, an Ali-Baba linen basket — and probably several other things I haven't thought of yet!

Although it is harder to work with, I prefer natural raffia to the artificial kind for mats and baskets, as the colour deepens with age to a beautiful gold, and it looks and feels better.

Bead and button items
From the enormous variety of beads and buttons available, numerous dolls'-house items can be made (Fig 52). Look around the local haberdashery department and art and craft shop, and raid friends' button-boxes for supplies. One of the super-glues is best to stick these bits and pieces together, as it will stick glass to plastic or metal, or practically anything else (including people, so use it with care).

Smaller glass beads, stuck together with a pin through the middle, make perfume bottles or decanters. Sand the bottom if necessary to make them stand properly. A large glass bead, with its bottom sanded, or stuck to a button base will make a crystal flower vase, with tiny dried or artificial flowers glued well into the hole. Coloured-glass or patterned beads can be used on their own or stuck together to make vases, bottles, paperweights, pots, jars or ornaments.

Wooden beads make excellent door knobs, feet for furniture, or finials for curtain poles. The barrel-shaped ones make good planters, biscuit barrels, flower vases or beer kegs. It is possible to wire and glue together a series of small wooden beads to make a turned leg for a piece of furniture or a newel post for the stairs.

Shallow, flat buttons with rims make good plates. Fill the holes with Polyfilla and give the buttons a coat of enamel paint and perhaps a tiny painted pattern or transfer. Bowl-shaped buttons treated the same way make bowls (sand the bottom if necessary); wooden ones make salad or fruit bowls. Crystal-glass buttons make ashtrays, glass dishes or serving dishes depending on size. Small black or coloured buttons make bases for bead vases or small ornaments. Buttons stuck one on top of another, perhaps a metal button with a crest on top of a plain-coloured one, make tobacco jars, storage jars or pill boxes. The large metal buttons with raised patterns make wall plaques, or, given a coat of copper enamel paint and a dowelling or cock-tail-stick handle, a warming pan to hang on the wall. The dome-shaped buttons with a raised pattern, with the shank cut off and painted the appropriate colour, make jelly moulds, cakes or puddings.

Fabric items

Scraps of fabric, ribbon and lace will provide the dolls' house with numerous small items of household linen. As with the soft furnishings, the choice of fabric is important. Natural cottons, lawn and silk are generally more use than heavier man-made fabrics, as they both hang and crease better.

Tablecloths can be made in lightweight cotton, cut either rectangular or round to suit the table and hemmed narrowly, or the edges could be frayed out. If you have difficulty getting the cloth to hang properly, damp it before putting it over the table and crease it firmly at the table edge. Tiny napkins can be made in matching or contrasting cotton fabric. Cut the squares carefully on the grain of the fabric and turn tiny hems, fray or blanket stitch the edges as preferred.

Towels are easily made from cotton tape, which comes in a variety of colours and widths. If the ends are cut carefully on the grain they can be neatly hemmed or frayed into a fringe. Crêpe bandage, calico and felt are also good to use as towels. If required,

coloured borders or patterns can be marked onto the fabric with felt pen. When making towels for the bathroom, don't forget to cut squares for flannels and bath mats as well. Tea-towels for the kitchen also look well made from coloured cotton tape; or look out for small rectangles of pattern in a cotton print to make modern tea-towels. If hemming these items is beyond you, paint a thin line of glue along the edge to prevent the fabric from fraying.

Small pieces of lace trimming can be used to make doilies, table mats and antimacassars. Round motifs cut from lace trimming make table mats suitable for any kind of house, and no Victorian parlour is complete without a selection of antimacassars on every chair and doilies under every potted plant! Scraps of pretty ribbon make excellent cushions. Don't stuff the cushion too much, or it will not tuck into the corner of a chair. Narrow embroidered ribbon would make a good bell pull to summon the maid from the Victorian kitchen. Plain-coloured ribbon gathered along one edge makes an ideal valance for the bed, a skirt for the dressing table or a pelmet frill for the curtains (embroidered ribbon also makes attractive pelmets if it matches the curtains). Wide ribbon is an excellent choice for curtains, needing hemming only at top and bottom.

Folding screen

A folding screen was generally found some-where in a Victorian house, either to block a draught or to undress modestly behind, and is easy to make and effective. Cut three or four panels of thick cardboard or thin obeche wood — approximately $4 \times 1\frac{1}{2}$in for a 1:16 scale house or $5\frac{1}{2} \times 2$in for a 1:12 scale house. The panels are hinged together with strips of $\frac{1}{2}$in wide black cotton tape, cut slightly shorter than the panels. Glue the tape to the panels, leaving a slight gap between each panel. Frame each panel on both sides with fine wood-strip, mitred at the corners. If required, paint or stain the wooden frame. The panels can be decorated with fabric or paper, cut to fit and stuck in place, or, more interestingly, with scraps of pictures. This last method is time consuming and fiddly, but rewarding, as the completed scrap screen is quite charming. Scraps on one side only, with a patterned

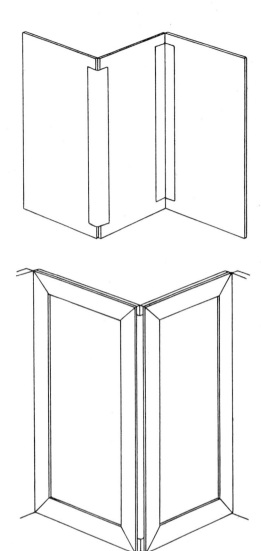

53 Making the folding screen

pieces, painting is often fiddly, but felt pens will colour wood effectively and are much easier to use.

A set of coloured pencils can be made from cocktail-sticks, by cutting lengths ½in long from the pointed ends of the sticks. Colour the points and most of the sticks with different coloured felt pens, leaving a small amount of bare wood around the point to represent the sharpened part of the pencil. A set of these pencils look effective in a mug or glass on the dolls'-house desk.

Square beading, ⅛in or ¼in thick, can be cut into cubes to make children's building blocks. Colour each face of the blocks in different coloured felt pens, perhaps drawing letters of the alphabet or simple pictures (an apple or fish) over the colour.

Fine round dowelling and obeche scraps can be used to make a roller towel for an old-fashioned kitchen, a set of coat pegs and wooden kitchen tools. The roller towel is a length of dowelling with a tiny gimp pin pushed into each end. This is supported by a piece of thin obeche wood, cut a little wider than the roller. Two small eye-screws are screwed into the obeche wood to hold the gimp pins at each end of the roller. A towel made from a length of cotton tape, 1in or 1½in wide, is seamed at the short ends and slipped onto the roller.

The set of coat pegs can be made in any length. Cut a board from obeche wood, as wide and deep as you require, and drill holes of the same diameter as the dowelling pegs at regular intervals. Cut the dowelling pegs to even lengths of approximately ¼in and glue them into the holes — the coat pegs can be stained. This set of pegs might also be used for hanging pots and pans or cooking tools in the kitchen.

With a little skill, a rolling pin with handles can be whittled from round dowelling, but if

paper on the other side, reduces the amount of work, and a coat of varnish (paper varnish is the best for this kind of work) will protect the end product.

Wooden items

Fine wooden dowelling, cocktail-sticks, square beading and scraps of thin obeche wood can be used to make a variety of wooden items. Use a craft knife with a sharp blade to cut the wooden pieces, with a metal ruler as a guide for cutting straight edges. With such small

(above right) The authors' first dolls' house — though badly proportioned and crudely built, it is still cherished and houses a collection of home-made furniture with home-made and bought accessories

(below right) Interior of the antique shop (Chapter 7) — designed to display craftsman-made pieces to good advantage

this is beyond you, glass-headed pins, cut short, can be glued into holes drilled into the ends of a length of fine dowelling. This rolling pin looks well on a pastry board cut from a piece of obeche wood. A similar board, cut to shape, will make a modern chopping board. Drill a fine hole through the handle, and cover one side with a picture, varnished to represent melamine. A square board of obeche wood could be ruled into squares and coloured to represent a draughts or chess board. Small slices of dowelling would make draughts, but whittling a chess set in this scale would be quite a task!

Mops and brooms

Very fine dowelling is used for the handles of mops and brooms, the top end sanded round. For the head of the mop, cut strands of soft white cotton thread such as crochet cotton about 3in long. Holding the bunch of cotton threads together in one hand, push the handle down into the middle of them. Bind the threads tightly to the handle halfway down their length, with cotton or fusewire. Shake the mop so that all the threads hang downwards and trim them to the required length. For a 'witch's' broom, use the finest twigs you can find and bind them to the handle close to the top of the bunch, then trim the twigs roughly to the right length (Fig 55).

A modern broom can be made by cutting the head off a toothbrush and sanding the cut end to match the other. A hole is drilled in the centre of the head and the dowelling handle glued into place. Small hand or hearth brushes can be made from mascara brushes or the small ones sold for cleaning sewing machines, cut down to the required size.

Food

Dolls'-house food can be modelled from bread-paste (equal amounts of flour and salt with a little water, baked in a slow oven) or Das or other clay. When modelling food, it is usually best to pick things which have simple recog-

(right) 54 A selection of small wooden items

(left) Exterior of the Tudor cottage (Chapter 9). The mellow red brick and roof tiles, oak timbers and small-paned casement windows make the dolls' house an attractive ornament

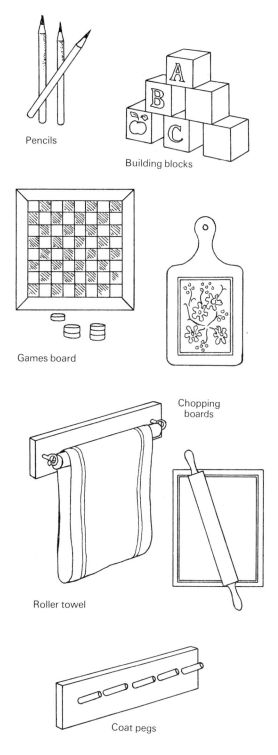

Pencils

Building blocks

Games board

Chopping boards

Roller towel

Coat pegs

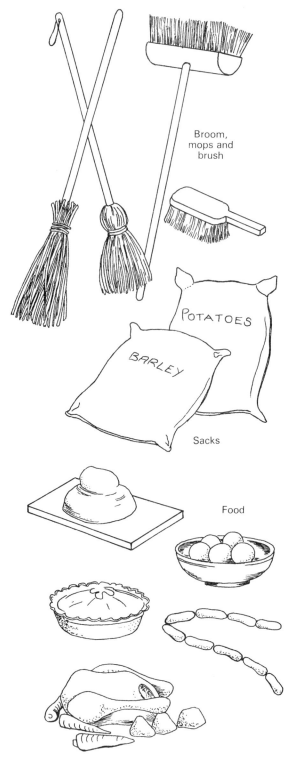

Broom,
mops and
brush

POTATOES

BARLEY

Sacks

Food

nisable shapes. A loaf of bread — perhaps a cottage loaf — stuck to a bread board is simple, and looks at home in any kitchen. A pie is easily made if it is modelled in the dish, lining the dish with clay as a real pie dish is lined with pastry, and using tiny beads or balls of clay for the fruit filling. Flute the edges of the pastry lid for the finishing touch. A string of sausages (joined by a cotton thread through the middle), eggs, a chicken or a ham, or a cake, are all good choices (Fig 55). When the piece is dry, paint it with poster colour and give it a coat of varnish, matt or gloss as you prefer, to preserve it.

Packets of foodstuffs such as corn flakes can be made by cutting labels and packet fronts from magazine advertisements and wrapping them around blocks of wood. Look out also for various seeds from garden plants, which look like miniature vegetables. Clarkia seed pods for example look exactly right as tiny cucumbers — these things are not suitable for childrens' houses.

Pasta, salt, flour, lentils, rice and other stuffs which will not deteriorate or go sticky can all be used as dolls' house foodstuffs in the appropriate containers, and miniature bottles can be filled with vinegar, cochineal, or paint and water for wine and milk.

Using 'found' items

The number of dolls'-house items which can be contrived from odds-and-ends is limitless. Lids and caps from bottles and pots, given a coat of paint, make a variety of containers or dishes. A toothpaste cap becomes a flower pot; a small tin lid, a tin tray. Washing-up-liquid bottle caps make flagons; shallow screw caps make dishes or baking tins. Oddments of metal, nails, screws, rivets, washers, cotter pins, etc can all be used. Washers make rings for kitchen stoves, cotter pins make firedogs for the hearth. A certain kind of rivet is perfect for a dolls'-house poker complete with handle. The secret is to look at all these bits and pieces with a dolls'-house maker's eye. What does the shape remind you of? What would it look like painted brass or copper or black?

Key rings often have useful things attached,

55 Brooms, mops, sacks and modelled foodstuffs

perhaps a tiny teddy bear or a pair of football boots. Pencil sharpeners are sometimes disguised as globes or cash registers, even kitchen stoves! Charm bracelets carry lots of things which would fit very happily into a dolls' house.

Cake ornaments can be used; from the white wedding-cake pillars, which make good pedestals for busts or jardinières, to the miniature trains or cars which will fit into the nursery. Cake-size bunches of artificial flowers fit dolls'-house vases, and tiny marzipan fruits will last quite well if you varnish them. Christmas-cake trees can be stood in tubs outside the front door, or decorated with beads for a Christmas tree.

Souvenir shops sell lots of tiny items — miniature Limoges vases or china potties, small brass kettles and candlesticks. Some games include pieces with dolls'-house possibilities (eg Monopoly), and odd wooden chess pieces with the tops cut off make excellent turned pedestals for tables. Knights from a very small chess set make ornaments or bookends. Miniature lead soldiers and horses for battles games look very effective polished up for ornaments. Clear greenish-glass marbles mounted on a black button stand make good crystal balls for the Victorian parlour. Tiny shells found on the beach make pretty dolls'-house collections.

Empty vaccine bottles (ask for them at your doctor's surgery) make storage jars for the kitchen, or a sweet shop. The smallest empty perfume bottles find a place as decanters. Pill boxes make pretty work or jewel boxes. Christmas crackers often contain miniature toys for the nursery. Broken jewellery might make brooch-mount picture frames, ear-ring ornaments or charm-bracelet door-bells. An empty lipstick case will make an umbrella stand to hold walking sticks, made from cocktail sticks with bead handles.

Half a ping-pong ball makes a good modern light fitting for the bathroom when stuck to the ceiling. Thin split-bamboo table mats can be cut down to make rush matting. Those perfumed sachets, about an inch square and prettily embroidered and lace trimmed, which are sold in haberdashery departments, make beautiful cushions or nightdress cases. Miniature china animals (Wade Whimsies, etc), especially a horse, look particularly good as dolls'-house ornaments.

The possibilities are endless!

PART TWO

7 The Antique Shop

This little shop was designed as a showcase for some of Martin's furniture. We chose an antique shop because his pieces are copies of antique furniture of various periods and they can be displayed to better advantage in this situation than in an ordinary room, where most pieces would be placed against a wall and obscured.

The miniature glass, metalware and china items which complete the shop's stock come from several sources. The best items are from the specialist shops (*see* Stockists) and though expensive, they are beautifully made. A few of these good pieces mixed with the cheaper commercial items and the home-made things make a realistic variety for an antique shop.

The furniture and the accessories are in 1:12 scale, so the shop is also built in this scale. If you plan to display a collection of craftsman-made miniatures, this is the scale of most pieces from the specialist shops. If, however, you plan to furnish your shop with furniture made from the patterns in this book, the shop plans should be reduced to 1:16 scale, by reducing the overall dimensions by ¼, including the door and window. A large number of 1:16 scale plans for furniture are given in the three following chapters and most, especially those from the Victorian and Tudor houses, would be appropriate. Accessories to fill the shop's shelves can be made from the instructions given in Chapter 6.

The design of the shop is simple — it is basically a box with the front divided into two pieces down the middle and hinged at each side. The square bay window, pediment and hipped roof give the structure some visual interest, but are easy to construct. It is important that the pieces are cut accurately, the right-angles exact and the measurements

precise, but once that is done, even an absolute beginner should have no trouble in assembling the shop.

We used Daler Board, as this was to be an adult's toy which would not receive rough treatment and because it is cheaper than plywood, but the shop can be built in plywood of the same thickness. You might find it helpful to read through the instructions in Chapter 2, before starting.

Materials

¼in Daler Board (or plywood) for the walls, floor and ceiling
⅛in Daler Board (or plywood) for the roof
length of picture-frame moulding for the cornice
³/₁₆in obeche wood for the door
¹/₁₆in perspex for the windows
two ½in hinges to hang the door and four 1in hinges to hang the fronts
length of fine wood-strip for door and window frames and glazing bars
UHU (or similar) glue, fine panel pins, masking tape

Cutting (Plans: Figs 56 and 57)
Draw all the pieces onto the Daler Board (or plywood) using a sharp pencil and ruler. Ensure that all the right-angles are correct and that measurements are precise. (It is a good idea to label each piece in pencil ie back, side, roof, etc to avoid confusion when assembling.) Cut out all the pieces, including the door and window holes, using a Stanley knife and metal ruler (plywood will need to be sawn). Before assembling, a dry run is advisable — tape the pieces together to check that they fit properly, and make any necessary adjustments.

Exterior of the antique shop, with its occupant

Assembly

Glue and pin the back onto the base, then glue and pin the sides onto the base, and to the back. The base protrudes slightly to allow for the fronts (Fig 58). Glue and pin the top to the sides and back, ensuring that all joins are square. The basic box is now complete — put it aside and assemble the bay window.

Window Glue the four pieces together to make a box frame, then glue and pin it around the window opening, taking care to line it up carefully around the window so that all the edges are flush. Assemble the window roof by sticking the two side pieces to the inside of the front piece, but do not stick it in place.

Exterior At this stage, the outside of the shop is papered. We chose a brick paper for the walls but any suitable paper will do, or you might prefer to paint the exterior (*see* Chapter 3). Cover the box part and the two fronts of the shop, lapping the paper over to the inside so that the edges are covered. Also, cover the front inch or two of the base, lapping the paper to the underside. If you use brick paper, ensure that the bricks line up correctly at the join in the two fronts and around the window bay. Paper the bay-window roof at this stage with the paper you intend to use for the roof. We chose grey slate paper as this seemed most appropriate to a hipped roof.

56 and 57   Plans for the antique shop (pages 93–4)

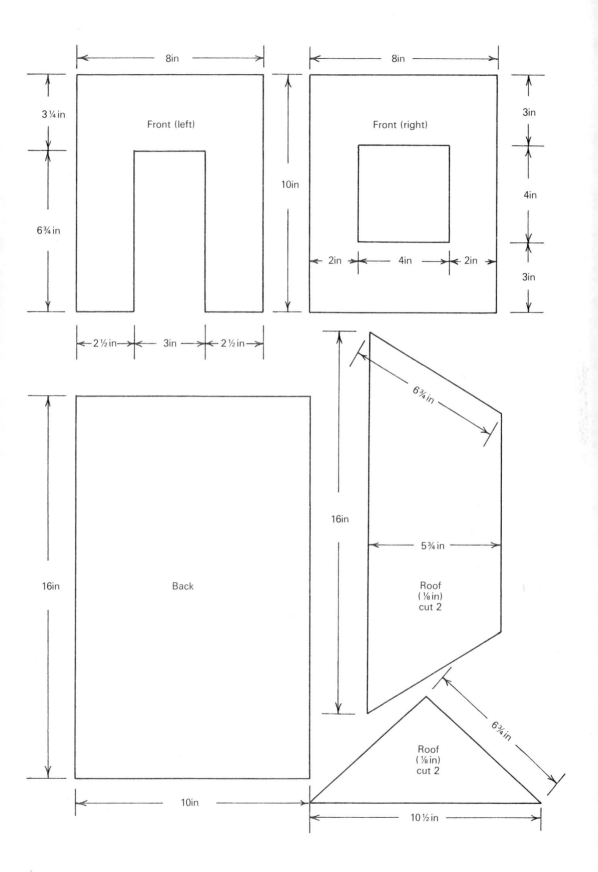

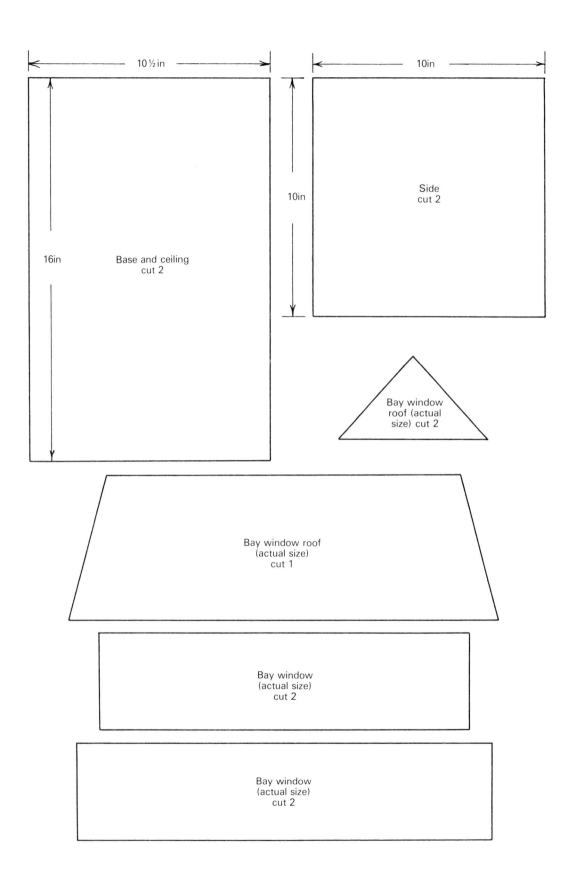

10½in

10in

16in   Base and ceiling
cut 2

10in

Side
cut 2

Bay window
roof (actual
size) cut 2

Bay window roof
(actual size)
cut 1

Bay window
(actual size)
cut 2

Bay window
(actual size)
cut 2

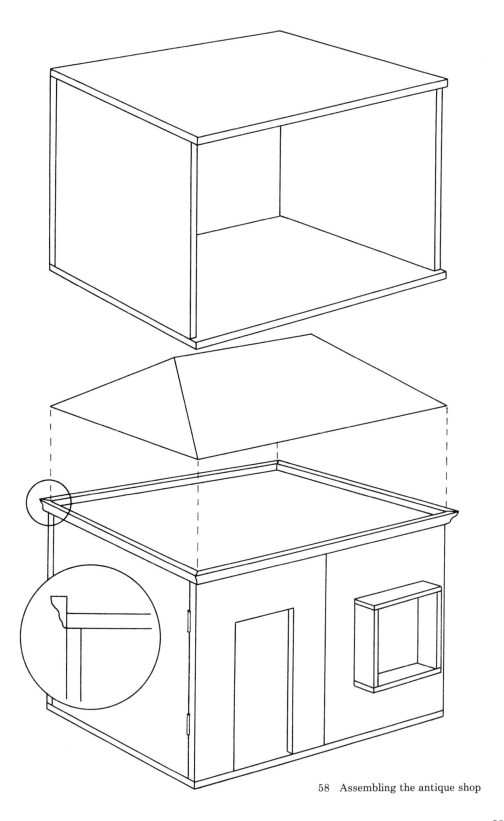

58 Assembling the antique shop

Window frame When the paper is thoroughly dry, cut and fix the window frame of 4–5mm fine square beading (stained or painted before being cut). It is easier to cut the pieces one at a time, using a mitre block for the mitred corners and glueing each piece in place before you measure and cut the next. When the frame is complete and stuck in place to the inside of the window's front edge, slip the perspex in place and hold it with a little glue. The window frame for the inside of this window is made in the same way, after the interior of the shop is papered as this gives a neater finish. The glazing bars are cut from very fine square beading, stained or painted before being cut. Cut and stick the vertical bars first, then the horizontal ones can be cut to fit between them. Ideally, glazing bars should be stuck to both the inside and outside of the window for the best effect. Fix the bay-window roof in place above the bay, sticking it to the top edges of the bay and to the wall above.

Door The door is cut in $^3/_{16}$in obeche wood to fit easily into the doorway. Allow sufficient clearance under the door for floor-coverings. Cut the small window in the door with a fretsaw, sand the whole piece carefully, then paint or stain on both sides. When the door is thoroughly dry, fit the small perspex window in the same way as the bay window, using the very fine square beading which was used for the glazing bars. Alternatively, omit the window in the door, or substitute a panelled door (*see* Chapter 2). Fix the ½in hinges to the left-hand side of the door, recessing them into the wood. These hinges are too small to be screwed in place, so we use fine pins. To avoid splitting the wood, mark the holes through the hinges onto the door and use a fine drill to drill the holes (if you do not have such a fine drill, bore the holes very carefully with a dressmaker's pin). Use super-glue to fix the hinge to the door and also on the pins pushed through the hinges. Repeat this process to hinge the door to the wall, recessing the hinges and securing them with super-glue. Make the outside door frame of ¼in wood-strip, mitred at the corners. The door frame should overlap the doorway slightly to cover the gaps between the door and the wall. Apply the inside door frame after the interior has been papered.

Fronts Hinge the fronts onto the shop, using two 1in hinges at each side. Fix them the same way as the door hinges, but use small screws. Super-glue both the hinges and the screws for extra strength. Make sure that the fronts line up correctly — a small cupboard hook can be screwed to the fronts at the join to close them.

Cornice The cornice is cut from picture-frame moulding and should be painted or stained before it is stuck in place. Cut and fix the front strip first, mitring the ends. Glue it in place to the top front edge of the shop, ensuring that the fronts swing open freely beneath it. Fix the sides and back pieces to line up with the front. The cornice rises above the top of the shop, providing a frame to hold the roof securely in place.

Roof The roof is cut to fit inside the cornice. Tape the back and front roof pieces together on the underside, then rest the two pieces in place inside the cornice and tape the join on the outside. Rest the two side roof pieces in place and tape them to the back and front. Reinforce the joins with several strips of tape both inside and outside so that the roof is rigid. Paper the roof, lapping the paper to the inside and taking care to line up the tiles or slates. When the paper is dry, glue the edges of the roof and fix it in place on top of the shop, inside the cornice.

Decorating
The interior of the shop can be papered or painted as you prefer (*see* Chapter 3). We used a brown-and-beige Laura Ashley wallpaper, but any decor suitable for a shop would be appropriate. Paint or paper the ceiling first. Bright white is a good choice here as it reflects the maximum light, but for a softer effect use any pale colour. Paper the walls, starting with the back wall, and not forgetting the insides of the fronts. If you intend to paint the interior, lining paper gives a better surface to paint on. The inside of the window bay can be papered

59 Pattern and assembly for the antique shop shelf unit

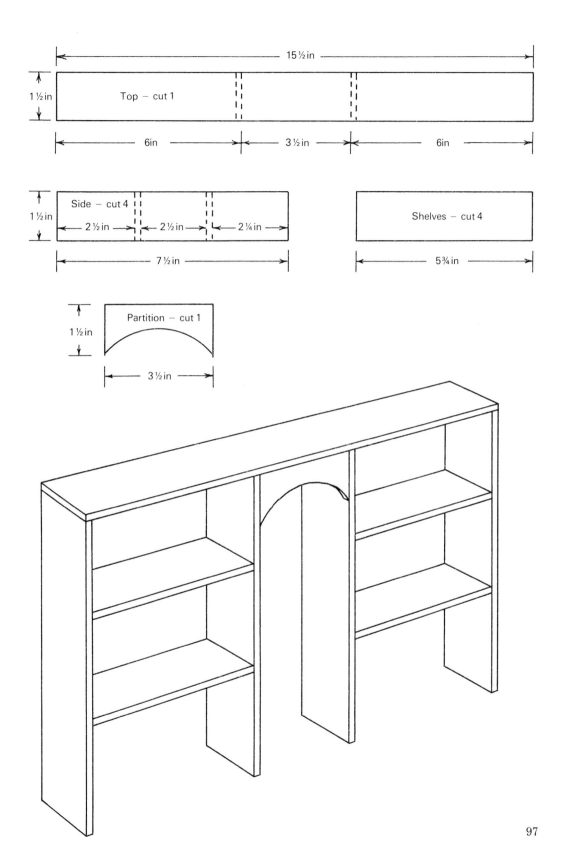

Top – cut 1

15½ in

1½ in

6in

3½ in

6in

Side – cut 4

1½ in

2½ in

2½ in

2¼ in

7½ in

Shelves – cut 4

5¾ in

Partition – cut 1

1½ in

3½ in

97

as the walls or treated separately. The floor can be papered or carpeted (*see* Chapter 3). We used a dark pink felt, backed with lightweight iron-on Vilene and stuck to the floor. The door frame, window frame and skirting boards, if required, are stuck in place when the wall-paper is dry. We used walnut wood stain on the woodwork both inside and outside, but you might prefer paint. As always, paint or stain before sticking in place. A lace curtain was stuck behind the window in the door, and, as the inside of the door was painted white, we papered the inside of the window bay white as well. A window sill cut from thin obeche wood and stained was stuck into the window bay to provide a display area.

Shelf unit (Fig 59) The fitted shelf unit at the back of the shop is made from ⅛in thick obeche wood, sanded smooth, but left unstained; though, if preferred, you could stain or paint it (stain before assembly, paint after assembly as for furniture).

To make the shelf unit, cut all the pieces from the pattern and check that the top shelf fits snugly across the back of the shop. Sand the pieces and stain them if required. Mark on the top and the side pieces where the uprights and shelves occur. Glue both sets of shelves to the outside upright pieces, then glue the inside uprights in place. Glue the top shelf across both units, ensuring that the outside edges line up correctly. Fit the arched centre piece and glue this in place slightly recessed into the space between the shelf units. If you are paint-ing the unit, wait until the glue is thoroughly dry, and sand carefully first. Fit the shelf unit

to the back wall of the shop and hold it in place with a little glue.

The shop is now complete, and awaits a tenant and stock. The doll in our shop is a 1:12 scale lady doll made from a bead and pipe-cleaners. Instructions for making her and her clothes are given in Chapter 11. The shop sign is painted onto stiff cardboard, 3½ × 1¼in, framed in fine wood-strip and mitred at the corners. Alternatively, a suitable sign could be cut from a magazine illustration or made with Letraset.

Variations
The shop described in this chapter is an antique shop but there is no reason why the same building could not be used for a variety of other shops. Suitably decorated, it could be a Victorian draper's shop — the shelves fitted with bolts of fabric, trimmings, tiny feathers and laces. You could make tailor's dummies with dresses, elegant chairs for the customers, a cheval mirror on a stand, elabor-ately trimmed bonnets and a shop counter with an old-fashioned till. A modern baker's or greengrocer's shop could be fitted with miniature goodies modelled in clay or bread-paste.

Alternatively, three or four basic shops could be made, without the roof, and stacked one on top of another, each one slotting inside the cornice of the one below, to make a dolls' house. If the upper stories had two plain windows on the front instead of the door and bay window, and the top storey had a roof, the result would be a sturdy dolls' house with large rooms.

8 The Victorian Town House

This house was designed as an eighteenth-birthday present for a young lady. We chose a Victorian town house for several reasons. Firstly, the tall narrow shape occupies only a little space (a distinct advantage in a teenager's room!). Secondly, the character of the period lends itself to pretty details like the half-tester bed and the lace curtains, but is sufficiently modern to suit items from the commercial dolls'-house ranges which the owner might want to add for herself. Another reason for choosing this design was its simplicity of construction — it has only three rooms, no internal doors or staircase and a fixed gable roof. Although it has only three rooms, they are a good size, and the absence of doors and stairs gives a lot of space and scope for decorating and furnishing. The windows in the side walls make the rooms light, and the fireplaces on the back wall provide focal points in each room. The house's narrow proportions allow for the typically high Victorian ceilings which make viewing and access to the rooms easy.

We decided we would not adhere rigidly to the Victorian concept of interior decor, which usually resulted in a gloomy, over-furnished atmosphere, but would concentrate on making the house attractive. After all, it was to be a toy, not an historical model. This attitude allows considerable freedom of choice in decorating and furnishing, though the purist might prefer greater accuracy in styles of wallpapers, paints, floor-coverings, and furnishings.

The contents of the house come from various sources — full details are given in this chapter. The furniture is made from the patterns given here, and full instructions for making the accessories are given in Chapter 6.

This house is in 1:16 scale (as are the patterns for the furniture) because it occupies less space and because the commercial dolls'-house furniture and accessories are made in this scale.

We used Daler Board, partly for economy and because it is easy to work with, but mainly because this style of house in this scale is sturdy enough in Daler Board, for an adult's toy. If you prefer plywood, choose the best quality you can afford and ensure that it is warp free. The instructions are the same for both Daler Board and plywood.

Before beginning, read Chapter 2.

Materials

¼in Daler Board (or plywood) for the house
⅛in Daler Board (or plywood) for the roof
narrow picture-frame moulding for the cornice ledges
$1/16$in perspex for the windows
⅛in and $1/16$in obeche wood for the front door
narrow wood-strip for the door and window frames and glazing bars
one $4 \times$ ½in block of balsa wood for chimney breast and stack
three wooden beads for the chimney pots
two ½in hinges for the door and three 1in hinges for the front
UHU (or similar) glue, panel pins, masking tape

Cutting (Plans: Figs 60 and 61)

Draw all the pieces onto the Daler Board (or plywood) using a sharp pencil and ruler. Ensure that all the right-angles are correct and the measurements precise. Label each piece in pencil, ie back, side, roof, etc, to avoid confusion when assembling. Cut out all the pieces, including doorway and window holes, using a Stanley knife and metal ruler (plywood

Bedroom of the Victorian town house, dominated
by the curtained half-tester bed

Victorian parlour, with aspidistras and lace

will need to be sawn). Draw lines on both the insides and outsides of the back and side pieces showing where the floors occur.

Tape the pieces together with masking tape to check that they fit properly, and make any minor adjustments.

Assembly

Glue and pin one side to the inside edge of the back. Glue and pin the base inside the side and back, then glue and pin the other side to the base and the back.

Tape the two roof pieces together at the apex, on the underside, and glue and pin the roof to the back and sides. The roof should overhang ¼in at the front, and fit flush with the wall at the back. When the roof is fixed in place, use several layers of masking tape on the outside of the apex to strengthen the join (Fig 63). Plane the back of the picture frame moulding so that it is flat.

Cut and fit the cornice ledges (plain picture-frame moulding for the kitchen and a more elaborate one for the parlour), mitring the

Victorian kitchen — the range made of a novelty pencil sharpener

corners, and glue them in place on the lines indicating the floor levels. Leave a 4in gap in the centre of the back wall of the kitchen to accommodate the chimney breast. Glue the side and back edges of the floors, and slide them in to rest on the cornice ledges — when the glue is dry, tap a few panel pins through from the outside, using the marked lines as a guide.

Cut the kitchen-fireplace opening out of a 4 × ½in block of balsa wood, and cut the balsa wood exactly the height of the kitchen. Glue the back of the balsa block and push it into place against the back wall. Cut a piece of picture-frame moulding the same width as the chimney breast and stick it to the ceiling and the front of the chimney breast.

60 and 61 Plans for the Victorian town house (pages 102–3)

101

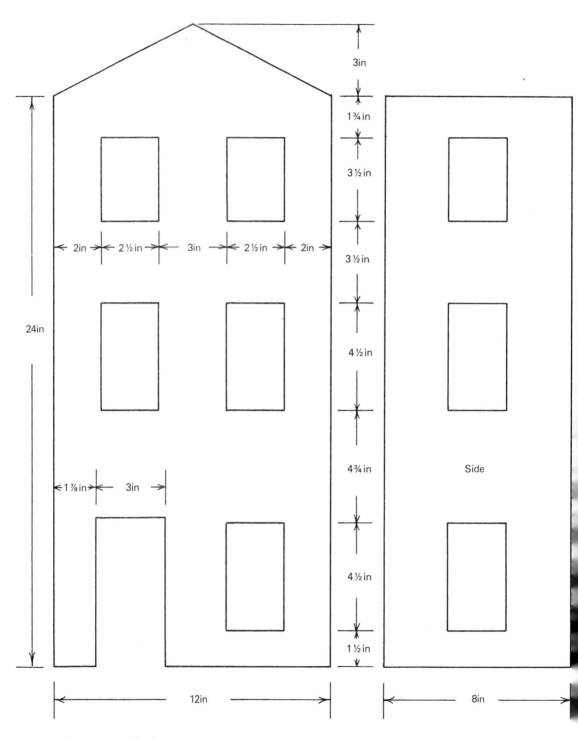

24in

3in

1¾ in

3½ in

3½ in

4½ in

4¾ in

Side

4½ in

1½ in

2in 2½ in 3in 2½ in 2in

1⅞ in 3in

12in

8in

Front — cut with windows
and door

Back — cut without windows
or door

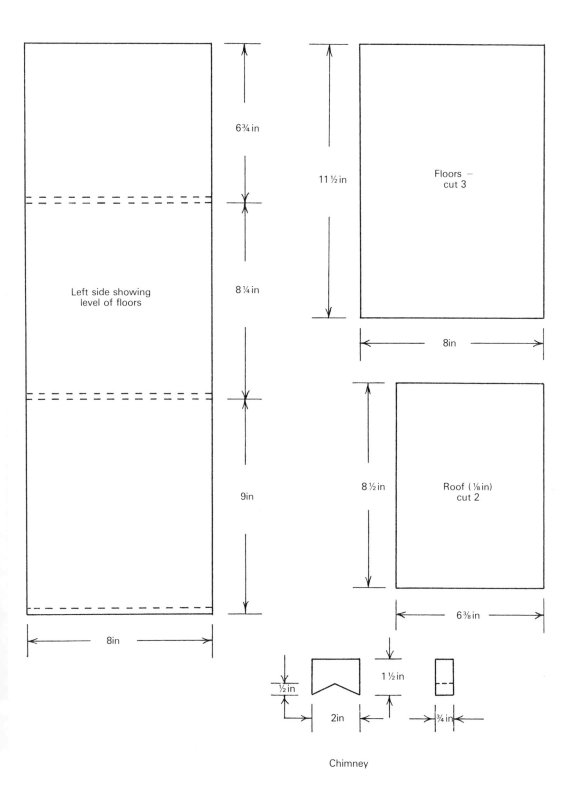

6¾ in

11½ in

Floors —
cut 3

Left side showing
level of floors

8¼ in

8in

9in

8½ in

Roof (⅛ in)
cut 2

8in

6⅜ in

½ in

1½ in

2in

¾ in

Chimney

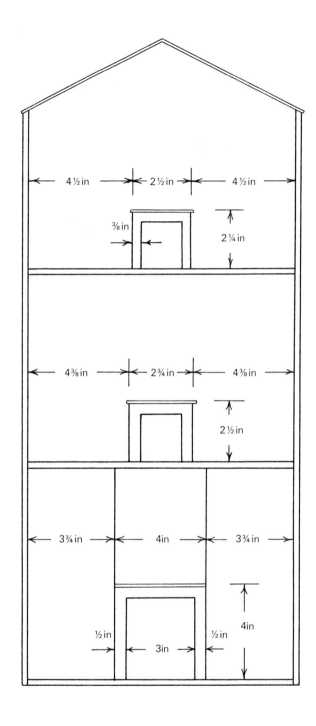

62 View from the front showing positions of
floors and chimney breasts

Exterior

At this stage, paper the exterior. We chose red brick and grey slate as typical of a Victorian town house, but you might prefer different papers or paint finishes. Consult Chapter 3. Paper the roof, lapping the paper round the front edge to the underside, and the house, lapping the paper round the sides to the inside. Cut strips of paper about 1½in wide to paper over the front edges of the floors, lapping them onto the floors and the ceilings, and underneath the base in the case of the bottom edge.

Paper the front of the house, lapping the paper round all sides to the inside, and through the door and window holes. Try to line up the bricks on the front with the bricks at the sides!

Windows

When the paper is thoroughly dry, fix all the windows in place. If the window frames are to be painted or stained, do this before cutting. Make a frame for each window from fine wood-strip, mitred in each corner and stuck to the inside front edge of the window hole. When each frame is complete, cut and insert the perspex window and make a similar frame on the inside to hold it in place. If you wish, the windows can be given an outer frame of fine wood-strip, mitred at each corner, (we have done this on the interior — after wallpapering — but not on the exterior). Stick on the glazing bars, firstly the horizontal ones, then the verticals, representing sash windows — for the best effect they should be stuck to both the outside and inside of each window.

Door

The edge of the doorway is faced with ¼in wood-strip (painted first) and the door is cut to fit easily into the faced opening, with sufficient clearance to open over the ground floor.

Make the door from ⅛in obeche wood, panelled with 1/16in obeche on both sides, sand carefully and paint it on both sides. Hang the door from ½in hinges fixed to the left-hand side and recessed into the wood. These hinges are too small to fix with screws so we use fine pins. To avoid splitting the wood, mark the holes through the hinges onto the door and use a fine drill or dressmaker's pin to drill the

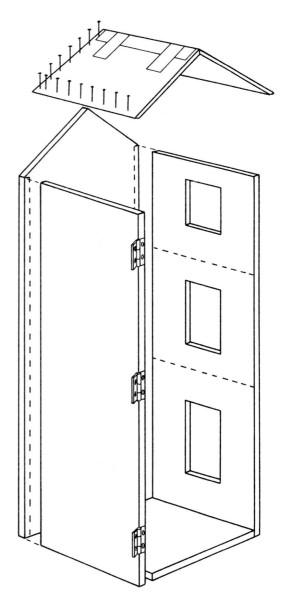

63 Assembling the Victorian town house

holes. Use super-glue to hold the hinge to the door and on the pins pushed through the hinges. Repeat this process to hinge the door to the doorway, recessing the hinges into the door frame.

Chimney

The chimney stack is made from a $2 \times$ ½in

105

block of balsa wood. The bottom edge is notched to fit the roof apex, it is covered in brick paper and stuck to the back edge of the roof. The chimney pots are three large wooden beads painted with terracotta-coloured poster paint and stuck to the top of the chimney stack.

Front
The front can be hinged in place at this stage, using three 1in hinges fixed in the same way as the door hinges but using screws instead of pins. You might prefer to wait until the interior has been decorated.

Exterior finishing
The exterior finishes can be added now or later. The brass door handle and numbers come from a dolls'-house shop. Alternative handles are suggested in Chapter 2, and the numerals could be cut from thin metal sheet or heavy-gauge aluminium foil. The keyhole is a brass eyelet flattened with a hammer and pushed into a hole drilled in the door.

The doorstep is a small block of obeche wood, cut to exactly the same width as the doorway and covered in brick paper. It is wedged into place and glued to each side of the door frame. The porch is also made of obeche wood, then stuck to brackets cut from picture-frame moulding, painted and stuck to the wall.

The left side wall of the house is decorated with several Victorian posters advertising soap, marmalade, etc, which were cut from a sheet of wrapping paper and stuck on with wallpaper paste. Similar posters can be found in magazines.

The first-floor window boxes are made of $^1/_{16}$in thick obeche wood (see Chapter 5 for instructions for making boxes). They are $3 \times \frac{1}{2}$in by $\frac{3}{4}$in deep, and the flowers are a mixture of fabric and plastic ones with a little lichen for greenery. Model-railway supply shops stock a range of miniature plants some of which are ideal.

Decorating
We chose to decorate this house in light pretty colours rather than traditionally Victorian dark colours and heavy patterns, using paper in the bedroom and parlour which was left over from our own home decorating. The pattern is the same in both rooms, tiny cream leaves, but in the bedroom it is on a pink background and in the parlour, beige. The kitchen is painted magnolia rather than a Victorian green or cream and brown which we felt would look rather gloomy.

Consult Chapter 3 for ideas, sources and detailed instructions for painting, papering and floor-coverings. As the house is small, the colour schemes in each room should harmonise so, unless you particularly want strict period accuracy, we recommend small patterns, and only two or three light colours, which also make a better background for the furnishings.

Before you begin decorating, check for tiny gaps, such as between cornice ledges and ceilings, or floors and walls. These gaps should be filled with Polyfilla — rub it in with the finger, and remove any surplus with a damp cloth. When the Polyfilla is quite dry, paint the ceilings. (The attic ceiling should be lined with paper first to cover the masking tape under the ridge and the slate paper at the front edge — bring the paper down an inch or two onto the side and back walls to cover any gaps under the roof.) Use magnolia-coloured emulsion which gives a softer effect than white, and include the cornices as part of the ceiling, so that they look like painted plaster. You will need two or three coats of emulsion to cover.

When the ceilings are dry, paper the walls, starting with the back wall. Even if you plan to paint the rooms, lining them with paper first will give a better finish. Divide the inside of the front into three sections and paint or paper each one to match the corresponding room. The flower border in the bedroom was cut from wrapping paper, and is also used on the inside front. If you wish to put in skirting boards or picture rails, paint or stain them first, then stick them in place at this stage.

Floor-coverings
The bedroom floor is papered with a dolls'-house parquet paper. The fitted carpet in the parlour is printed needlecord, backed with Vilene, and stuck to the floor with the selvedge to the front edge. On the kitchen floor is a tile-design Fablon pattern, the original bright-yellow colour toned down with brown shoe polish.

Curtains

The bedroom and parlour curtains are made from 2in wide lace edging, hung from thin wood-strip mounted on wooden blocks stuck to the wall. The pelmets are fringed upholstery braid, stuck to wood blocks above the windows. Similar curtains and pelmets are hung at the front windows in the same way. The kitchen curtains are small pieces of the same lace stuck to thin wood-strip over the bottom half of the windows, and cream-linen roller blinds are hung from tiny eye-screws at the top of the windows.

Fireplaces

The pattern given (Fig 64) is for the parlour fireplace. It is made from ½in square wooden beading, with a mantelshelf of obeche wood. The brackets which hold the mantelshelf are pieces of picture-frame moulding.

Cut the two uprights, the horizontal piece, the two brackets and the mantelshelf and assemble the pieces, sticking them to a backing of thin cardboard and to each other (Fig 65). When the glue is thoroughly dry, cut away the surplus cardboard from the outside using a sharp craft knife and sand the fireplace smooth. Paint it white, using gloss enamel paint over an undercoat of matt enamel paint and leave to dry. Line the cardboard-back of the fireplace opening with brick paper, and decorate the fireplace surround with tiny paper tiles, varnished with colourless nail varnish. (The paper tiles in this house came from a specialist shop, see Stockists, but similar tiles can be found in magazine illustrations and leaflets.) When the fireplace is assembled, glue the cardboard backing to the wall, holding it in place until firmly stuck. The bedroom fireplace is made in the same way, a little narrower and lower.

The kitchen fireplace is made from ¹/₁₆in thick obeche wood, stained rosewood colour. Paper the opening, back, sides, and floor with brick paper. Cut two uprights and a crosspiece from obeche wood, stain them and stick around the opening. Cut two brackets from the cornice moulding, stain, and stick them to the front top edges of the side pieces. Cut and stain an obeche-wood mantelshelf, ½in wide, and stick it to the brackets. (If you plan to use the built-in dresser, page 121, in the kitchen

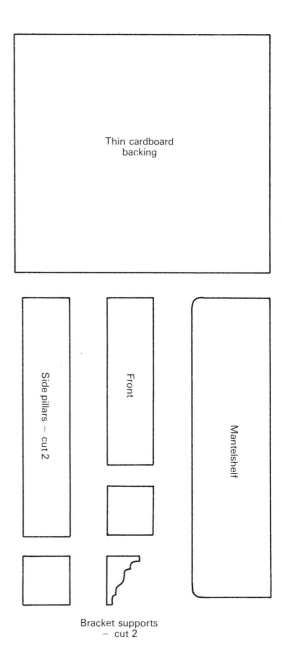

64   Scale pattern for the parlour fireplace

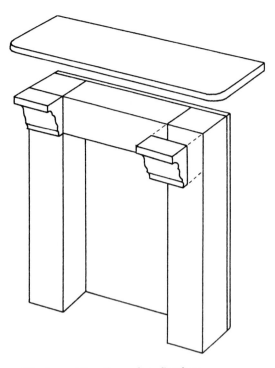

65   Assembling the parlour fireplace

Victorian looks make it remarkably realistic. Failing such a pencil sharpener, see Chapter 4 for instructions on making a kitchen range.

The sink in this house is made from the lid of a Vaseline jar, given several coats of ivory-gloss enamel paint and mounted on two wood-block piers covered in brick paper. The piers are stuck to the floor and the back wall and the sink is stuck to the piers. A small gap between the sink and the wall due to the slight curve of the lid was filled with Polyfilla and, before this dried, a piece of wire was pushed through it to represent the pipe. The tap is made up from plastic oddments, glued together and fixed to the bent pipe with fine fuse wire and glue. The draining board is obeche wood, sanded smooth, mounted on a small bracket on the wall and glued to the bracket and the edge of the sink. A rail of fine square beading is glued under the sink and the draining board for the tea-towel. A sheet of paper tiles coated with colourless nail varnish is stuck to the wall above the sink, and although the sink has no plug-hole, a waste pipe of bent wire leads from under the sink to the floor.

The bedroom furniture

The patterns for the Victorian house's furniture are drawn actual size, so that they can be traced from the book. Read the detailed instructions in Chapter 5 before beginning, and refer to them when necessary.

The chest of drawers (Fig 66)   This is made of ⅛in thick obeche wood, stained mahogany, and the handles are brass gimp pins.

Draw the pattern pieces onto the wood, ensuring that the grain lines are consistent, the measurements and right-angles precise. Cut the pieces with a razor-toothed saw and chamfer the edges of the top and base pieces. Sand all the parts with fine abrasive paper and stain them. Assemble the shell by sticking the shelves to the back, then sticking the sides in place, lining them up with the front edges of the shelves. Stick the top and the base pieces in place, and then the feet, set slightly back from the edges. Check that the drawer fronts fit snugly into the drawer spaces. Cut the bottom and sides of the drawers from un-stained wood and assemble the drawers to fit the drawer space.

alcove, make sure that the mantelshelf does not jut out into the alcove.)

The fender in the bedroom is made from ⅛in square beading, stuck to a piece of thin cardboard and painted white, with a hearth of paper tiles stuck on the cardboard. The whole thing is then stuck to the floor in front of the fireplace. A grate — made from lead strip folded around a wooden block and painted gloss black — is glued into the fireplace opening and filled with a paper fan.

The fender in the parlour is made of metallic-gold upholstery braid glued to a strip of metal, bent to shape and stuck to the carpet. The braid is varnished with several coats of colour-less nail varnish to prevent it tarnishing. The grate is again made from lead strip painted black, and a fire of coal, wood and paper is laid in the grate. The brass knobs used on the front of the grates are from a dolls'-house shop, but a similar effect could be achieved with map pins pushed through the grate and given a touch of brass-coloured enamel paint.

The elaborate cooking range in the kitchen is in fact an unusual pencil sharpener, whose

Sand the shell and the drawer fronts gently with fine abrasive paper and apply a coat of amateur French polish. Allow this to dry thoroughly, then gently sand again, Apply several coats of wax polish, well-buffed between each coat. Mark the positions of the drawer handles and drill holes with a $^1/_{16}$in drill. Cut the shanks of the gimp pins to $^3/_{32}$in long and push them into the holes — secure with a dab of glue over the pinhole on the inside of the drawer.

The washstand (Figs 67 and 68) This is made from $^3/_{32}$in obeche wood, with legs of 5mm square beading, stained mahogany. Draw the

Nursing chair, chest of drawers and plaited-raffia cradle from the Victorian bedroom

pieces onto the wood and cut them with a razor-toothed saw. Sand the legs with fine sandpaper wrapped around a small wood block, tapering them towards the bottom. Sand all the pieces with fine abrasive paper and stain them.

Stick the back and side pieces onto the top, matching the corners carefully. Stick one frieze piece between the two front legs, slightly recessed, and the other between the two back legs, again slightly recessed. Stick the two side-frieze pieces between the back

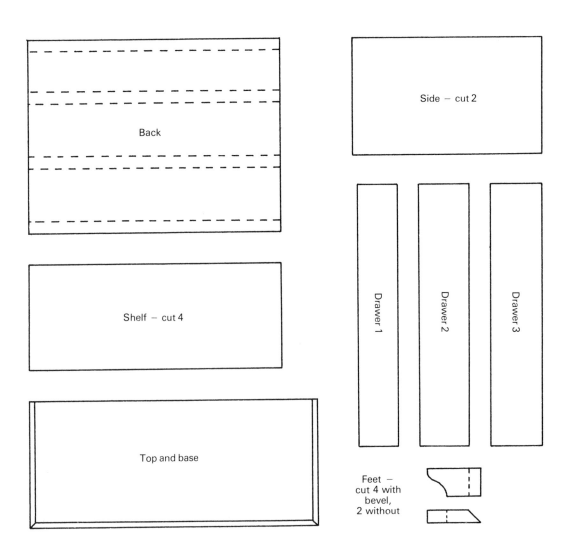

Back

Side — cut 2

Shelf — cut 4

Drawer 1

Drawer 2

Drawer 3

Top and base

Feet —
cut 4 with
bevel,
2 without

66 Scale pattern for the chest of drawers

and front legs, also slightly recessed. If necessary, support the legs in place while the glue dries. Stick the assembled legs under the top, so that the front overhangs by $^1/_{16}$ in.

When the glue is thoroughly dry, sand the washstand carefully until perfectly smooth, apply one coat of amateur French polish and sand again. Apply several coats of wax polish and buff well between each coat.

The half-tester bed (Figs 69 and 70) The half-tester bed is made from $^1/_8$ in thick obeche wood and 5mm square beading, stained walnut. The bedcover and curtains are rose-pink figured satin.

Draw the pieces onto the wood, ensuring that the measurements and right-angles are precise. Cut the pieces with a razor-toothed saw, taking particular care to cut the two pairs of bedposts of equal length with perfectly square ends. Whittle the knobs on the bottom bedposts with a craft knife, and sandpaper smooth. Sand all pieces with fine abrasive paper and stain them.

Stick the side rails to the base. Stick the headboard to the top edge of the base and the footboard to the bottom edge. Glue the bed-posts into the corners between the head and

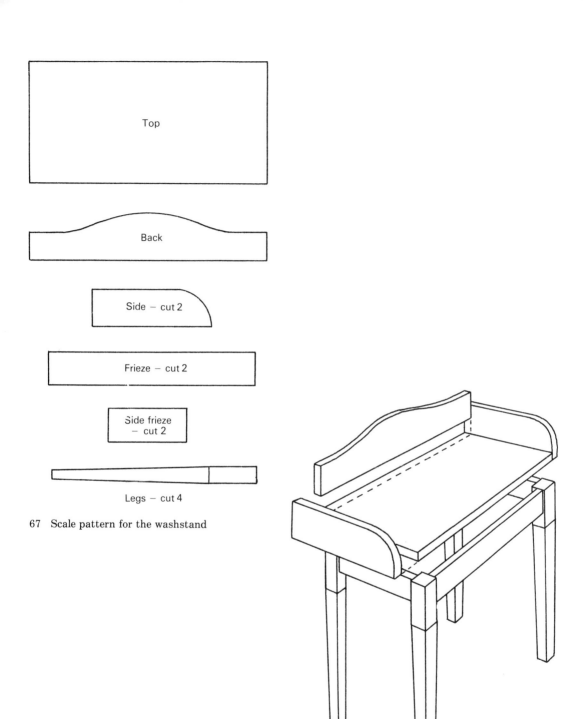

Top

Back

Side – cut 2

Frieze – cut 2

Side frieze
– cut 2

Legs – cut 4

67 Scale pattern for the washstand

68 Assembling the washstand

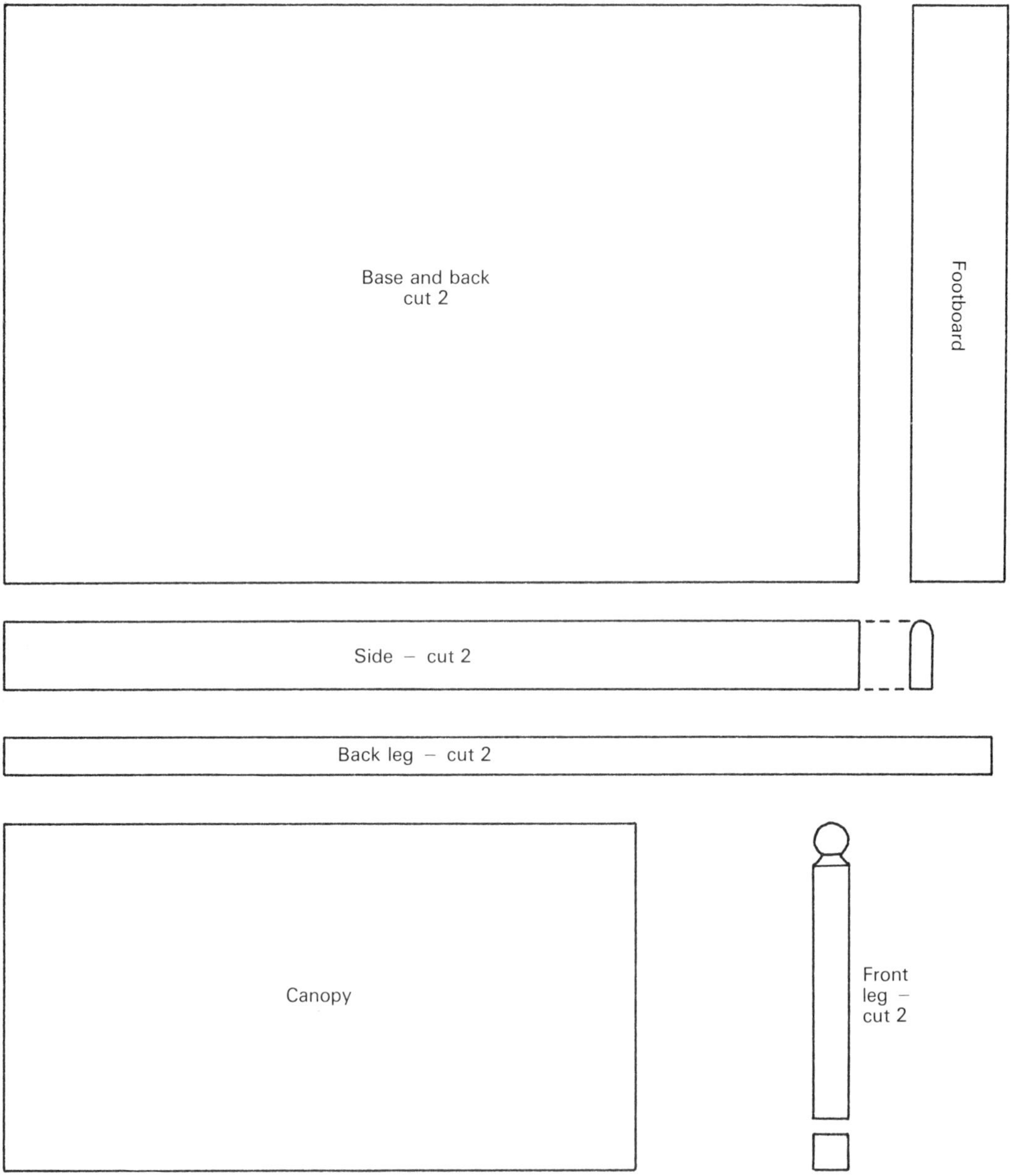

Base and back
cut 2

Footboard

Side — cut 2

Back leg — cut 2

Canopy

Front
leg —
cut 2

69 Scale pattern for the half-tester bed

footboards and the sides. Ensure that the bed-posts stand square, supporting them if necessary until the glue is dry. Stick the canopy (tester) to the top of the headboard and posts.

Cut a piece of thin cardboard the same size as the headboard and cover it with fabric, glueing the raw edges firmly on the underside of the card. Glue the back of the covered card and stick it to the headboard (not the bedposts). Cut and hem the bed curtains. Gather the top edges and stick them to the sides of the tester and glue the sides of the curtains to the bedposts if they do not hang well. Cut, hem and gather the frill and glue it around the

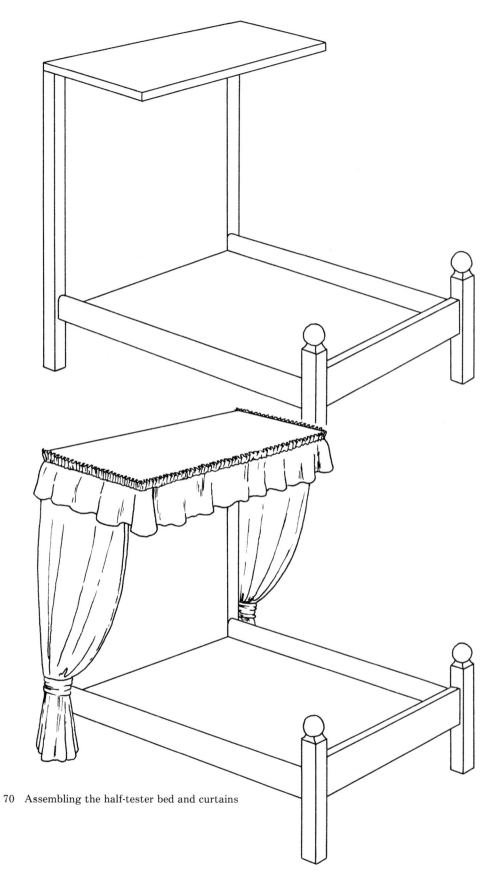

70   Assembling the half-tester bed and curtains

sides and front of the tester, over the curtains. Make small ties from embroidery silk and tie the curtains back to the bedposts.

Bedclothes Make a mattress (using the bed base as a pattern), two pillows, sheets and a blanket.

Cut a bedspread ½in wider and 1in longer than the bed, for seam allowances. Cut the frill in three pieces, two sides and the bottom, to allow for the bedposts. Hem and gather the frills and sew them to the bedspread. Line the bedspread with a fine fabric, oversewn in place under the frill and slipstitched along the top edge. Press carefully. Put the bedspread onto the bed and push pins through each side into the mattress to hold the frills in place until they hang properly.

The nursing chair (Fig 71) This is made of cardboard, padded with foam and covered with printed cotton.

Cut the cardboard back. Cut the foam and cover ½in larger all-round than the pattern to allow for seams. Stick the foam padding to the cardboard, rolling the edges over to the back. Sew the cover, turn through and slip onto the padded cardboard. Pulling the cover taut, slip-stitch the bottom edge closed. Cut the round seat from a 1in thick balsa block. Pad and cover the seat. Curve the back of the chair

around the seat and stick in place, holding the pieces together with pins until the glue is dry. A small piece of upholstery braid is used to finish the bottom edge of the chair, and four small wooden beads are glued to the underside for feet. A loose cushion, made in the same fabric is tucked into the back of the chair.

The cradle This is made from half of an egg-shaped plastic sweet container covered with plaited raffia.

Plait sufficient lengths of raffia to cover the sweet container. Coat the outside of the container with glue, and, starting at the centre working outwards, coil and stick down the raffia until the whole of the outside is covered. Cut a strip of broderie-anglaise trimming and glue this carefully to the inside to line the cradle. Cut an oval cushion, and stuff it lightly for a mattress. Make a tiny sheet and coverlet from fine fabrics and tuck these in around the mattress.

For the stand, use 4mm square beading. Cut two uprights approximately 2in high, and a cross-bar the same length as the cradle. Cut two feet 1in long. Stain or paint the pieces if required and stick them together. When the stand is thoroughly dry, stick the cradle between the two uprights. No specific pattern is given, because the size of the cradle will depend on the size of the container used.

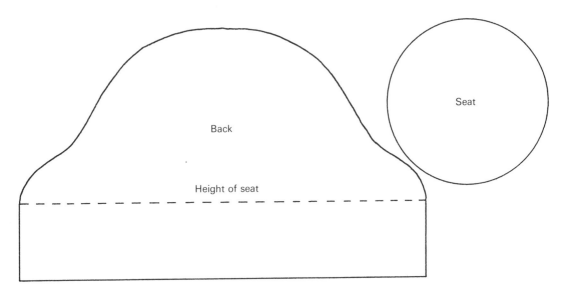

Back

Seat

Height of seat

71   Scale pattern for the bedroom chair

(It is possible to make this cradle from half of a large eggshell, cut lengthwise — a light touch is necessary when glueing the raffia in place.)

The bedside table This is made from a chess piece with the top sawn off and sanded flat, and a circle of obeche wood for the table top.

Use a cut-down chess piece, or any similar piece of turned wood, for a pedestal. If it is varnished, remove the varnish with paint-stripper first. From ⅛in obeche wood, cut a circle 1½in in diameter, and sand with fine sandpaper. Stain both pieces, then stick the pedestal to the underside of the top, taking care to centre it exactly. (We used button polish to stain the top, as the chess piece was this colour). Finish the table with a coat of varnish or wax polish. It can be covered with a circular lace cloth.

Glass-fronted bookcase, wing chair, footstool and chess-piece wine table

The parlour furniture

The bookcase (Figs 72 and 73) This is made of ⅛in obeche wood, stained mahogany. The glass panels in the doors are ¹/₁₆in perspex.

Draw the pattern pieces onto the wood, ensuring that the grain lines are consistent, the measurements and the right-angles correct. Cut the pieces with a razor-toothed saw. Chamfer the underside front and side edges of the top piece. Stick the two base pieces together, and chamfer the top side and front edges. Sand all the pieces with fine abrasive paper and stain them. (At this stage, we painted the inside of the back piece matt dark green.)

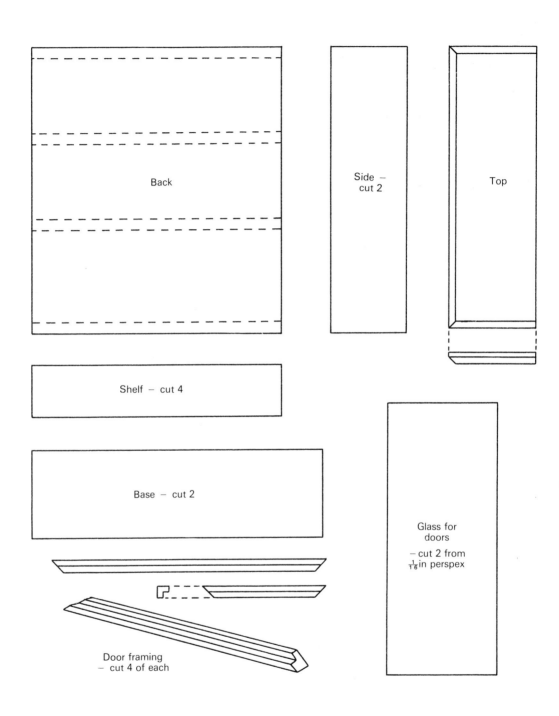

Back

Side –
cut 2

Top

Shelf – cut 4

Base – cut 2

Glass for
doors

– cut 2 from
$\frac{1}{16}$ in perspex

Door framing
– cut 4 of each

72 Scale pattern for the glass-fronted bookcase

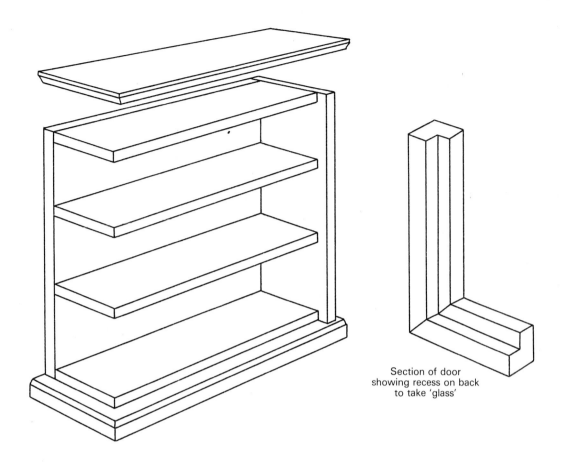

Section of door
showing recess on back
to take 'glass'

Assemble the shell by sticking one side to the back, then sticking the shelves to this side and back. The shelves are not as deep as the sides, to allow for the doors. Stick the other side in place, then glue the assembled shelf unit to the base. Do not fix the top in place yet.

The door frames are made by cutting rabbetting in each piece using a craft knife and steel ruler, and making up the frames with mitred corners. If you cut a cardboard template the exact size of the door, and use this as a guide when cutting and mitring, building the frame on the cardboard template, this fiddly process becomes less difficult. When the frames are complete, cut the perspex to fit and put it into the frames with a little glue around the edges. Use brass pins with the shanks cut short for cupboard-door handles. Drill a tiny hole into the door frames, and glue the pins in place. Bore holes with a dress-

73 Assembling the glass-fronted bookcase

maker's pin into the bottom and top edges of the doors, and the base and the top to receive the pin hinges. If necessary, sand the hinged door edges slightly round with fine abrasive paper to allow the doors to swing open freely. When the pin hinges are properly aligned, glue the top in place. Sand the bookcase, apply one coat of amateur French polish, sand again and apply several coats of wax polish, well-buffed between coats.

The pedestal table (Figs 74 and 75) This is made of $^3/_{32}$in obeche wood for the top and the feet, with a pedestal of ¼in diameter dowelling. It is stained walnut.

Draw the pattern pieces onto the wood, using a compass to ensure accurate circles and, with the point, marking the centre on the underside of the smaller top piece. (A pencil

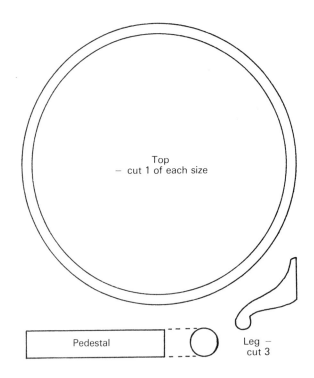

Top
— cut 1 of each size

Pedestal

Leg —
cut 3

74 Scale pattern for the pedestal table

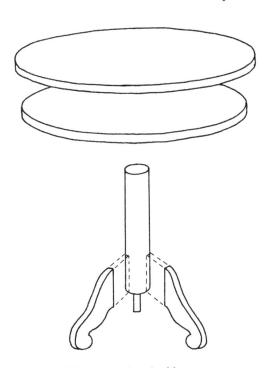

75 Assembling the pedestal table

mark would not show when the wood was stained.) Sand the pieces with fine abrasive paper and stain them.

Glue the smaller top to the underside of the larger top, centring it carefully. Glue the three feet to the bottom of the pedestal, ensuring that they are evenly spaced and that the pedestal stands upright. Centre the top end of the pedestal carefully over the mark on the underside of the top and glue it firmly in place, leaving upside-down until the glue is completely dry.

Sand the table with fine abrasive paper and apply one coat of amateur French polish. Sand again and apply several coats of wax polish, building up a good finish, especially if you do not intend to cover with a tablecloth.

The dining chairs (see Fig 41) Full instructions and patterns for these dining chairs (and other alternatives) are given in Chapter 5. For this parlour they are made of $^3/_{32}$in obeche wood, stained walnut, and finished with wax

polish. The seat pads are covered in dark-green silk.

It is essential when making these chairs to cut the two side pieces with the grain of the wood running vertically, and to handle them carefully until they are fully assembled as the pieces are fragile.

The sofa (Fig 76) This is made of cardboard, padded with foam, and covered with printed cotton.

Cut the cardboard back from the pattern and score the fold lines. Cut the foam and covers ½in larger than the pattern to allow for seams. Stick the foam padding to the cardboard, rolling the edges over to the back

The pedestal table and dining chairs, simple but elegant pieces for a Victorian house

(use a slightly thicker foam for an overstuffed effect). Stitch the cover, clip the curves, turn through and slip it over the padded cardboard. Pulling the cover taut, slipstitch the bottom edges closed.

Cut the seat from a block of balsa wood, pad with foam and cover with fabric. Fold the arms forward, and fit the back around the seat. Stick the back and arms to the seat, and hold in place with pins until the glue dries. Stick four round wooden beads to the underside for feet, and make several loose cushions to tuck along the back of the sofa. An anti-

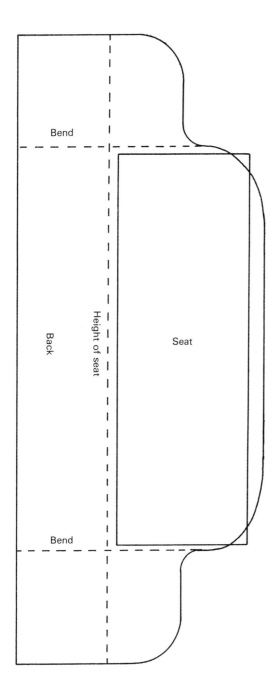

Back

Height of seat

Bend

Bend

Seat

76 Scale pattern for the sofa

macassar of broderie anglaise or lace adds the finishing touch.

The wing chair (Fig 77) This is made of cardboard, padded with foam and covered with brown felt.

Cut the cardboard back for the chair from the pattern and score the fold lines. Cut the padding and the felt ½in larger all-round than the pattern to allow for seams. Glue the foam to the cardboard, rolling the edges over to the back. Stitch the cover, clip the curves and turn through. Slip the cover over the padded cardboard, pulling it taut, and slipstitch the bottom edges closed.

Cut the seat from a balsa block, pad with foam and cover with felt. Fold the sides of the chair forward and fit the seat in place. Glue the seat to the back and sides of the chair, holding it in place with pins until the glue dries. Stick four square wooden beads to the underside for feet, and cut a scrap of broderie anglaise for an antimacassar.

The wine table The wine table is a black chess piece with a circular top 1½in in diameter cut from ⅛in obeche wood, stained mahogany. The top is cut, sanded, stained, and glued to the chess-piece pedestal. The table is varnished with one coat of polyurethane varnish.

(Any similar piece of turned wood can be used for the pedestal. If such a piece is unavailable, the pattern given for the pedestal table could be used with the dowelling cut to 2in long.)

The footstool This is made from a piece of cotton reel padded with foam and covered with beige silk.

Cut a ½in piece from one end of a cotton reel with a razor-toothed saw (or use a circle of balsa wood or cork). Cut a circle of fabric 3in in diameter. Glue a little padding to the top of the cotton reel. Run a gathering thread around the edge of the fabric circle and draw it over the padded cotton reel, with the thread under the base. Pull the gathers as tightly as possible, distributing them evenly, so that the cover is taut. Fasten off the thread and trim the excess fabric. Cut a circle of felt and glue it to the underside of the stool to cover the raw

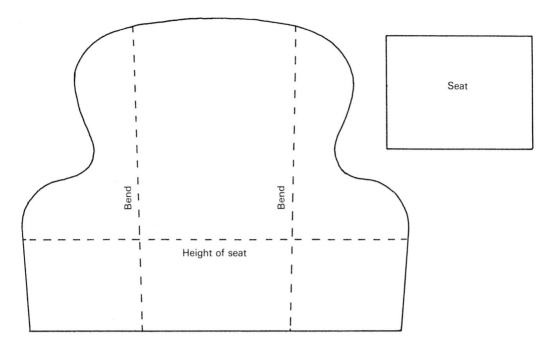

Bend

Bend

Height of seat

Seat

edges. Glue a piece of narrow upholstery braid or ribbon around the sides of the stool to trim.

The kitchen furniture

The dresser (Figs 78, 79 and 80)   The kitchen dresser was designed to fit into the alcove on the right side of the chimney breast, but it could equally well be free-standing. It is made from $^3/_{32}$in thick obeche wood, coloured with button polish to a pine colour.

Firstly, assemble the top unit. Draw the pattern pieces onto the wood, ensuring that the measurements and the right-angles are precise. Cut out the pieces with a razor-toothed saw. Score the lines on the back piece with a scissor blade to represent planking. Chamfer the front edge of the top. Sand all pieces with fine abrasive paper. Glue one side piece to the back. Stick the shelves to the side and back, and then stick the other side in place. Glue the top in place, then the frieze under its front edge.

Secondly, the lower unit. Glue one side piece to the back. Glue the drawer shelf in place, then the upper and lower partitions. Glue in the bottom shelf, then the other side piece. Stick the top in place, then the frieze strips under the drawer shelf.

77   Scale pattern for the wing chair

Check that the drawer fronts fit snugly into the drawer spaces. Cut bottom, back and side pieces from unstained wood for the drawers and assemble the drawers to fit the drawer spaces. Make drawer handles from blocks of fine square beading stuck to the drawer fronts. Sand both units of the dresser with fine abrasive paper and stain them with a coat of button polish painted on with an artist's paintbrush. Sand both units, and polish them with wax polish. The top unit can be stuck to the base unit for extra stability (a good idea if the dresser is to be free-standing).

The table (Fig 81)   This is made of $^3/_{32}$in thick obeche wood, with legs of 5mm square beading. It is stained with button polish to represent pine. Draw the pattern pieces onto the wood, ensuring that measurements and right-angles are correct. Shape the table legs by sandpapering. Glue the four frieze pieces between the legs, ensuring that the table legs stand square. Support them if necessary until the glue is dry. Glue the table top accurately in place, the edges overhanging slightly all-round. Leave the table upside-down while the glue dries.

121

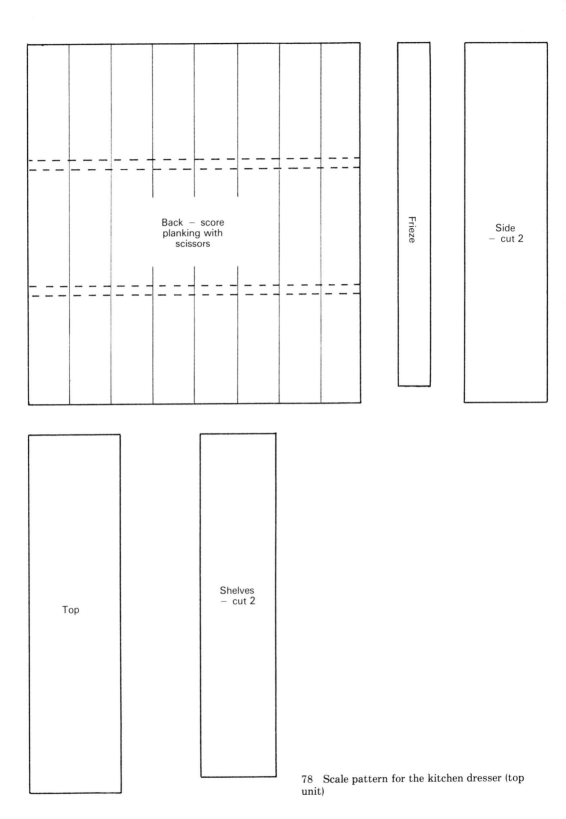

Back – score
planking with
scissors

Frieze

Side
– cut 2

Top

Shelves
– cut 2

78   Scale pattern for the kitchen dresser (top unit)

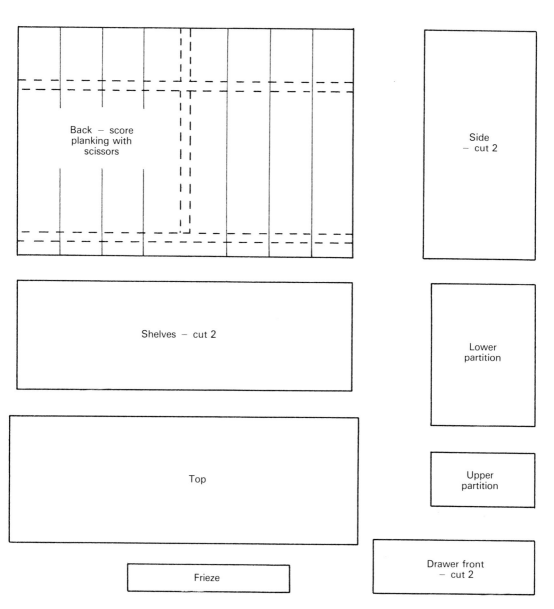

Back − score
planking with
scissors

Side
− cut 2

Shelves − cut 2

Lower
partition

Top

Upper
partition

Frieze

Drawer front
− cut 2

79   Scale pattern for the kitchen dresser (base unit)

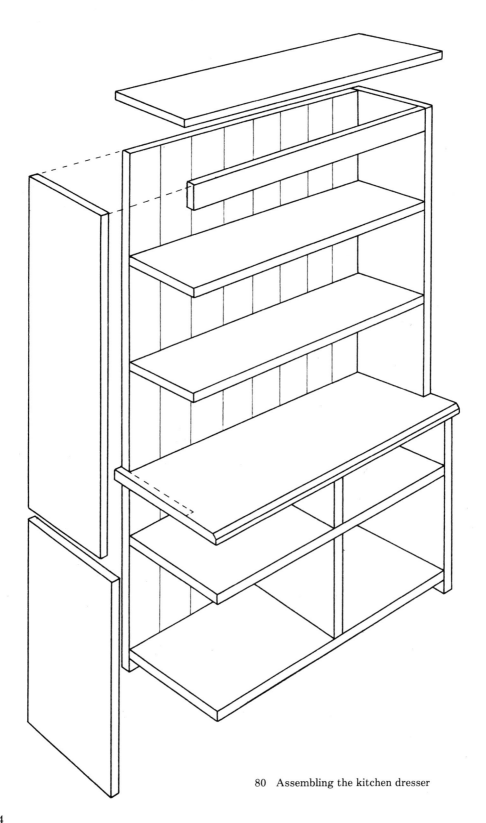

80   Assembling the kitchen dresser

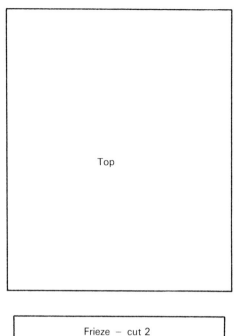

Top

Frieze – cut 2

Side frieze – cut 2

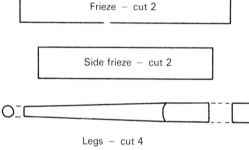

Legs – cut 4

81 Scale pattern for the kitchen table

Sand the table with fine abrasive paper, and stain it with a coat of button polish, painted on with an artist's paintbrush. Sand again, and polish with wax polish.

Kitchen chairs (*see* Fig 42) Full instructions and patterns for these chairs (and others) are given in Chapter 5.

The chairs in the kitchen are made of 4mm square beading with obeche-wood seats. They are stained with button polish to pine colour. Square loose cushions are held in place with thread ties.

Wall shelves (Fig 82) These are made of $^3/_{32}$in thick obeche wood, stained light oak.

Draw the pieces onto the wood and cut them out with a razor-toothed saw and a fretsaw. Sand the pieces with fine abrasive paper and stain them. Stick one side to the back, then stick the shelves to the back and side. Stick the other side in place. Sand the shelves, and apply one coat of amateur French polish to the sides and the shelves. Sand again, and wax

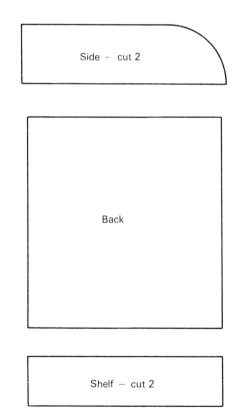

Side – cut 2

Back

Shelf – cut 2

82 Scale pattern for the wall shelves

polish the sides and shelves. Glue the shelf unit to the wall, or fix it with double-sided tape or small pieces of Blu-Tac.

Alcove shelf The shelf in the alcove above the sink is made from ³/₃₂in thick obeche wood, the same width and depth as the alcove. Cut the shelf and sand it. Cut two brackets from picture-frame moulding or triangular pieces of obeche wood. Stain the shelf and the brackets (we used light oak) and sand it again. Stick the brackets under the shelf, lining up the back edges, and glue brackets and shelf to the wall.

Stool The three-legged stool has a ⅛in obeche-wood top with fine-dowelling legs. The top is a circle one inch in diameter. Three evenly spaced holes are drilled at a slight outward angle in the under-side of the seat. The seat and three 1in lengths of dowelling are sanded and stained light oak. The legs are glued into the holes. When the glue is dry, the stool is finely sanded and left unpolished.

Accessories
Full details of how to make all the home-made accessories used in the house are given in Chapter 6. Most of the bought items are from the commercial dolls'-house ranges, available from good toy shops. A few items were bought from specialist dolls'-house shops (*see* Stockists).

Rugs The large rug in the bedroom, 7½ × 6½in, is beige felt, coloured with pink, red and green felt pens, and backed with carpet tape. The small rugs in the parlour and kitchen are both bought (Lundby).

Lights The brass candlesticks in the bedroom (holding home-made wax candles) and the brass-and-glass oil lamp in the kitchen are from a dolls'-house shop. The gas brackets in the parlour are made from picture hooks and Christmas-tree bulbs, and the parlour oil lamp is made from green-glass beads and jewellery findings.

Mirrors and pictures The mirrors in the bedroom (Caroline's Home) and the parlour (Lundby) are both from the commercial ranges. The rectangular picture frames in the

bedroom were both bought (the brown one was painted) and fitted with pictures cut from magazines.

In the parlour, the rectangular frames are made from wood-strip; the one holding a miniature embroidery print is stained oak colour, the other, holding a photograph, is painted dull gold. The elaborate gilt-framed picture over the sofa is a bought one (Lundby). The large picture over the kitchen mantelpiece is cut from a magazine and framed with thin wood-strip stained oak colour. The tiny 'Bless this House' by the window was framed with thicker wood-strip, oak stained. The round frames in the bedroom and parlour are all made of flat buttons, painted shiny black, with pictures cut from magazines. The miniature by the bed is a Victorian button. The Gainsborough lady by the bedroom window is an old brooch.

The washstand set and chamber pot (under the bed!) were bought from a dolls'-house shop. The glass jar and dish on the chest of drawers are made of glass buttons, and the white pot on the mantelpiece is a button with a pretty bead lid. The linen basket under the washstand was a holiday souvenir from France. The flowers are velvet ones in a white-painted plastic goblet. The clock under a dome on the parlour mantelshelf is from a toyshop (Lundby) and the metal grenadier on the bookcase, from a model shop. The plants are cut from plastic leaves in white-painted wooden-bead pots. The dried flowers are in a pretty glass-bead pot. The crystal ball on the bookcase, from a model shop. The plants, cut from plastic leaves, are in white-painted wooden-buttons, and the books are picture-covered wooden blocks. On the mantelpiece are a pretty pebble paperweight and a silver, plastic sugar bowl. The miniature books, magazine and photographs are from a dolls'-house shop. The poker at the fireplace is a rivet, the hearthbrush from a dolls'-house shop.

In the kitchen, the crockery on the dresser, the cutlery and the small wine bottles are from a toy shop. The kettle, saucepans and bucket were bought in yellow plastic, and painted with copper enamel paint. The red plastic flowers on the mantelpiece are in a painted

83 Variations on the Victorian town house plans

126

toothpaste cap. The soup ladle is made up of brass oddments super-glued together, and the flat iron is made of a piece of wood painted black with a brass oddment handle. The food-stuffs are modelled in clay and breadpaste, and the linen potato sack is filled with irregular-shaped beads. The glass storage jars are from a specialist shop, as is the earthen-ware jar on the dresser. The blue honey pot on the mantelshelf is made of wood and painted with enamel paint, as is the white jug on the table. The miniature tins of food are plastic and come from a toy shop. The roller towel and the washboard are made from obeche wood, dowelling and toothpicks. The towel is cream cotton tape. The wooden armchair is American (Shackmans), a present from a friend.

The master and mistress of the house, their baby and their cook are made from beads and pipecleaners. Full instructions for making them and patterns for their clothes are in Chapter 11. The cat on the kitchen hearth rug is modelled in clay and painted with gouache colours.

Variations
Although the tall, narrow design of this house is typical of a Victorian town house, the design could be adapted to other periods (Fig 83).

For example, with casement windows rather than sashes and an exterior of brick paper and timbering, the basic design could be trans-formed into a Tudor merchant's house. Also the roof should be covered with red tiles, the woodwork stained oak colour, and a planked door should be fitted for the complete Tudor effect. Inside, the house could be whitewashed or panelled, with planked floors upstairs and stone flags downstairs. The ground floor might be the merchant's shop, with a living room above and a sleeping chamber in the attic. In such a house, large heavy furniture such as a refectory table, benches and a four-poster bed would be appropriate. Tudor details such as leaded windows, elaborate chimney pots and tapestry wallhangings will enhance the effect.

Alternatively, the Victorian house might be inhabited by a modern family and decorated in modern colours and styles. The outside might be colour washed, perhaps cream or blue, with white paintwork and a brightly coloured front door. Inside, the fireplaces might have been blocked up, with electric fires in front of them and an Aga cooker in the kitchen fireplace. The wallpapers would be modern and the furniture in the latest style (see Chapter 10 for ideas). The kitchen would have fitted units and vinyl flooring. Upstairs, the modern sitting room would have a fitted carpet, wall units and a television. The bedroom would have a divan bed and built-in cupboards.

Two of these houses, fixed side-by-side, would make a large dolls' house with six rooms. Cut the side-window holes full length, to make doorways (on the opposite side in the second house) to give access from one part of the house to the other. The door on the front of the second house should be replaced with a window, and the whole front hinged to open on the right side rather than the left. The two houses could be made separately, then glued and screwed together before decorating the exterior.

You might fit a staircase into one half of the double-fronted house, making smaller rooms in the remaining space. Or a small building could be constructed, to house the staircase, the same height and depth as the houses with about a six inch frontage. This could have a flat roof, and doorholes on each floor, to line-up with the doorholes in the two wings. Sand-wiched between the two wings, and glued and screwed in place before the house is decorated, this staircase section would have its own front panel, either hinged to one side or made to lift off completely. This large house, with its central hall and staircase and two gabled wings, would make a typical large Victorian house, and provide a lot of space and scope for decorating and furnishing.

The basic Victorian-town-house design is also a good choice if you want to make a pair of semi-detached houses. It might be amusing to decorate and furnish one in the style of the 1880s and next-door in the style of the 1980s.

9 The Tudor Cottage

This house was commissioned by a lady as a present to herself. We were asked to build an old-fashioned cottage, but the design of the house and its furnishings were left to us. As the house was to be kept in the drawing room, and would obviously be closed much of the time, we felt that the exterior should be as attractive as possible, and chose the Tudor style for this reason. Tudor architecture, with its mellow red brick and roof tiles, oak beams and small-paned casement windows, gives plenty of scope for making the dolls' house an attractive ornament.

The interior of the house is decorated and furnished in the style of the early years of this century. We felt that a Tudor interior would greatly limit the number of things which could go into the house, and prove visually dull. Therefore, the cottage is an old one, built several hundred years before its present inhabitants were born. The red roof tiles have a weathered look, and the old timbers are sagging just a little.

The design of the cottage is fairly simple, with four rooms, two larger, two smaller. The staircase leads up from the kitchen and comes out behind a partition wall in one bedroom (a fairly common practice in small cottages, where space could not be wasted on halls and landings). There is a door between the kitchen and parlour and another between the two bedrooms, and a fireplace in each room. The rooms are not large, and the ceilings are fairly low and beamed both upstairs and down.

We chose subdued colours for the wallpapers and furnishings, and a dark stained finish for all the woodwork. Colour is important when planning an old house — natural colours in subdued shades and dark colours give a soft, mellow effect. Strong primary colours should be avoided, and large areas of pastel colour, although they look well in a Georgian or Regency house, are not appropriate to this period. This sort of cottage calls for simple, slightly rustic furniture, and offers the perfect home for miniature handicrafts such as patchwork or crochet bedspreads, raffia baskets, simple pottery and dipped candles.

The gable roof is hinged at the ridge, which allows the roof space to be used as an attic. We chose to use the attic space for storage, but it could be decorated and furnished as a room (in which case a small trapdoor should be cut in the bedroom ceiling and supplied with a ladder). The Tudor house is in the 1:16 scale and we built it of plywood (though Daler Board would be perfectly suitable, especially if the house is for an adult).

Before beginning, read Chapter 2.

Materials

¼in plywood (or Daler Board) for the house
⅛in plywood (or Daler Board) for the roof
thin cardboard for the roof tiles
narrow picture-frame moulding for the bargeboards
⅛in obeche wood for the doors
narrow wood-strip for door and window frames and glazing bars
$1/16$in perspex for the windows
one 4 × 1⅛in and three 3 × ¾in balsa blocks for chimney breasts
½in wide triangular beading for the stairs
½in square beading for the ridgepole
six 1in hinges for the roof and fronts
two ½in hinges for the front door
four ½in hinges for the interior doors (or use cloth hinges)
white woodwork glue, panel pins, masking tape

(above) Left-hand bedroom of the Tudor cottage, with matching curtains and bedspread

(below) Right-hand bedroom of the cottage, showing beamed ceiling

Cutting (Plans: Figs 84—7)

Draw all the pattern pieces onto the plywood, using a sharp pencil and ruler. Ensure that all the right-angles and measurements are precise. Label each piece in pencil ie back, side, roof, etc to avoid confusion when assembling. Cut out all the pieces with a saw, including the doorways, window holes and stairwell. Tape the pieces together with masking tape, to ensure that they fit properly and make any minor adjustments.

Assembly

Glue and pin one side onto the base (Fig 88). Glue and pin the back and second side onto the base and to each other. Glue and pin the top ceiling onto the side and back walls. Mark the positions of the floor and partition walls on the inside and outside of the sides, back, base and ceiling. The floor and partition walls (with the doorways and stairwell previously cut out) are cross-halved and fitted into the house. Glue and pin through the back and sides, base and top ceiling (full instructions for

Cosy cottage parlour, with antimacassars and oil lamp

cross-halving and other building methods are given in Chapter 2). The small partition wall in the bedroom is cut, assembled and fitted, but not fixed in place, at this stage.

(overleaf) Tudor cottage kitchen, with refectory table and benches, wooden dresser, and the farmer with his wife (Jonathon Bosley)

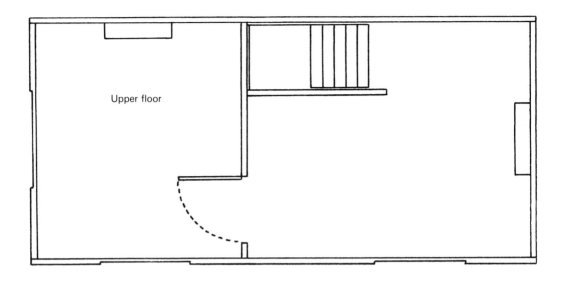

Upper floor

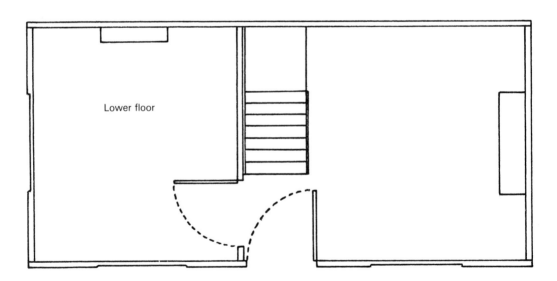

Lower floor

84   Floor plans for the Tudor cottage

85 86 and 87   Plans for the Tudor cottage
(pages 135–7)

134

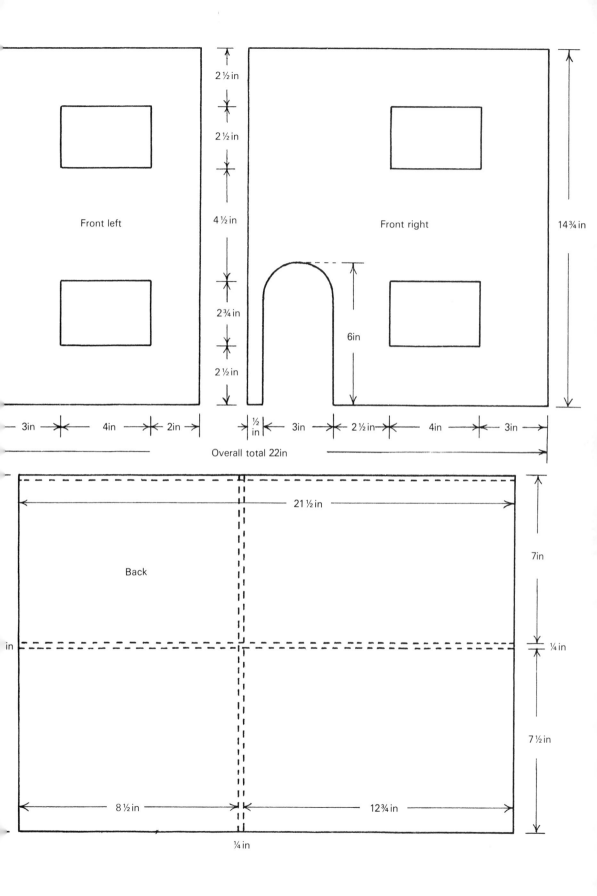

Front left

Front right

14¾ in

2½ in

2½ in

4½ in

2¾ in

2½ in

½ in

6in

3in → 4in → 2in →

½ in → 3in → 2½ in → 4in → 3in →

Overall total 22in

Back

21½ in

7in

¼ in

7½ in

in

8½ in

12¾ in

¼ in

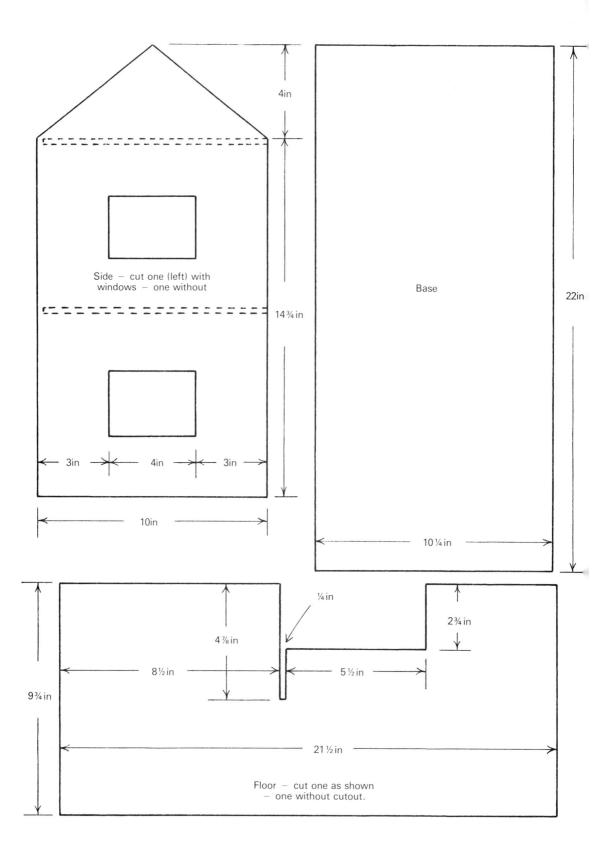

4in

14¾ in

Side — cut one (left) with
windows — one without

3in 4in 3in

10in

Base

22in

10¼ in

¼ in

4⅞ in

2¾ in

8½ in

5½ in

9¾ in

21½ in

Floor — cut one as shown
— one without cutout.

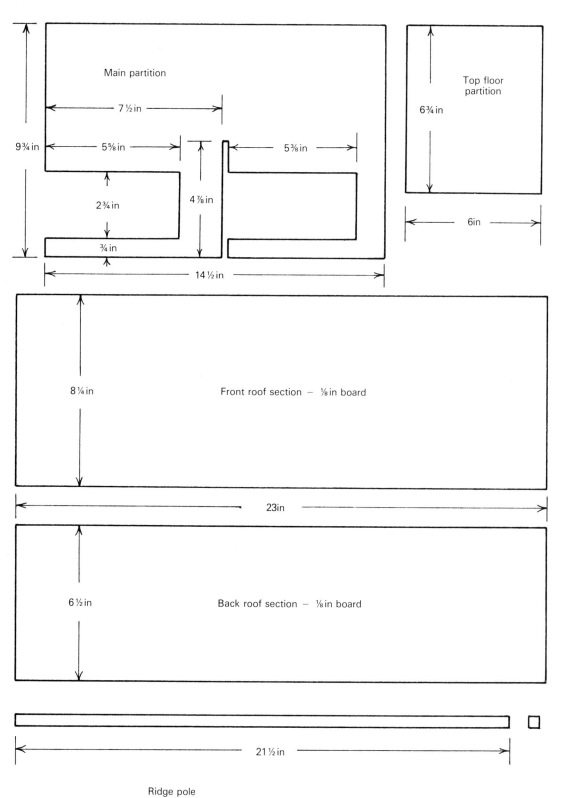

Main partition

7½in

9¾in 5⅝in 5⅜in

2¾in 4⅞in

¾in

14½in

Top floor partition

6¾in

6in

Front roof section — ⅛in board

8¼in

23in

Back roof section — ⅛in board

6½in

21½in

Ridge pole

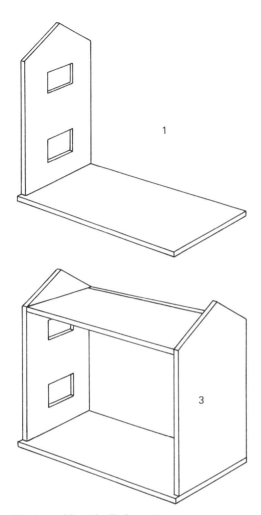
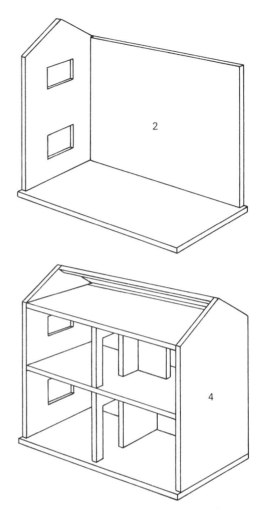

88   Assembling the Tudor cottage

Stairs

The stairs are made of ½in triangular beading on a backing of ⅛in obeche wood. The half landing is ⅛in thick obeche wood and the skirting boards ³/₃₂in obeche. The staircase is stained dark oak.

Draw the pattern pieces for the landing, skirting boards and backing for both flights onto the wood, ensuring that the measurements and angles are precise (Fig 89). Cut the pieces with a razor-toothed saw, sand them with fine abrasive paper and stain. Cut thirteen steps from triangular beading, ensuring that each step is exactly the same width as the backing. Sand the steps and stain them. Cut a fourteenth step from triangular beading, and plane one side of it down by ⅛in to fit the pattern for the top stair of the

bottom flight. Sand and stain this step as the others.

To assemble the staircase, begin with the bottom flight. Glue the stairs to the backing, beginning with the bottom step, and butting each step tightly against the next so that the top step fits where the chamfered edge of the backing begins.

Make the top flight in the same way, but starting with the top step, and ending with the bottom step against the chamfered edge of the backing. Glue this edge of the top flight to the edge of the half landing. This is temporarily a weak joint, so allow it to dry thoroughly before you proceed. Glue the top step of the bottom flight under the half landing. Glue the skirting boards in place on the outsides of each flight and the half landing

89   Scale pattern for the staircase

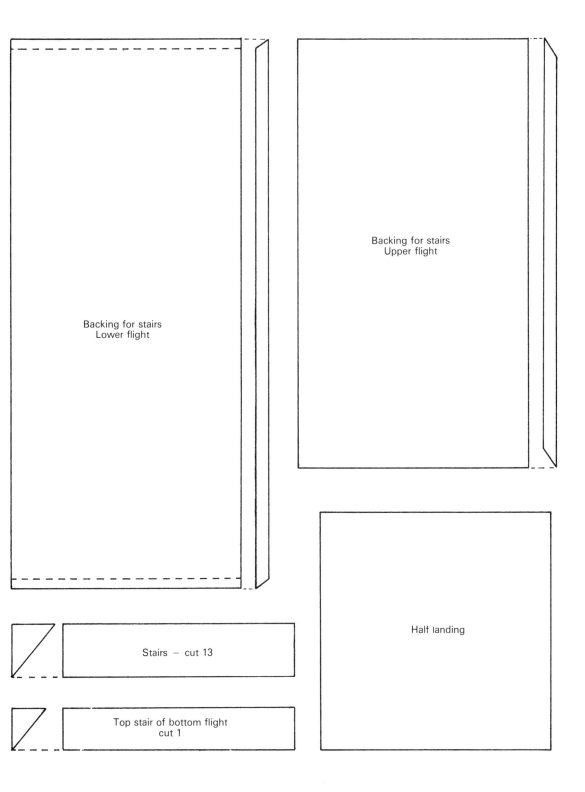

Backing for stairs
Lower flight

Backing for stairs
Upper flight

Half landing

Stairs — cut 13

Top stair of bottom flight
cut 1

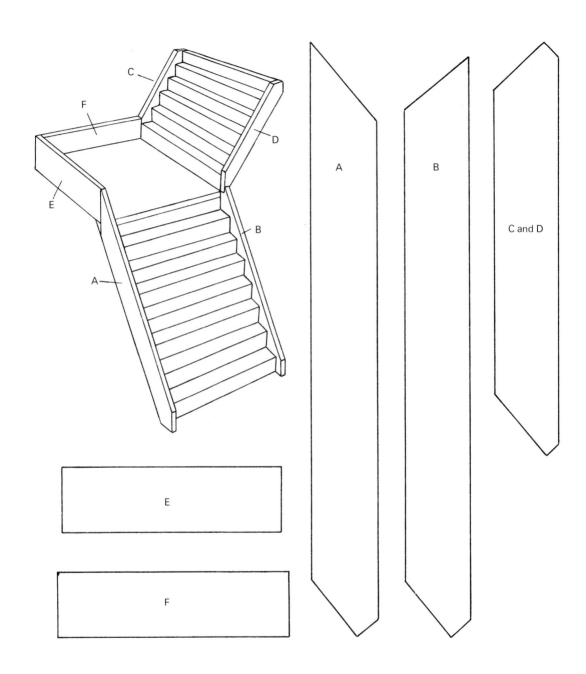

90 Scale pattern and assembly for the staircase
skirting boards

as shown in the pattern (Fig 90), ensuring that the joints match correctly.

The staircase is carpeted with a strip of felt, glued in place, and tucked firmly into the angle of each step. Do not fix the staircase in place until the house has been decorated.

Chimney breasts

Cut the chimney breasts to fit each room from balsa-wood block. The kitchen breast is 4in wide × 1⅛in deep, the parlour and bedrooms, 3in wide × ¾in deep. Cut out the fireplace openings: the kitchen has an arched opening, 3in wide and 3½in at the centre of the arch; the parlour 2in wide by 2½in high, and the bedrooms 2in wide by 2in high. Stick the balsa chimney breasts to the wall in each room, lining them up carefully, one above the other.

Doors

Cut, stain and assemble the two planked interior doors and hang them in the doorways with ½in hinges recessed into the door and the doorway (or cloth hinges). We used large loops from hook and loop fastenings for door handles, painted with black enamel paint and stuck to the doors with super-glue.

Exterior

Paper the exterior and the fronts. We chose red-brick paper, but a white woodchip wallpaper looks like whitewashed plaster or you might prefer to paint the exterior (Consult Chapter 3 for ideas). Paper the house, lapping the paper around the edges onto the walls inside. Cut strips of paper about 1½in wide to paper over the front edges of the floors and partition walls, lapping the paper onto the floors, ceilings and into the rooms. Paper the fronts, lapping the paper round all sides and through the door and window holes. Make sure that the paper is straight and line up the bricks at the centre-front join. Do not stick the timbering in place at this stage.

Windows

When the paper is thoroughly dry, you can fix all the windows in place. Stain the lengths of wood-strip before cutting — we used walnut stain, but dark oak or rosewood would also be suitable. Make a frame for each window from wood-strip, mitred at each corner, and stick to the inside front edge of the window hole. Cut the perspex and fix in place. Make a similar frame on the inside back edge of each window to hold the perspex in place. The glazing bars are stuck to the window, both inside and out. Firstly, divide each window down the centre to make two casements, and make a frame for each half, mitred at the corners. The vertical bars are stuck in place first, then the horizontal bars are cut to fit and stuck in place. Although time consuming, glazing bars stuck to both sides of the window are very realistic, and worth the effort. The handles on the windows are large loops from hook and loop fastenings, pulled open with pliers, painted black and stuck to the window frame at the centre with super-glue.

Front door

Cut and assemble the planked front door from obeche wood, sand, paint or stain it on both sides. Hang the door from ½in hinges on the right-hand side, recessed into the wood. These hinges are too small to fix with screws so we use fine pins. To avoid splitting the wood, mark the holes through the hinges onto the door and use a fine drill or dressmaker's pin to drill the holes. Use super-glue to hold both the hinges and the pins. Repeat this process to hinge the door to the doorway, recessing the hinges into the door frame and holding them with super-glue and pins. Before hanging the door, the doorway can be faced with fine wood-strip, ⅛in wide. The wood-strip should be stained, then steamed over a kettle until it is pliable. The arched top of the door frame is formed by taping the wood-strip around a jam jar until it is dry. The strip is then glued into the doorway and the door is cut to fit.

Roof

The ridgepole is fitted between the tops of the gable-end walls, and screwed in place. The back-roof section is glued and pinned to the top of the gable-end walls and the ridgepole, with an overhang at each side. The front-roof section is hinged to the ridgepole, with an overhang at each side and the bottom edge (full instructions are given in Chapter 2).

The roof tiles are cut from strips of thin cardboard and stuck to each side of the roof in overlapping layers. The tiles are then painted a dark brownish-red to represent old clay roof tiles. The bargeboards are cut from picture-frame moulding, stained and stuck to the underside of the gable ends of the roof, with the apex join mitred to fit.

This house does not have chimneys, because the space it was to occupy was not big enough. But chimneys can be cut from balsa block, covered in brick paper and stuck to the roof above the chimney breasts. Clay or bead chimney pots should be stuck to the chimneys — one pot for each room.

Fronts

The fronts can be hinged in place at this stage, using two 1in hinges at each side, fixed in the same way as the door hinges but using super-glue and screws rather than pins. You might prefer to leave this until the interior has been decorated. The timbering effect and the front porch are fitted after the fronts have been fixed onto the house.

Timbering

Mark lightly in pencil on the front and sides of the house where the timbers are to go, ensuring that the horizontal beams line up (Fig 91).

Using any thin wood-veneer sheets (available from art and craft shops), stained to the appropriate colour, cut strips, roughly ½in wide for the main beams and ⅜in wide for the smaller beams. Cut the strips with scissors so that they are not too straight and even. Stick the veneer strips in place using UHU or similar glue. The large horizontal beams are fixed first, and the vertical beams cut to fit around them.

Porch

The gabled porch is made from ⅛in thick obeche wood (Fig 92). Cut the roof pieces, chamfer their top edges, stick them together and then stick the porch roof to the house, above the front door. Cut the brackets from ¼in thick wood with a fretsaw, stain and stick in place either side of the door, under the porch. Cut the bargeboards from 5mm square beading, stain and stick to the underside front edges of the porch roof, with the apex join mitred to fit. The porch-roof tiles are made from painted cardboard as for the roof, with a narrow strip of card folded down the middle to cover the ridge.

91 Design for the timbering on front and sides

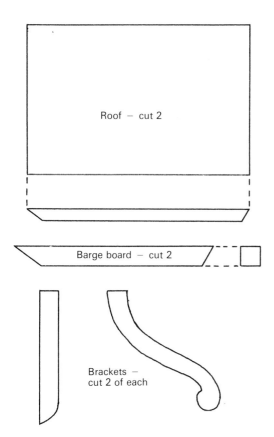

Roof — cut 2

Barge board — cut 2

Brackets —
cut 2 of each

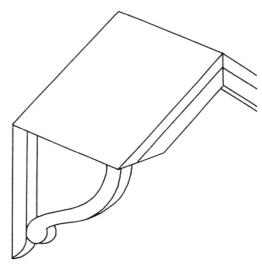

92 Scale pattern and assembly for the gable
porch

Finishing
The plaque or datestone above the front door is modelled in Das. This is rolled flat about ⅛in thick, and a rectangle cut with a knife. The name of the house and the date (Aragon House 1980) are incised with a pointed instrument. When the plaque is dry, it is stuck to the front of the house with UHU.

The metal door furniture we used for this house came from a specialist dolls'-house shop (*see* Stockists), but similar elaborate hinges could be cut from thin metal sheet or even cardboard, painted black and stuck in place. The door knocker could be made from a broken ear-ring and small brass or plastic ring, and the door knob from a map pin.

You might wish to add window boxes or a creeper climbing over the front porch (*see* Chapter 3), a porch lantern or a letterbox. If you have used white woodchip wallpaper instead of brick paper, you might like to give it the effect of pargetting by painting a shadowy design in the plaster panels between the timbers. Grey poster paint and a fine artist's paintbrush will do this efficiently, and choose simple patterns, birds, stylised flowers, etc, for the pargetting designs.

Tie-rods were often used on old houses when the brick walls started to lean outwards or bulge. A tie-rod runs through the house (usually from gable to gable) and is held with tie-plates on the outside walls. The tie-plates can be decorative, often an S or X shape in wrought iron. Dolls'-house tie-plates can be made from thin metal, cut to shape and painted matt black. They can be stuck to the wall, and look more realistic if a nut or washer is stuck to the centre to represent the end of the tie-rod.

Interior
The wallpapers used in this house are ordinary household wallpapers with small designs. The two bedrooms were papered with sample

143

pieces begged from the local wallpaper shop, and the parlour with a remnant from our own home decorating. The kitchen is painted with two coats of magnolia emulsion paint. Green, brown and light cream are the only colours used for the walls in this house, so that the general effect is harmonious and subdued. The bedroom above the parlour has a cream paper with a tracery of brown flowers and leaves, the other has cream paper with light-brown stripes and green roses. The paper in the parlour is a darker green, heavily patterned with cream flowers. All three papers are very similar to late-Victorian wallpaper patterns, especially the striped design, and all have the right 'cottagey' feel about them. The rich flocked and gilded papers which were fashionable in opulent houses would look out of place in a cottage.

Before you begin decorating, fill any small gaps with Polyfilla rubbed in with a finger, and wipe off any surplus filler with a damp cloth. When the Polyfilla is dry, begin by painting the ceilings. These can be papered with lining paper first but in a cottage a slightly rough texture is appropriate. Use household emulsion paint for the ceilings, two or three coats as necessary. Magnolia gives a softer effect than white, which would be too garish for this sort of house.

When the ceilings are dry, paper the rooms (except the right-hand bedroom). Even if you plan to paint the walls, lining them with paper first will give a better finish. Start with the back wall of each room (see Chapter 3). When the paste is thoroughly dry, paint the kitchen with two coats of emulsion paint, continuing the paint up into that part of the bedroom which will be behind the partition wall above the stairs. When the paint is dry, glue and pin this partition wall in place, before wallpapering the bedroom. The insides of the fronts can be papered to match one of the rooms or in a harmonising colour. We used a plain-beige paper.

The kitchen floor is papered with the same red-brick we used for the outside of the house, but stone flags would look equally good. The parlour and bedroom floors are covered with plain-brown wrapping paper.

When the walls and floors are papered, cut, stain and fix the door and window frames made from fine wood-strip and the skirting boards made from ½in wide strips of $^{1}/_{16}$in thick obeche wood.

The staircase, stained and carpeted, is then glued into place in the kitchen, followed by the banister rail, if required.

Fireplace surrounds (Figs 93 and 94) The fireplace surrounds in the bedrooms are cut from the pattern given, using $^{3}/_{32}$in thick obeche wood. Assemble, paint with ivory enamel paint, and use varnished paper tiles for decoration. Glue the surrounds in place over the fireplace openings on the chimney breasts. The grates are pieces of thin metal, curved and glued into the fireplace openings.

The parlour fireplace surround (Figs 95 and 96) is cut from obeche wood and stained walnut. The brackets which support the mantelshelf are cut from picture-frame moulding, and the rope-twist decoration is cut from a piece of fancy wood moulding. The sides and back of the opening are papered with brick paper. Full instructions for making the log basket and fireback are given in Chapter 4.

The mantelshelf above the kitchen fireplace is cut from ⅛in thick obeche wood, stained and mounted on picture-frame-moulding brackets stuck to the wall. The kitchen stove, made from a Colman's-mustard tin, is fully described in Chapter 6.

Ceiling beams The ceiling beams in this cottage run from back to front. There are two in each of the larger rooms and one in each of the smaller rooms. They are made from lengths of wood ½in wide and ¼in deep. Each beam is cut to fit, 'aged' with a hammer, then stained walnut and stuck to the ceiling with UHU glue. The beam in the parlour is placed to the right of the chimney breast, in the bedroom above to the left of the chimney breast. In the other bedroom, one beam is about half-way along the small partition wall, the other is about 3in in front of the chimney breast. In the kitchen, one beam runs under the head of the stairs, the other across the front of the chimney breast. These beams are not essential, but they give a period effect, and are simple to fix. Smaller beams about ¼in square could be glued to the ceiling instead, evenly spaced about 2in apart.

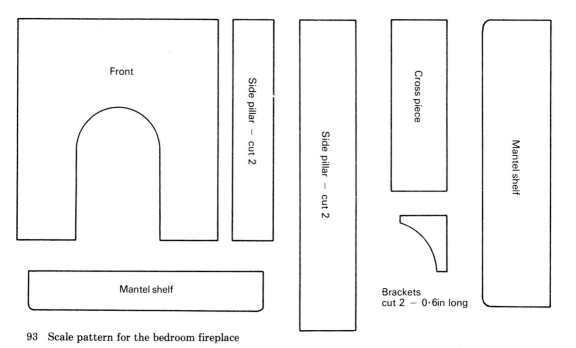

Front

Side pillar — cut 2

Side pillar — cut 2

Cross piece

Mantel shelf

Mantel shelf

Brackets
cut 2 — 0·6in long

93   Scale pattern for the bedroom fireplace

95   Scale pattern for the parlour fireplace

96   Assembling the parlour fireplace

94   Assembling the bedroom fireplace

Attic The attic in this cottage is used as storage space rather than a room. The underside of the roof is painted with magnolia emulsion paint, the gable walls are papered with red-brick paper, and the floor with brown wrapping paper. This provides a useful place to put surplus pieces of furniture and junk, as in real houses. It can also be a convenient place, if the house is to be wired, for the wiring connections, batteries or transformer. When the roof is opened, it is supported on two 4½in posts made of ½in square wood, which are hinged to the attic floor. When the roof is closed, the supports fold down.

Curtains There are net curtains at each window, made from pieces of an old curtain — modern white nets can be dyed to the appropriate cream colour by soaking them in cold tea. The net curtains are hung from wood-strip battens, glued to the top of the window frame. The printed-cotton curtains in the bedroom, and the velveteen ones in the parlour are gathered onto wood-strip battens mounted on wooden blocks stuck to the wall at each side of the window. This means that the net curtains

are fixed permanently, but the heavier curtains open and close.

The windows on the fronts of the house have only net curtains, although you could hang two sets at these windows as well.

Furniture for the left-hand bedroom
The patterns for the Tudor house's furniture are drawn actual size, so that they can be traced from the book. Before beginning, read Chapter 5, and refer to it when necessary.

Chest of drawers (Fig 97) This is made of $^3/_{32}$in thick obeche wood, stained light oak. The handles were bought from a specialist shop, but brass gimp pins would be a good alternative.

Draw the pattern pieces onto the wood, ensuring that the grain lines are consistent, the measurements and right-angles are correct. Cut the pieces with a razor-toothed saw and chamfer the edges of the top and base pieces. Sand all the parts with fine abrasive paper and stain them.

97 Scale pattern for the chest of drawers

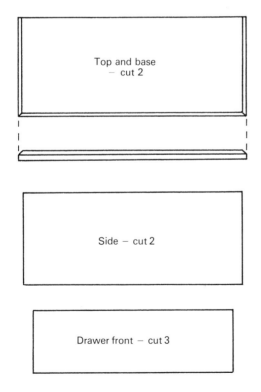

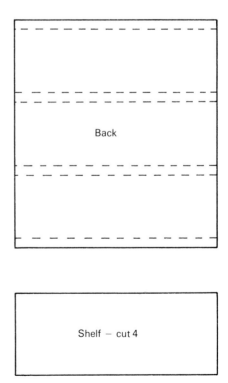

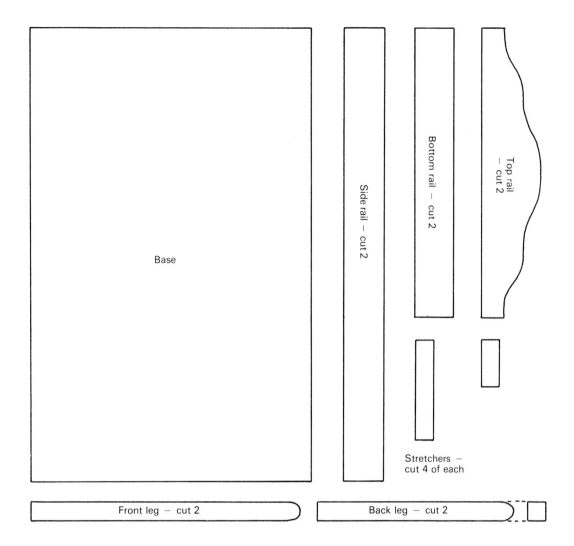

Base

Side rail – cut 2

Bottom rail – cut 2

Top rail – cut 2

Stretchers –
cut 4 of each

Front leg – cut 2

Back leg – cut 2

Assemble the shell by sticking the shelves to the back, then sticking the sides in place, lining them up with the front edges of the shelves. Stick the top and base in place. Check that the drawer fronts fit snugly into the spaces. Cut the bottoms and sides of the drawers from unstained wood and assemble the drawers to fit the drawer spaces.

Sand the shell and the drawer fronts gently with fine abrasive paper and apply one coat of amateur French polish. Allow this to dry thoroughly, then gently sand again. Apply several coats of wax polish, well-buffed between each coat. Mark the position of the drawer handles, and drill fine holes to take the

98 Scale pattern for the double bed

shanks of the handles or gimp pins. If you are using gimp pins cut the shanks to $^3/_{16}$in long. Push the handles into the holes and fix with a small dab of glue over the pin hole on the inside of the drawer.

Double bed (Figs 98 and 99) This is made from $^1/_8$in thick obeche wood, and 5mm square beading stained mahogany.

Draw the pieces onto the wood, ensuring that the measurements and right-angles are precise. Cut the pieces with a razor-toothed saw, taking particular care to cut the pairs of

147

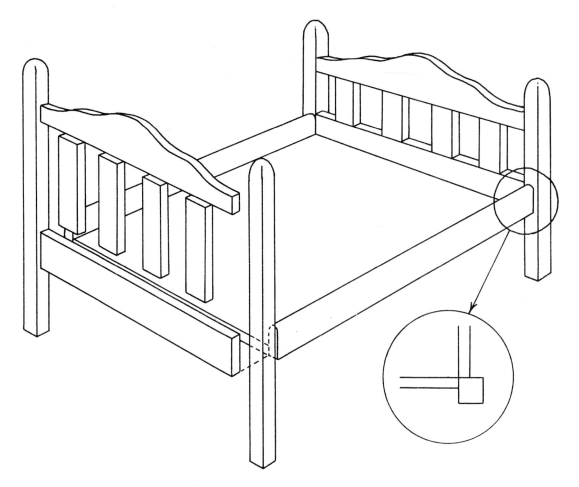

99 Assembling the double bed

bedposts of equal lengths with perfectly square ends. Cut the top rails for the head and foot of the bed with a fretsaw.

Assemble the head and foot by glueing the upright stretchers between the top and bottom rails, and the bedposts onto each side. Ensure that the leg part of each post is exactly ¾in, so that the bed will stand square. Glue the side rails to the base. Glue the head and foot onto the base so that the bedposts line up with the side rails. Ensure that the legs stand square, supporting them if necessary until the glue is dry. Sand the bed carefully with fine abrasive paper and apply one coat of amateur French polish with an artist's paintbrush. Sand again with very fine abrasive paper and apply several coats of wax polish, well-buffed between each coat.

(above right) Right-hand bedroom in the Tudor cottage, with flowery wallpaper, chintz chair and tiny patchwork quilt. The staircase emerges behind the partition wall on the left, as shown in the jacket picture

(below right) The country kitchen of the Tudor cottage, with brick floor, beamed ceiling and open staircase. The well-polished furniture reflects the gleam of brass and copper pans

(overleaf) Interior of the modern house (Chapter 10), designed to take full advantage of the commercial ranges of dolls'-house accessories, and have all modern conveniences

148

Make a mattress using the bed base as a pattern, two pillows, sheets and a blanket. Cut a bedspread ½in wider and 1in longer than the bed, to give seam allowances. Hem the top and bottom edges. Cut two strips for the frilled sides; hem the bottom and side edges of each frill and gather the top edges. Sew them to either side of the bedspread. Put the bedspread onto the bed, and, if necessary, push pins through each side into the mattress to hold the frills in place until they hang properly. (We used the same printed cotton for the bedspread and curtains here, though any lightweight natural fabric could be used.)

Washstand (Figs 100 and 101) This is made of ³/₃₂in thick obeche wood, stained walnut. The towel rail is a fine wooden toothpick and the tiles are varnished paper.

Draw the pattern pieces onto the wood, ensuring that the measurements and right-angles are correct. Cut the pieces with a razor-toothed saw, the curved side pieces with a fretsaw. Sand the pieces with fine abrasive paper and stain them, including the wooden toothpick. Drill fine holes in the side pieces where indicated, to take the towel rail.

Glue one side piece to the back, then glue the two shelves to the side and back. Glue the other side in place. Push the toothpick into the holes drilled in the sides, trimming the ends if necessary so that they do not protrude.

Sand the washstand with fine abrasive paper and apply one coat of amateur French polish. Sand again with very fine abrasive paper and apply several coats of wax polish, buffing well between each coat. Cut the paper tiles (we used tiles cut from a magazine illustration) to fit the back and the top shelf and stick them in place with UHU or similar glue. A coat of varnish (colourless nail varnish works well) gives the tiles a more realistic effect. Cut a towel and hang it from the rail. The top shelf of the washstand holds a washbowl and jug, the bottom shelf a chamber pot.

(above left) The lounge/dining room of the modern house, the parents listening to their hi-fi

(below left) The dolls (Chapter 11), simply made from beads and pipecleaners, but, when suitably dressed, quite at home in any period or modern house

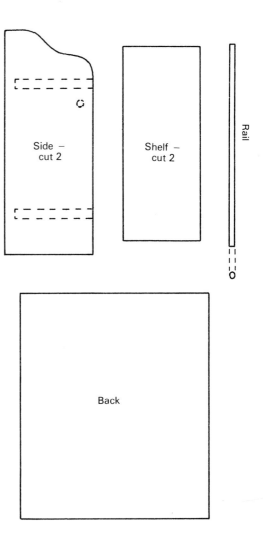

100   Scale pattern for the washstand

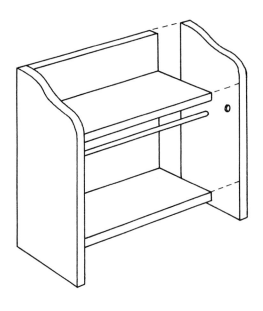

101 Assembling the washstand

102 Scale pattern for the dower chest

Dower chest (Figs 102 and 103)   This is made of ⅛in thick obeche wood stained medium oak. The panelling is made with fine wood-strip.

Draw the pattern pieces onto the wood, ensuring that the measurements and right-angles are precise. Cut the pieces with a razor-toothed saw, sand with fine abrasive paper and stain them, including the wood-strip. The top edges of the lid should be chamfered slightly before staining if the chest is to look old.

Glue the front and back to the base, with the base inside. Glue the ends to the back, front and base, to form the box. The under-lid piece is glued to the underside of the lid, leaving a larger overhang at the front edge than the back to allow for the panelling. Make a frame of fine wood-strip on the front of the box, mitring the corners. Divide the panel into three equal sections with two small uprights of wood-strip, fitting exactly into the frame.

Sand the box and the lid carefully with fine abrasive paper. Apply one coat of amateur French polish to the outside of the box and the top of the lid. Sand again with fine abrasive

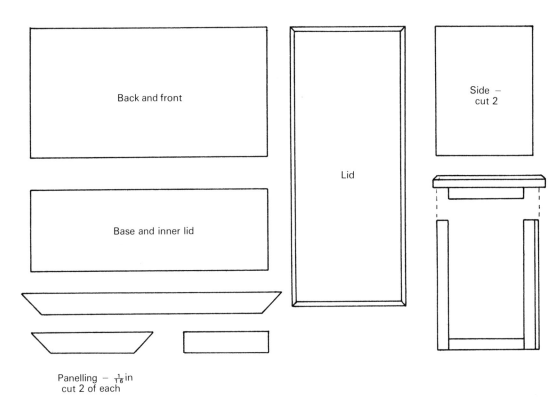

Back and front

Base and inner lid

Side –
cut 2

Lid

Panelling – $\frac{1}{16}$in
cut 2 of each

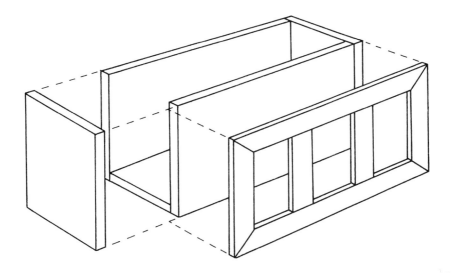

103   Assembling the dower chest

paper and apply several coats of wax polish, well-buffed between coats.

The dower chest in this house holds the deeds of the house but it might contain folded linen or small treasures.

Chair   The chair in the bedroom is an adaptation of the ladderback chair fully described in Chapter 5. It is made in mahogany, the legs and rails carved with a craft knife to represent turning. This particular chair is rather difficult to make, but a simpler alternative can be made from the instructions given in Chapter 5 (*see* Fig 42).

Furniture for the right-hand bedroom

Wardrobe (Figs 104 and 105)   This is made of $^3/_{32}$in thick obeche wood stained light oak. The handles on this piece were bought from a specialist shop, but brass gimp pins would be a good alternative. The rail inside is made of fine dowelling.

Draw the pattern pieces onto the wood, ensuring that the measurements and right-angles are precise. Score outlines of door panels on the door fronts with a sharp instrument, using a metal ruler as a guide. Cut the pieces, using a razor-toothed saw. Drill shallow holes on the insides of the side pieces, where marked, to hold the hanging rail. Glue the two base pieces together and press under a weight until the glue is dry. Chamfer the underside of the top piece at the front and sides. Sand all pieces with fine abrasive paper and stain them. Assemble the wardrobe by glueing one side to the back. Glue the inner top inside the back and side, and the base inside the back and side, as marked on the pattern. Glue the other side in place, fixing the rail into the holes. Pin hinge the doors into the base, then into the top (with the chamfered edge to the underside). Glue the top in place. Assemble the cornice with mitred corners and glue to the top, overhanging slightly. Glue the sides of the plinth to the bottom of the wardrobe sides and the front of the plinth to the front of the wardrobe below the doors.

Sand the wardrobe carefully with fine-grade abrasive paper and apply one coat of amateur French polish. Sand again with very fine abrasive paper and apply several coats of wax polish, well-buffed between coats. Mark the positions of the door handles and fix in place.

Single bed (Fig 106)   The bed is made from $^1/_8$in thick obeche wood with 5mm square-beading posts, stained walnut.

Draw the pattern pieces onto the wood, ensuring that the measurements and right-angles are precise. Cut the pieces with a razor-toothed saw, and the curved tops of head and footboards with a fretsaw. Take particular care to cut the two pairs of bedposts of equal

155

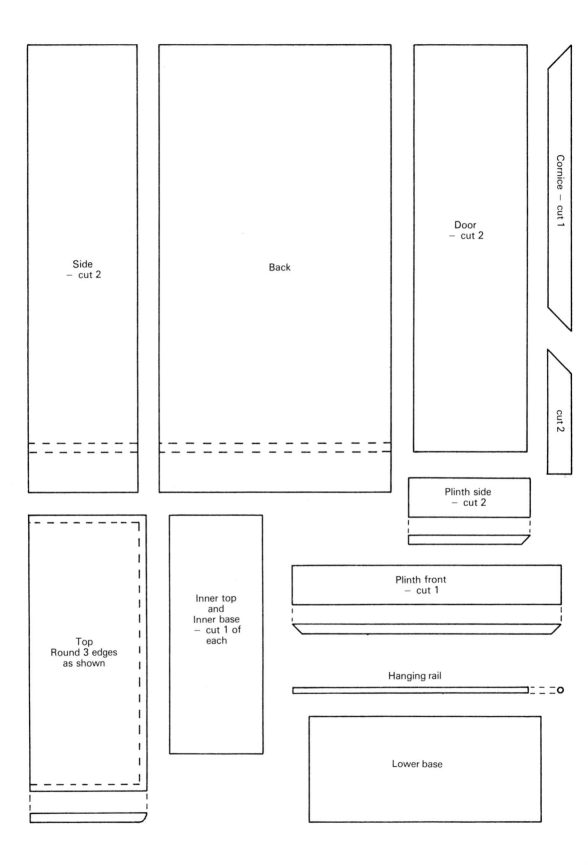

Side
— cut 2

Back

Door
— cut 2

Cornice — cut 1

cut 2

Plinth side
— cut 2

Plinth front
— cut 1

Top
Round 3 edges
as shown

Inner top
and
Inner base
— cut 1 of
each

Hanging rail

Lower base

105   Assembling the wardrobe

(left) 104   Scale pattern for the wardrobe

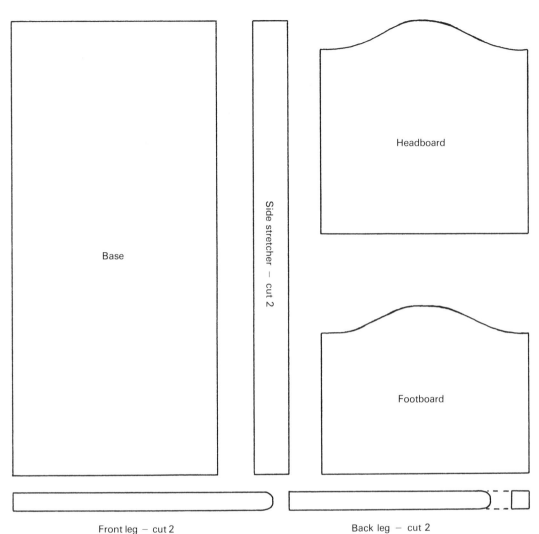

Base

Side stretcher — cut 2

Headboard

Footboard

Front leg — cut 2

Back leg — cut 2

106 Scale pattern for the single bed

lengths with perfectly square ends. Sand the pieces with fine abrasive paper and stain them.

Glue the headboard and footboard between the bedposts, ensuring that the leg parts of the posts are exactly ¾in so that the bed will stand square (*see* Fig 99). Glue the side rails to the base. Glue the headboard and footboard onto the base so that the bedposts line up with the side rails. Ensure that the legs stand square, supporting them if necessary until the glue is dry.

Sand the bed carefully with fine abrasive paper and apply one coat of amateur French polish. Sand again with very fine abrasive paper and apply several coats of wax polish, buffing well between coats.

Make a mattress using the bed base as a pattern, plus a pillow, sheets and a blanket. The patchwork bedspread on this bed is a real one — the squares are 1cm each, sewn nine on each side to form a 9cm square (Fig 107). The quilt is backed with a piece of lawn, and the edges bound with a narrow strip of one of the fabrics used in the quilt. The sides and bottom are edged with rough cotton lace. Four patterns,

107 Design for the patchwork quilt

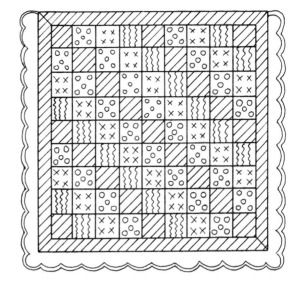

Single bed (plus chamber pot) and panelled dower
chest

all cotton prints in shades of pink, blue and gold, were used to make the quilt. A fake patchwork or alternative bedspread could be used instead.

Armchair (Fig 108) This is made of cardboard, padded with foam and covered with printed cotton.

Cut the cardboard back for the chair from the pattern and score the fold lines. Cut the padding and the fabric cover ½in larger allround than the pattern, to allow for seams. Glue the foam to the cardboard, rolling the excess foam to the back, and glueing the edges to the back of the cardboard. Stitch the cover, clip the corners and curves and then turn through to the right side. Slip the cover over the padded cardboard, pulling it taut, and slipstitch the bottom edges closed.

Cut the seat from balsa block, pad with foam and cover with fabric. Fold the sides of the chair forward and fit the seat in place. Glue the seat to the back and sides of the chair, holding it in place with pins until the glue dries. Glue four square wooden beads to the underside for feet. Make a loose cushion in the same fabric for the seat, and a small cushion in a plain, toning fabric to tuck into the corner of the chair.

Book shelf (Fig 109) This is made of $^3/_{32}$in thick obeche wood, stained with button polish to pine colour.

Draw the pieces onto the wood, and cut them with a razor-toothed saw, and fretsaw for the curved side pieces. Sand the pieces carefully with fine abrasive paper.

Assemble the shelves by sticking one side to the back, then sticking the shelves to the back and side. Stick the other side in place. Sand the shelves with very fine abrasive paper and stain them with a coat of button polish, applied with an artist's paintbrush. Sand again, and polish with wax polish. The shelf is stuck to the wall with double-sided tape.

Small table (Fig 110) This is made of $^1/_{16}$in thick obeche wood with 4mm square beading for legs. It is stained walnut.

Draw the pattern pieces onto the wood, ensuring that the right-angles are precise, and the legs are exactly the same length with square ends. Sand the pieces with fine abrasive paper and stain them. Glue the four frieze pieces to the underside of the table top to form a closed box. Glue the legs into the corners of this box, supporting them if necessary to keep them straight whilst the glue dries. Glue the notched corners of the shelf

108 Scale pattern for the bedroom chair

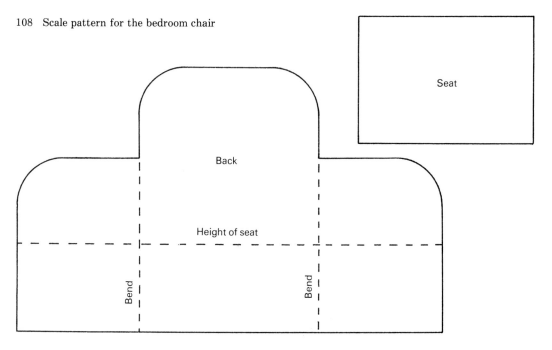

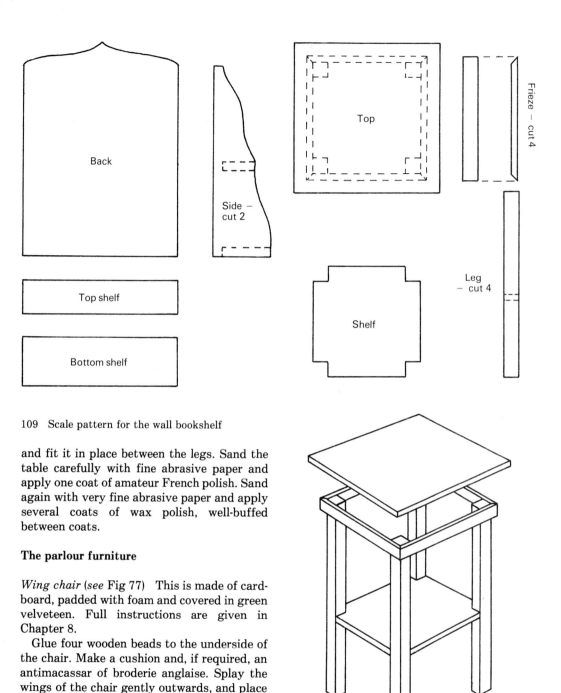

109 Scale pattern for the wall bookshelf

and fit it in place between the legs. Sand the table carefully with fine abrasive paper and apply one coat of amateur French polish. Sand again with very fine abrasive paper and apply several coats of wax polish, well-buffed between coats.

The parlour furniture

Wing chair (see Fig 77) This is made of cardboard, padded with foam and covered in green velveteen. Full instructions are given in Chapter 8.

Glue four wooden beads to the underside of the chair. Make a cushion and, if required, an antimacassar of broderie anglaise. Splay the wings of the chair gently outwards, and place the cushion in the back of the chair.

Footstool This is made of a ½in piece sawn from one end of a cotton reel. It is padded with foam and covered with brown velveteen.

Cut a ½in piece from one end of a cotton reel (or use a circle of balsa wood or cork) with a

110 Scale pattern and assembly for the bedroom table

razor-toothed saw. Cut a circle of fabric 3in in diameter. Glue a little padding to the top of the cotton reel. Run a gathering thread around the edge of the fabric circle and draw it over the padded cotton reel with the gathered edge under the base. Pull the gathers up as tightly as possible, distributing them evenly so that the cover is taut. Fasten off and trim the excess fabric. Cut a circle of felt and glue it to the underside to cover the raw edges. Glue a piece of narrow upholstery braid or ribbon around the sides of the stool to trim.

Shelf unit (Figs 111 and 112) This is made of $^3/_{32}$in thick obeche wood, stained walnut.

Draw the pattern pieces onto the wood, ensuring that the measurements and right-angles are precise. Cut the straight-edged pieces with a razor-toothed saw, and the curved side pieces and pediment with a fretsaw. Glue the three base pieces together, one on top of another, and press under a weight until firmly stuck. Sand the pieces with fine abrasive paper and stain them.

Assemble the shelf unit by glueing one side to the back, then the shelves to the back and side, then the other side to the back and shelves. Glue the shelves onto the base, lining them up carefully so that the base protrudes slightly at the front and sides. Glue the curved front pediment to the front edge of the top and glue the top in place. Glue the two pediment sides to the top, behind the pediment front.

Sand the shelf unit carefully with fine abrasive paper and apply one coat of amateur French polish. Sand again with very fine abrasive paper and apply several coats of wax polish, buffing well between coats.

Sofa (*see* Fig 47) The sofa is made of cardboard, padded with foam and covered with printed cotton. Full instructions are given in Chapter 5.

Cupboard This particular cupboard was bought from a dolls'-house shop, but a similar cupboard could be made from the pattern for the wardrobe, reduced to 2½in high. Follow

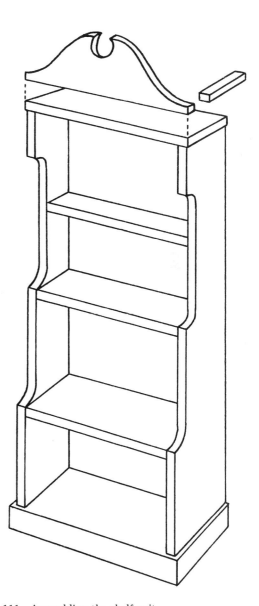

111 Assembling the shelf unit

(above and below left) Various pieces from the Tudor parlour — wooden and upholstered furniture, a printed felt rug and several life-like accessories

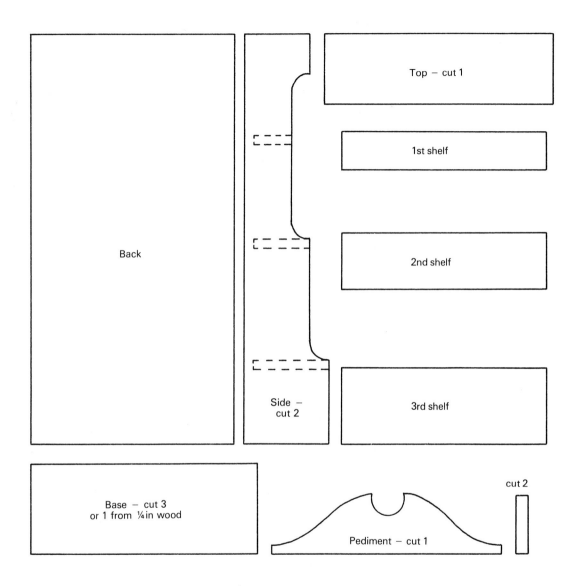

Back

Top – cut 1

1st shelf

2nd shelf

Side –
cut 2

3rd shelf

Base – cut 3
or 1 from ¼ in wood

Pediment – cut 1

cut 2

112   Scale pattern for the shelf unit

the directions given for the wardrobe, using ⅛in thick obeche wood and rosewood stain. In place of the wardrobe cornice, cut a flat top to overhang the front and sides slightly. Brass gimp pins would make suitable handles.

Armchair (see Fig 108) The armchair in the parlour is made in exactly the same way as the armchair in the bedroom. When the chair is complete, cut a strip of the same fabric 1in wide and 7in long to make the frill. Seam the two short ends together and sew a narrow hem along the bottom edge. Turn in the raw top edge and press the fold. Run a gathering thread along the fold line, and pull tightly around the chair. Distribute the gathers evenly and fasten off. Slipstitch the top edge of the frill to the chair as neatly as possible. This chair has matching loose cushions.

Sofa table (Fig 113) This is made in ⅛in thick obeche wood, stained mahogany. Draw the pattern pieces onto the wood, ensuring that the two legs are exactly alike. Cut the top and the stretcher with a razor-toothed saw, the legs with a fretsaw, omitting cut-outs on the legs if you prefer. Sand the pieces carefully with fine abrasive paper and stain them. Glue the stretcher and the two legs in place to the underside of the top, positioning them carefully while the glue is wet and supporting them if necessary until the glue is dry. Sand the table with fine abrasive paper and apply one coat of amateur French polish. Sand again with very fine abrasive paper and apply several coats of wax polish, well-buffed between coats.

Wine table This is made from a black chess piece, with a circular top 1½in in diameter, cut from ⅛in thick obeche wood stained walnut.

The top is cut, sanded and stained, and glued to the chess-piece pedestal. The table top is varnished with one coat of polyurethane varnish. Any similar piece of turned wood could be used for the pedestal, or use the pedestal table in the Victorian town house reduced to 2in high.

The kitchen furniture

Dresser (Figs 114, 115 and 116) The kitchen

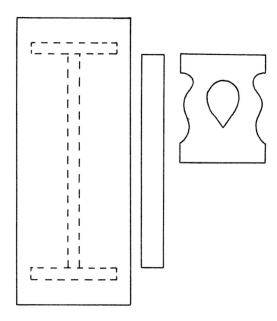

113   Scale pattern for the sofa table

dresser is made in the traditional manner as two separate units. It is made of ³/₃₂in thick obeche wood, stained dark oak. The handles on this piece were bought from a specialist shop, but brass gimp pins or the loop part of hook and loop fasteners would make suitable alternatives.

Draw the pattern pieces onto the wood, ensuring that the measurements and right-angles are precise. Cut the straight-edged pieces with a razor-toothed saw, and the curved sides and frieze pieces with a fretsaw. Score the back pieces with a sharp instrument (eg scissor blade) to represent planking. Chamfer the top front and side edges of the base-unit top. Sand all the pieces with fine abrasive paper and stain them.

Firstly, the base unit: glue one side piece to the back. Glue the drawer shelf in place, then the drawer divider and the lower partition. Glue the bottom shelf then the other side piece. Stick the top in place, overhanging at the front and sides, then the small curved frieze pieces under the drawer shelf. Check that the drawer fronts fit snugly into the drawer spaces. Cut bottom, back and side pieces from unstained wood and assemble the drawers to fit into the spaces.

Oak-stained rustic pieces fit perfectly into an old cottage

Secondly, the top unit: glue one side piece to the back. Stick the shelves to the side and back, then stick the other side in place. Glue the top in place, overhanging the front and sides, then the frieze under the top.

Sand the top and base units carefully with fine abrasive paper and apply one coat of amateur French polish. Sand again with very fine abrasive paper and apply several coats of wax polish, well-buffed between each coat. Mark the positions of the handles on the drawer fronts and fit the handles. If you prefer, the top unit can be glued to the base unit for extra stability.

Wooden wing chair (Figs 117 and 118) This is made of ⅛in thick obeche wood, stained dark oak. Draw the pattern pieces onto the wood and cut them with a fretsaw. Sand the pieces with fine abrasive paper and stain them. Glue one side to the outer edge of the back. Glue the seat into the side and back, and

the seatboard, at a backward-tilted angle, under the front of the seat. Glue the other side in place. Sand the chair with fine-grade abrasive paper and apply one coat of amateur French polish. Sand again with very fine abrasive paper and apply several coats of wax polish, buffing well between coats. Make a fabric cushion for the chair seat.

Refectory table (Figs 119 and 120) This is made of ⅛in thick obeche wood, stained dark oak.

Draw the pattern pieces onto the wood, choosing wood with a clear grain for the top. Cut the top and stretchers with a razor-toothed saw, and the legs with a fretsaw. Sand the pieces with fine-grade abrasive paper, rounding the corners and sides of the top. Stain the pieces. Glue the support stretchers to the underside of the top as marked on the pattern. Glue the legs inside the stretchers to the underside of the top. Glue one stretcher between the legs ¼in below the table top, and the other ½in below the top stretcher.

Sand the table with fine-grade abrasive

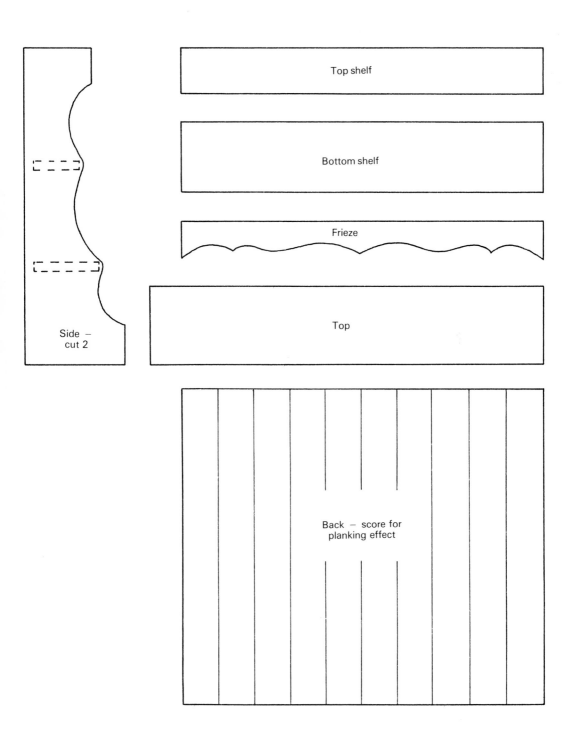

Top shelf

Bottom shelf

Frieze

Top

Side –
cut 2

Back – score for
planking effect

114 Scale pattern for the kitchen dresser (top
unit)

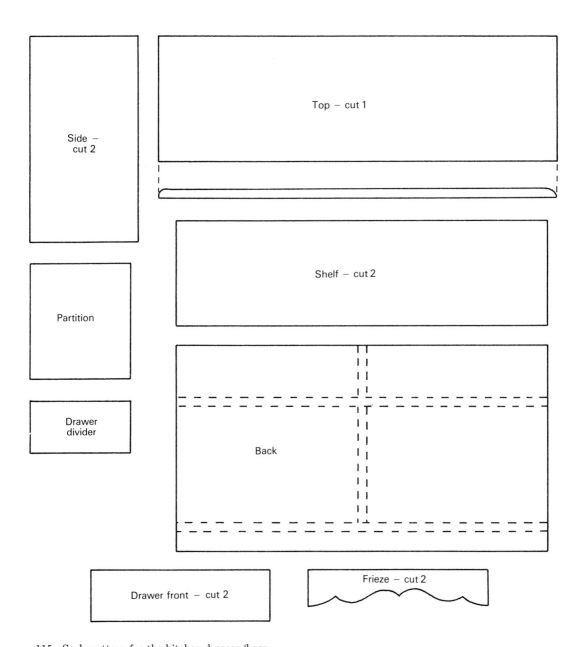

Side –
cut 2

Top – cut 1

Partition

Shelf – cut 2

Drawer
divider

Back

Drawer front – cut 2

Frieze – cut 2

115   Scale pattern for the kitchen dresser (base
unit)

168

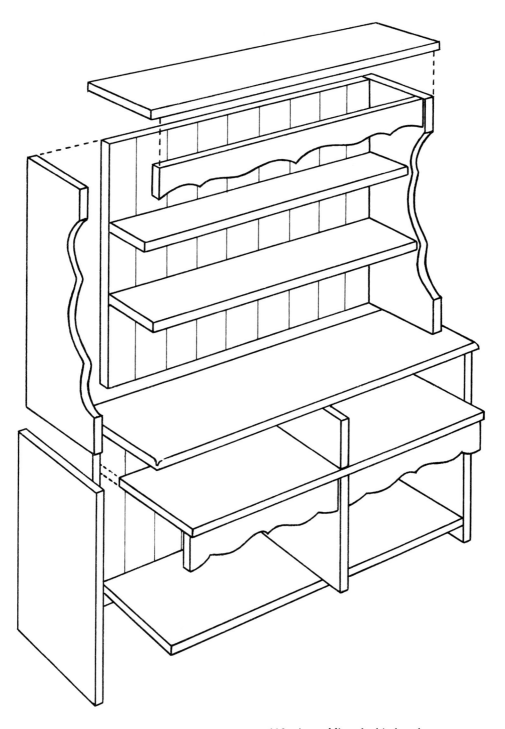

116   Assembling the kitchen dresser

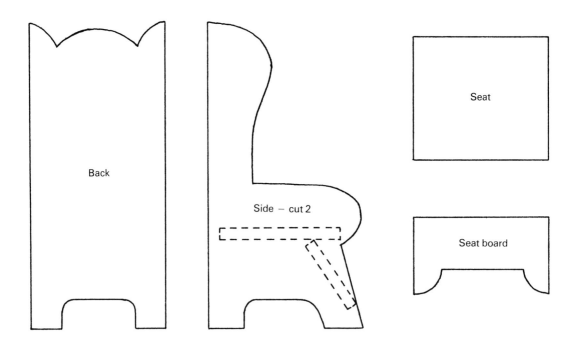

Back   Side – cut 2

Seat

Seat board

117   Scale pattern for the wooden wing chair

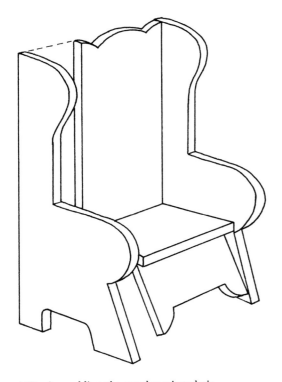

118   Assembling the wooden wing chair

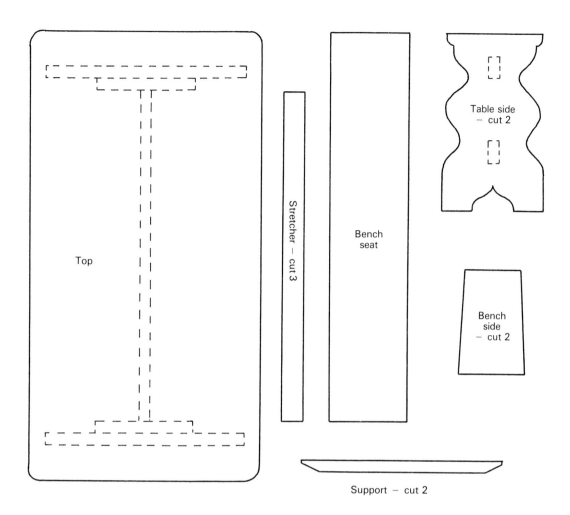

Top

Stretcher — cut 3

Bench
seat

Table side
— cut 2

Bench
side
— cut 2

Support — cut 2

paper and apply one coat of amateur French polish. Sand again with very fine abrasive paper and apply several coats of wax polish, well-buffed between each coat.

Benches (Figs 119 and 120) The benches are made of ⅛in thick obeche wood stained dark oak. Draw the pattern pieces onto the wood and cut them with a razor-toothed saw. Sand the pieces with fine abrasive paper, rounding the sides and corners of the bench seat. Stain the pieces. Glue the legs to the underside of the seat, and the stretcher to the underside of the seat between the legs. Sand the bench with fine abrasive paper and apply one coat of amateur French polish. Sand again with very fine abrasive paper and polish with wax polish.

119 Scale pattern for the refectory table and bench

Accessories
Many of the accessories used in this house were bought from the specialist dolls'-house shops (*see* Stockists) and a few from the commercial dolls'-house ranges available from most good toy shops. Full instructions for all the home-made items are given in Chapter 6, where alternatives to the bought items will also be found.

Rugs All the rugs in the Tudor cottage are home-made, of felt, with the designs in felt pen, and backed with iron-on carpet tape. The rug in the left-hand bedroom is 5½in square. The design is in beige, cream, pink and green.

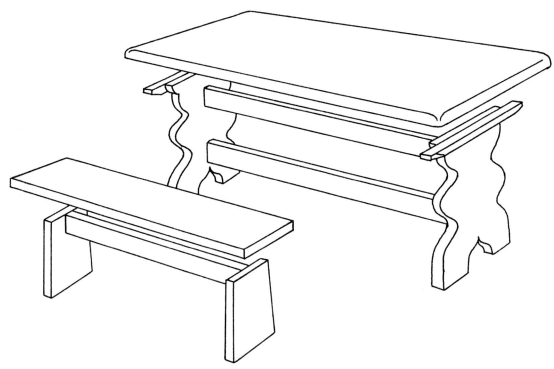

120 Assembling the refectory table and bench

There is also a cream fur-fabric rug by the fire. In the other bedroom, both rugs are coloured in pink and green on a beige background. The larger one is 6 × 4½in, the smaller by the bed is 4½ × 2½in. The large rug in the parlour, 7½in square is coloured in rust, greens and cream. The small rug by the stove in the kitchen, 3 × 1½in is dark red and brown on beige.

Lights The light fittings include brass candlesticks (with home-made wax candles), a brass-and-glass oil lamp from a specialist shop and a plastic hanging oil lamp from one of the commercial ranges (Lundby).

Mirrors and pictures The small bedroom mirror, framed in wood-strip, and the oval mirror in the parlour, framed with a brooch mount, were both cut by a glass merchant to the required size. The mirror in the single bedroom is a commercial one (Caroline's Home), as are the plastic-gilt picture frames in the bedroom and above the sofa in the parlour (Lundby). All the rest are made of narrow wood-strip with mitred corners, stained oak or walnut. The pictures are from magazines. The miniature Victorian photographs are from a specialist shop, one framed with wood-strip, one with a broken locket.

In the left-hand bedroom, the washstand set and chamber pot were bought from a specialist shop; the other items — the pot of flowers, perfume bottle, jewel box, etc — are made from beads and buttons. The shell on the mantelshelf is a perfect tiny shell found on the beach.

In the right-hand bedroom, the chamber pot came from a specialist shop; the perfume bottle, flower vase, and trinket box are made of beads and buttons. The little lead soldier comes from a toy shop, the coloured pencils are made from toothpicks, the books from typing paper. The workbasket, with its miniature knitting, and the wastepaper basket are plaited raffia.

The parlour contains many bead, button and shell trinkets, including glass-button ashtrays, a tobacco jar made of beads, and a button rose-bowl. The pretty flower vase on the mantelpiece is a glass bead filled with dried flowers. The viking and the lovebirds both come from a toy shop, as does the brass wine set. The plastic copper kettle and brass pestle and mortar are both from a commercial dolls'-house range (Lundby). The books in the bookshelf are a picture-covered block, the miniature magazine is from a specialist shop.

In the kitchen, the pewter plates, mugs and tea service, brass horseshoes, glass storage jars and cakestand are all from a specialist shop. The saucepans and kettle are commercial plastic ones, painted with copper enamel paint. The tea set, a commercial one (Caroline's Home), is decorated with flower transfers. The bread is modelled in bread paste; the Dundee cake and mince pies, in clay. The sacks of barley and potatoes are made of coarse linen and filled with sand and beads. The mop and broom are made of fine dowelling, soft cotton and twigs. The log basket of plaited raffia is filled with sawn lengths of twig. The carpet beater is from a specialist shop. The hedgehog (to eat the ants) is from a gift shop. The mousetrap is made of a little piece of obeche wood with a spring from a retractable ball point pen.

The old couple and their daughter who live in the house are made from beads and pipe-cleaners. Full instructions for the dolls and their clothes are in Chapter 11.

Variations

When decorated with red-brick paper and timbering, this house is typically Tudor, but with different decorating schemes the basic design could be used to make other houses (Fig 121).

The proportions of the exterior make the basic design suitable for a small Queen-Anne house. The windows should be paned sashes rather than casements and the doors should be panelled rather than planked. The red-brick paper is suitable, but the paintwork should be cream, and typical features such as a pediment and fanlight over the front door should be added. Inside the house, the lower floor should be partitioned into two equal-sized rooms with a central hall and staircase. Upstairs, the bedrooms could be partitioned as for the Tudor house, or divided to correspond with the rooms below, the stairs emerging on a central landing. The interior

decor would follow contemporary fashion, with pastel colours on the walls, polished wood floors and white or cream paintwork. Although modest in size, its furnishings might include an elegant four-poster bed, with a dressing chest and mirror. The smaller bedroom might be a nursery, with a hooded cradle on rockers and a truckle bed for an older child. The parlour might be panelled in wood with a gilt-framed mirror above an elaborate marble fireplace, and a polished wood floor covered by a rug. The parlour furnishings could include a gate-legged table and several tall-backed chairs, a cabinet to store and display silver or china and a lightly upholstered settee with cabriole legs. The kitchen would have a stone-flagged floor with a large fireplace where food was cooked over an open fire — there would be a clockwork jack to turn the spit and a crane in the chimney to hold the cooking pots over the fire. There might be a water pump (though this was more commonly outdoors) over a stone sink. A wooden table and a few stools and shelves would complete the kitchen furnishings in Queen Anne's day! Accessories such as a warming pan, a spinning wheel and collections of miniature stoneware, Delft or silver would find a perfect home here.

Alternatively, you might decorate and furnish the interior to correspond with its Tudor exterior. The walls would be lime washed (magnolia emulsion paint over a wood-chip paper would give the right rough texture), or panelled with wood. In a Tudor house, the front door would open into the hall — a large room with stone-flagged floor strewn with rushes (dried grasses) and a large stone fireplace. The furniture would be sparse, perhaps a large table, a buffet, a few stools or chests, and one chair for the master of the house! There might be a display of pewter cups and plates on the buffet, candles in sconces on the walls and a decorative stag's head or pieces of tapestry. The other room downstairs would be the kitchen. Again, the floor would be stone flagged and the fireplace very large. There would be a spit by the fire (turned by a boy or a dog) and a crane in the chimney to hold the cooking pots. There might be a brick oven for baking and a brazier for cooking smaller amounts. The furniture would include a trestle table, benches, a few shelves

121 Variations on the Tudor cottage plans

and stools. Upstairs, the main bedchamber would have a planked floor and, possibly, wood-panelled walls. The large four-poster bed would occupy most of the available space with a chest and stool. The other room upstairs might be furnished as a bedroom, or a parlour — here there might be a hooded cradle, an armchair or two, a stool, a chest and the lady's spinning wheel. The Tudors were fond of music (even the owner of a modest house might have a lute), and embroidery, such as wall-hangings, bed-hangings, covers and cushions.

While this house would have provided ample accommodation for the Tudors who built it, or even the Georgians who lived there later, modern tenants would find it rather cramped. As with a similar life-sized cottage, they would probably build an extension to house a bathroom. This could be done by building a single storey or lean-to extension onto the kitchen side of the house and cutting a doorway through the alcove to the rear of the kitchen chimney breast. The extension might have a hinged roof or front and need only be 6—8in wide. The modern tenants might also find the inter-communicating bedrooms inconvenient, and build a landing.

10 The Modern House

This house was designed for a pair of eight-year-old twin girls. They live in a modern house on a new estate and we planned the dolls' house as a loose copy of their own home.

This is the largest house in this section of the book. It has two bedrooms and a bathroom (which open onto a small landing), a kitchen, large lounge/dining room and garage. Our original intention was to use the commercial doors and windows, available from craft and model shops, but we found that the doors were unsuitable — they are under scale, the equivalent of 5ft 3ins in life size, and do not open and close freely! The windows, however, are a good size and available in several styles, including our mock Georgian. We decided, therefore, to use the commercial windows, but to make our own doors.

The interior of the house we intended to be typical of a small modern house of the 1980s, and planned to use the commercial dolls'-house furniture available from most good toy shops. Again, we had to change our plans! Although many of the commercial pieces are well designed and realistic, especially the bathroom and kitchen fittings, we found the bedroom furniture particularly disappointing. It looks very 'dolls' house', not like miniature versions of real furniture, so we decided to make the beds, wardrobes and other items. We wanted everything about the house to be as typical of its time as possible, with many miniature copies of things found in the owners' own home.

For accessories, the commercial dolls'-house ranges are invaluable — you will find the pop-up toaster, the coffee percolator, the latest-model vacuum cleaner and much more — designed in the latest style with excellent detail. Here too, you will find a selection of light fittings and a transformer to wire the dolls' house for electricity. See Chapter 3 for further details.

All the wallpapers and the 'carpet' floor papers in this house were taken from a sample book begged from a local shop, which contains hundreds of sheets of wallpaper, many patterns repeated two or three times. It is essential to choose carefully, though, as most of the patterns are too large — only the plain colours, textured or small-patterned papers are suitable. We used the Habitat catalogue as inspiration for designing the furniture, helped by the fact that it gives measurements for the furniture it illustrates. We also found the catalogue useful for pictures of clock faces, bulletin boards and posters.

The modern house is in 1:16 scale to accommodate the commercial furniture and accessories, and is made in plywood. Daler Board could be used if the house is for an older child or an adult. The front opens in two sections, the roof is a fixed gable with a fixed top-front edge. The garage is built separately, on a base which makes a small garden area, and is glued to the side of the house, by the kitchen door.

Full instructions and plans are given for the house and the home-made pieces of furniture, and details of the bought items are also given. Instructions for making the home-made accessories can be found in Chapter 6. Before beginning, read Chapter 2.

Materials
¼in plywood (or Daler Board) for the house
⅛in plywood (or Daler Board) for the roof
½in square beading for the ridgepole
¼in square beading for the bargeboards
⅛in obeche wood for the doors and stairs
fine wood-strip for the door frames

Exterior of the modern house, with its doll family

six 1in hinges for the fronts
twelve ½in hinges for the doors (or use cloth
  hinges)
5 triple, 1 double and 1 single commercial
  windows
woodwork glue, panel pins, masking tape
¼in thick wood (eg spruce) for the stair stringers

Cutting (Plans: Figs 122–5)

Draw the pattern pieces onto the plywood
using a sharp pencil and ruler, and ensuring
that the right-angles and measurements are
precise. Label each piece in pencil, ie floor,
back, roof, etc, to avoid confusion when
assembling. Cut out the pieces with a saw,
including the door and window holes and stairwells. Draw lines onto the inside and outside
of the relevant pieces to mark where the upper
floor and partition walls occur.

Assembly

Tape the pieces together to check that they all
fit properly (Fig 126). If necessary, make any
minor adjustments. Sand all the house pieces
thoroughly. Glue and pin the back onto the

Exterior of the modern house, with its doll family

base. Glue and pin the sides to the back and
the base. Glue and pin the lower partition wall
(kitchen/lounge) in place, pinning through the
base and back. Glue and pin the upstairs floor
in place, pinning through the side and back
walls. Pin through the floor into the lower
partition wall. Glue and pin the partition wall
in the left-hand (parents') bedroom, lining it up
above the lower partition and pinning through
the back.

Glue and pin the top ceiling in place, inside
(and pinned through) the side and back walls.
Pin through the top ceiling into the parents'
bedroom partition wall. Assemble the partition walls for the right-hand (childrens')
bedroom by glueing and pinning the side-
partition (bathroom/bedroom) to the back-
partition (bedroom/stairwell). Wallpaper the
rear of the back-partition with the wallpaper
chosen for the landing and stairwell before
putting these walls in place. Glue and pin the
partition walls in place, pinning through the
top ceiling and the side wall. Pin up through

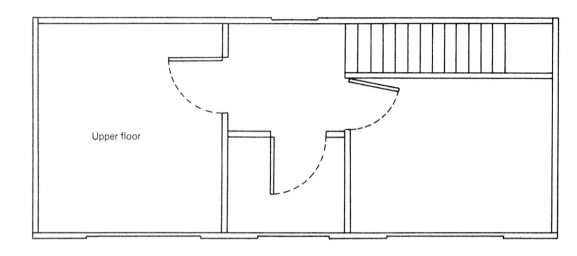

Upper floor

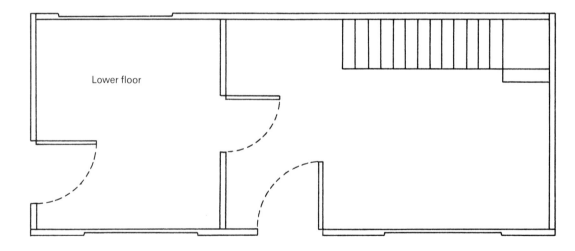

Lower floor

122 Floor plans for the modern house

123 124 and 125   Plans for the modern house
(pages 179–81)

178

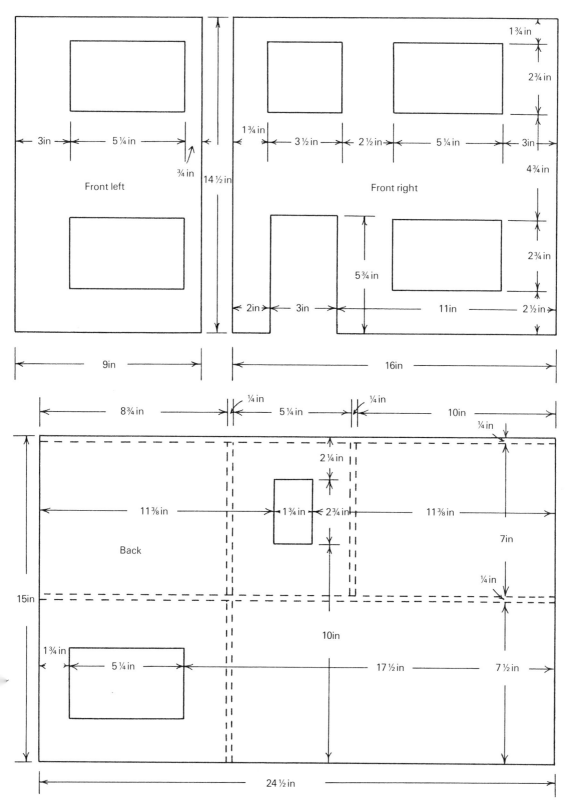

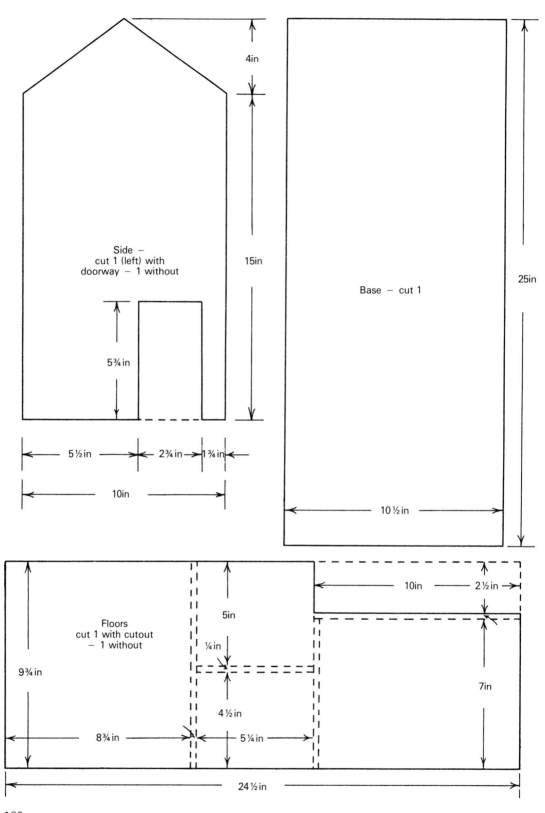

Side –
cut 1 (left) with
doorway – 1 without

4in

15in

5¾ in

5½ in   2¾ in   1¾ in

10in

Base – cut 1

25in

10½ in

Floors
cut 1 with cutout
– 1 without

9¾ in

5in

¼ in

4½ in

8¾ in   5¼ in

24½ in

10in   2½ in

7in

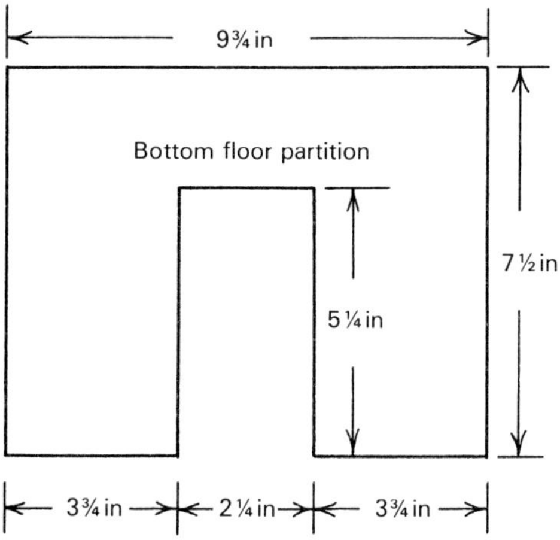
9¾ in
Bottom floor partition
7½ in
5¼ in
3¾ in
2¼ in
3¾ in

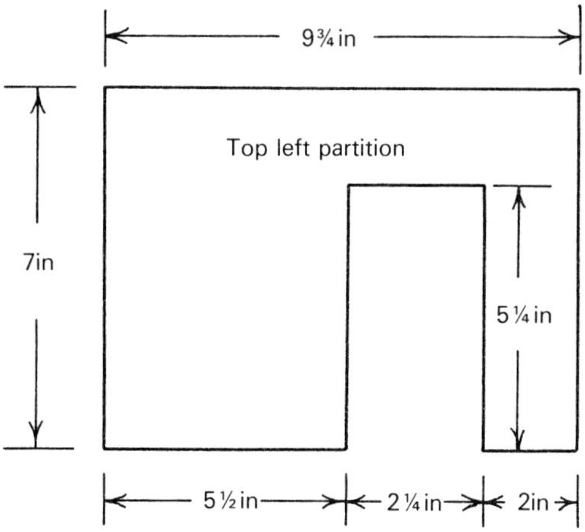
9¾ in
7in
Top left partition
5¼ in
5½ in
2¼ in
2in

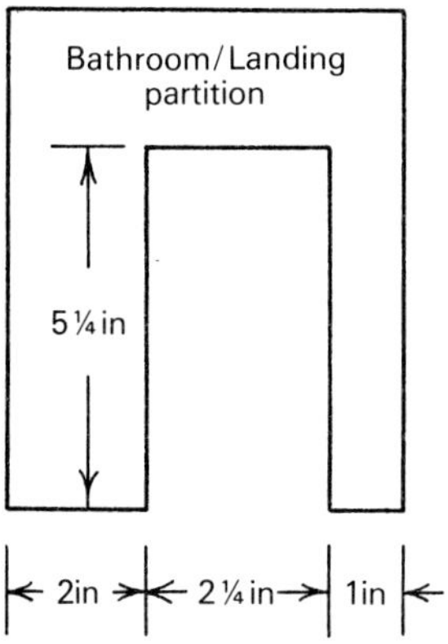
Bathroom/Landing partition
5¼ in
2in
2¼ in
1in

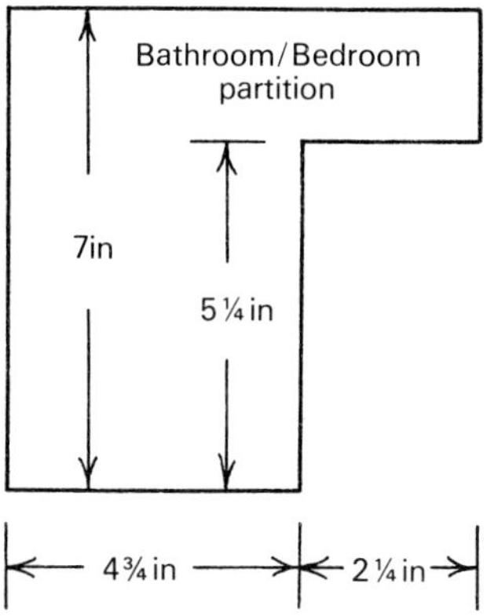
Bathroom/Bedroom partition
7in
5¼ in
4¾ in
2¼ in

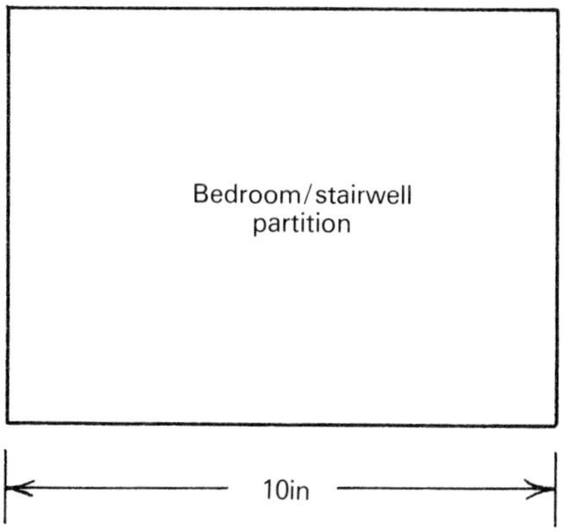
Bedroom/stairwell partition
10in

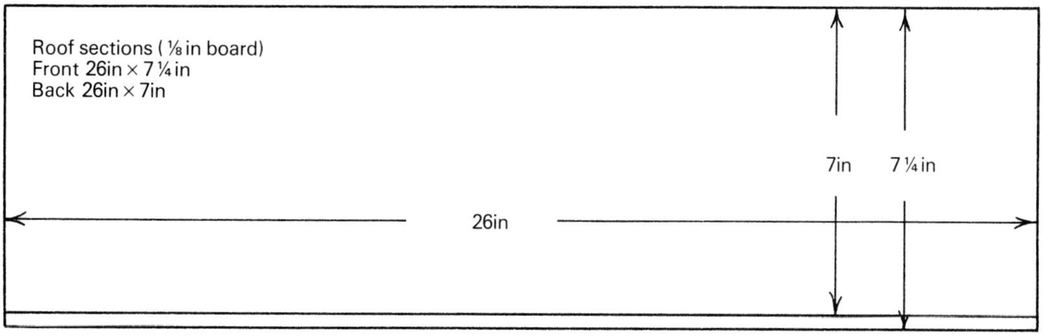
Roof sections (⅛ in board)
Front 26in × 7¼ in
Back 26in × 7in
7in
7¼ in
26in

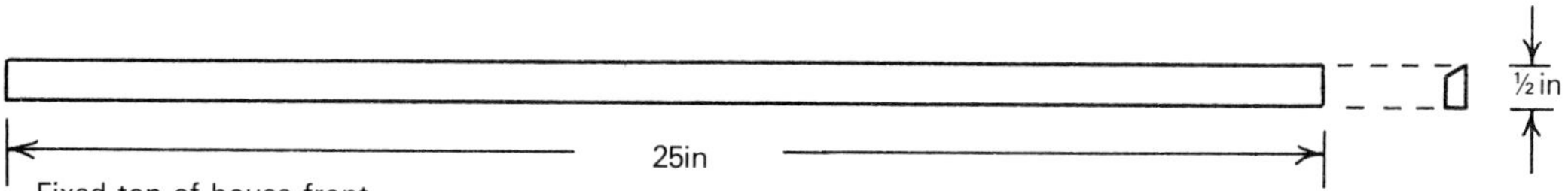
½ in
25in

Fixed top of house front

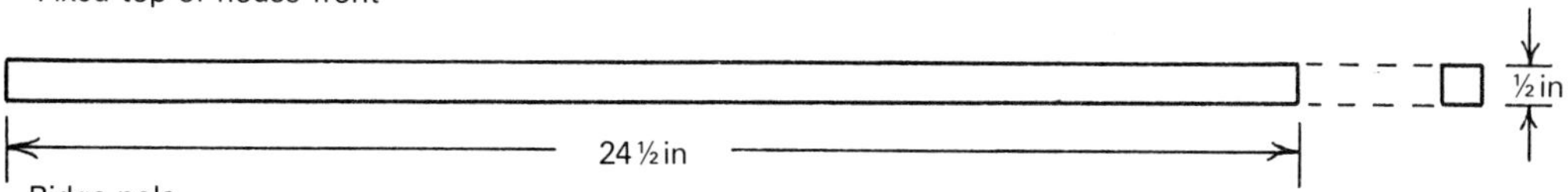
½ in
24½ in

Ridge pole

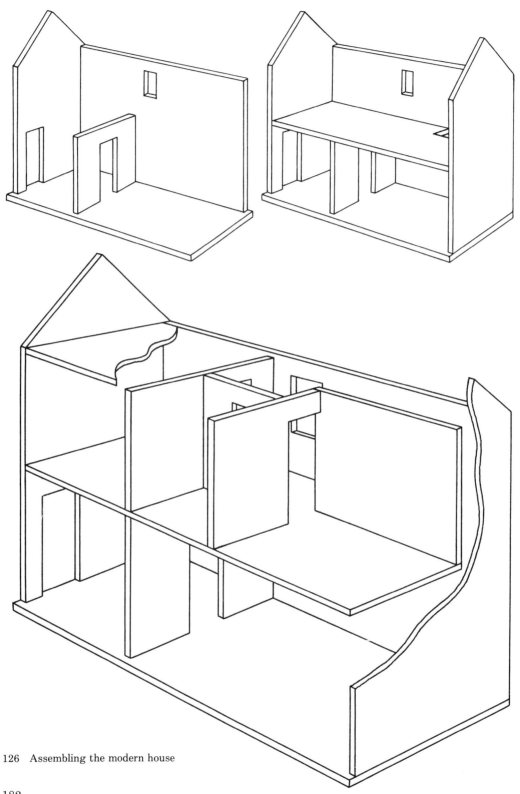

126 Assembling the modern house

the floor, along the stairwell edge and under the side-partition wall. The bathroom/landing partition is not fixed in place until the house is decorated.

Glue and pin the front-edge strip (chamfered edge uppermost), to the front edge of the top ceiling. Fix the ridgepole by screwing it in place between the tops of the two gables. Pin and glue the back-roof section to the ridgepole and to the top of the gable walls. The back roof overhangs the back and sides of the house by ½in. Glue and pin the front-roof section to the ridgepole (butted against the back-roof section), the top of the gable walls and the front-edge strip. The front-roof section overhangs the front of the house in line with the bottom of the front-edge strip, so the fronts open freely when they are hinged in place.

Exterior

The exterior of the house is decorated at this stage. We chose red-brick and green-pantile papers. Consult Chapter 3 for suggestions.

Paper the roof, lapping the paper under the gable edges, and the front and back. Paper the house, cutting the paper around the window and door holes, and lapping the sides around to the inside of the house. Cut strips of paper to cover the front edges of the floors and partition walls, lapping them onto the walls, floor, ceiling, and base. Paper the fronts of the house, lapping the paper around all sides to the inside. Cut the paper around the door and window holes. Make sure that the bricks are lined up at the centre join.

Windows

Glue and pin the windows over the window holes. We painted the window frames with a coat of white-gloss enamel paint before fixing to match the doors. When the windows are fixed, paint the inside edges of the window holes with white-gloss enamel paint over an undercoat of matt enamel paint. Paint the inside edges of the doorway holes in the same way. Paint the bargeboards and glue them under the gables, mitring the apex join.

Exterior doors

Cut the front door and the kitchen door in ⅛in obeche wood. The perspex windows are cut to fit into the larger window space on the inside

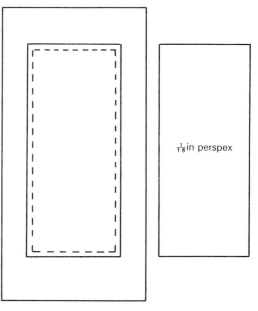

$\frac{1}{8}$in perspex

Cut two door halves
– one on solid line –
one on dotted

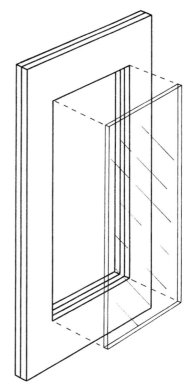

127 Pattern (not to scale) and assembly for the exterior doors

of the door (Fig 127). Cut the two door pieces with a razor-toothed saw, the window space with a fretsaw. Glue the two pieces together, sandwiching the cloth hinge if you are using one, and press them under a weight until the glue dries. Sand the door with fine abrasive paper and paint both sides. Fit the window into the window hole, using a little UHU or similar glue at the edges.

Hinge the front door on the right-hand side, the kitchen door on the left-hand side, using ½in hinges recessed into the wood. These hinges are too small to fix with screws so we use fine pins. To avoid splitting the wood, mark the holes through the hinge onto the door and use a fine drill or dressmaker's pin to drill the holes. Super-glue the hinge to the door, and the pins pushed through the hinges. Repeat this process to hinge the door to the doorway, recessing the hinges into the frame and holding them with super-glue and pins. The handles are map pins — the shanks cut short, glued into fine holes drilled in the doors.

We used transparent Fablon with a ridged pattern over the perspex panels in the doors and bathroom windows to give a reeded-glass effect.

Fronts

The fronts can be hinged in place at this stage, using three 1in hinges at each side, recessed into the wood. You might prefer to wait until the interior has been decorated.

Stairs

The open-plan staircase is made of ⅛in thick obeche wood for the stairs, and ¼in thick wood (eg spruce, obtainable from craft shops) for the stringers. It is stained pine colour with button polish and left unwaxed, though you might prefer other finishes. Draw to full size the patterns for the long-flight stringers, using the half-scale diagrams as a guide (Fig 128). Cut one left and one right-hand stringer from your patterns. The two-step stringers which support the bottom flight have full-sized patterns. Cut all the stringers in ¼in thick wood. Cut fourteen steps in ⅛in thick obeche wood, using the pattern, and round off the front and left-hand edges of each step with abrasive paper. Cut the half-landing from ⅛in thick obeche wood, using the pattern, and

sand the front edge round. Sand all the pieces with fine abrasive paper and stain if you wish.

To assemble the stairs, glue the top and bottom steps to the stringers of the main flight, followed by the other steps, with the treads overhanging slightly at the left-hand side and fitting flush with the stringer at the right-hand side (Fig 129). The overall width of the stringers is exactly 2½in. Assemble the bottom stair and half-landing in the same way, glueing the stringers under the half-landing as shown on the pattern. Glue the left side of the half-landing onto the stringers of the main flight.

Paint with button polish to represent pine and sand gently with fine abrasive paper. Do not fix the stairs in place until the interior of the house is decorated. Then fit the banister post of 5mm square beading. Whittle the top of the post to form a knob, or sand it round, stain it to match the stairs and glue it to the half-landing by the bottom step of the main flight. The banister rail is made of fine wood-strip, sanded, stained and glued to the banister post and into the edge of the stair-well.

Interior doors

The interior doors are made of ⅛in thick obeche wood. Cut two pieces for each door and glue them together (sandwiching cloth hinges, if used), pressing them under a weight until the glue dries. Sand with fine abrasive paper and check that they fit easily into the doorway holes, allowing for two coats of paint. Paint both sides with a matt undercoat followed by gloss enamel paint, ensuring that the edges are covered. Glue the tape-hinged doors to the walls, or use two ½in hinges as described for the front door. The handles are coloured map pins, with shanks cut short, glued into tiny holes drilled into the door.

Hang all the doors as described. The bedroom and bathroom doors open into the rooms; the communicating door downstairs, into the lounge. Do not forget to hang the door on the bathroom/landing partition which is not yet fixed in place.

128 Patterns for the open-plan staircase

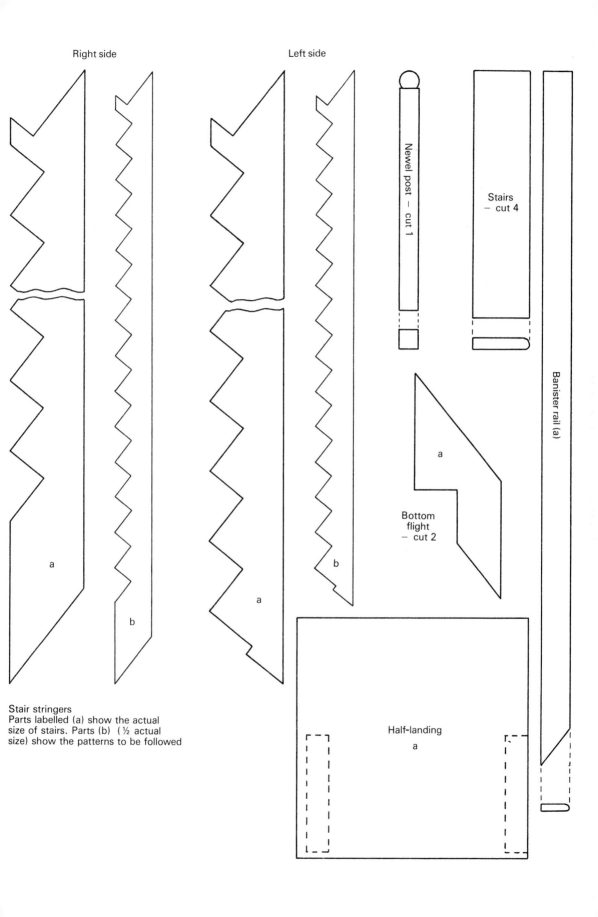

Right side

Left side

Newel post — cut 1

Stairs
— cut 4

a

Bottom
flight
— cut 2

Banister rail (a)

a

b

a

b

a

b

Half-landing

a

Stair stringers
Parts labelled (a) show the actual
size of stairs. Parts (b) (½ actual
size) show the patterns to be followed

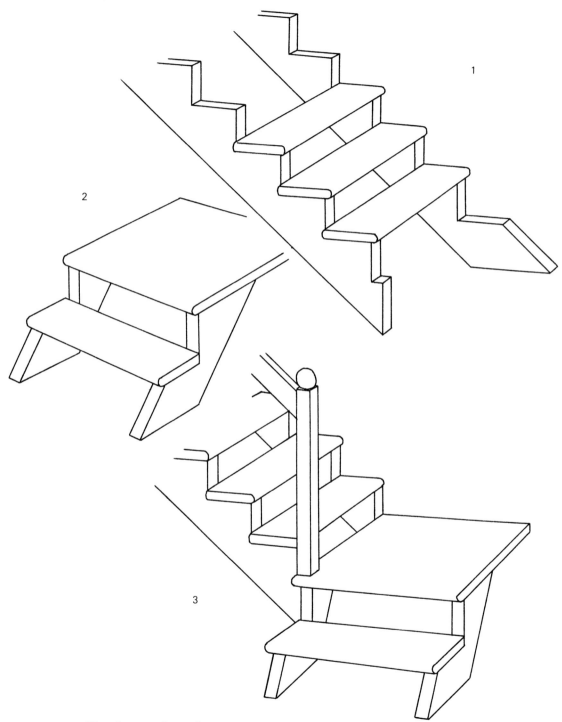

1

2

3

129   Assembling the open-plan staircase

Decorating

We tried to choose wall and floor papers typical of the 1980s (given the limitations of the wallpaper sample book). The paintwork is all brilliant-white gloss enamel paint and the ceilings have two coats of brilliant-white emulsion. The parents' bedroom has a silk-effect wallpaper in shades of beige on a cream background. The floor is covered with a dark-brown hessian-textured paper which makes a realistic fitted carpet. The twins' bedroom has a white paper with a tracery of blue flowers and leaves. The carpet is pale-blue hessian-textured paper. The bathroom wallpaper is vinyl, a cream background with brown and orange flowers. The floor is covered with Fablon in a brown-leather effect which in this scale looks like cork tiles. The kitchen has a linen-textured wallpaper in brown and white. The floor paper is vinyl with a tile design. The lounge/dining room wallpaper has a striped pattern in yellow, beige and white. The carpet is a brown hessian-textured paper.

Before decorating, check for any tiny gaps and fill these with Polyfilla rubbed in with a finger, removing any surplus filler with a damp cloth. Start by painting the ceilings, which can be papered with lining paper first for a better finish.

The bedrooms and kitchen are straight-forward — paper the back wall first, then the side walls. Paper them with lining paper if you intend to paint. Next, paper the floors; then cut, paint and fit the door and window frames and skirting boards. We used fine wood-strip for door and window frames and ¼in wide wood-strip for skirting boards. Chapter 3 gives full instructions.

The lounge, bathroom and landing are a little more difficult. As the bathroom/landing partition wall is not yet in place, there is access to the landing, though restricted. We used the same wallpaper as for the lounge, to make the procedure as simple as possible. Paper the back wall of the lounge, continuing up the stairwell to the top of the house (reaching up through the stairwell), and include the landing walls beside and above the bedroom doors. Paper the side walls of the lounge, again continuing up the stairwell to the top of the house on the right wall. Make a window frame for the landing window from fine wood-strip, with mitred corners — paint it white and glue in place. In the same way, make door frames for the bedrooms. Cut, paint and fix skirting boards under the landing window and to each side of the parents'-bedroom door. Cut and stick a piece of carpet paper to the landing floor.

Decorate the back of the bathroom/landing partition to match the other landing walls. Cut the wallpaper to fit exactly, with no overlap, and make and fix the door frame and skirting board as before. Glue the edges of the partition and push it into place. Ensure that it is properly positioned (peep through the landing window to check) and leave until the glue is thoroughly dry. Paper the back wall of the bathroom, lapping the wallpaper an inch onto the side walls and the floor, to strengthen the joins. Then paper the side walls of the bathroom. Cut the bathroom floor and stick it in place. Cut, paint and fix the door frame. Small pieces of skirting board are fitted around the bathroom fixtures when they are fixed in place.

This procedure means that the entire house is decorated, not just those areas which can be seen from the front — most satisfactory when peeping through the landing window! When the decorating is complete, the stairs can be glued into the stairwell, and against the back and side walls.

Fronts The insides of both fronts are papered with the same beige silk-effect wallpaper which was used in the parents' bedroom. It is the most neutral of those used, and the wallpaper sample book contained several sheets in this pattern.

Curtains The bedroom curtains are of the same printed-cotton fabrics as used for the duvet covers in each room. They are gathered onto white-painted, narrow wood-strip tracks, mounted on blocks of wood glued to the wall at each side of the windows. The bathroom has a rust-coloured, linen roller blind, hung from tiny eyes screwed into the wall at either side of the window. A similar roller blind hangs at the rear kitchen window, made of brown-and-orange-printed cotton. The same fabric is used for the curtains at the front kitchen window, hung in the same way as the bedroom curtains. The lounge curtains are rust-coloured velveteen, hung from a curtain pole made of fine dowelling with bead finials stained walnut. The landing window is left uncurtained.

The parents'-bedroom furniture

The patterns given here are drawn actual size so they can be traced from the book. Before beginning, read Chapter 5, and refer to it when necessary.

Bed The divan bed is made from a 5¼ × 3¾in block of balsa wood ¾in thick, covered in brown cotton. The raw edges of fabric are glued firmly underneath and covered by a rectangle of felt 4¾ × 3¼in. The bed legs are 1in lengths of fine dowelling or square beading, coloured with black felt pen and tapped gently into the balsa wood with a hammer.

Cut a rectangle of foam 5¼ × 3¾ × ½in for a mattress and make a cotton cover for it. Make a sheet and two pillows (ours are cream-coloured lawn) and put the sheet over the mattress, if necessary holding the mattress on the divan with double-sided tape. The duvet is a cotton bag 6in square, filled with terylene wadding, and slip-stitched closed. We used a cotton print in pink, black and cream for our duvet cover, but any small print or plain colour would be appropriate. Co-ordinate the room by having matching duvet cover and curtains.

The headboard is made of obeche wood; ³⁄₃₂in thick for the centre panel, ⅛in thick for the frame. For the panel cut a piece 3¼ × 1¼in. For the frame cut two strips 1¼ × ¼in and one strip 3¾ × ¼in. Glue the short lengths to either side of the panel, and the longer length to these, across the top, so that the panel is slightly recessed. Sand the headboard with fine abrasive paper and stain with button polish. Sand again, and wax polish. The headboard is fixed on by two upright battens of fine wood-strip which are glued to the back of the headboard and pinned or glued to the divan base.

Bedside table (Fig 130) This is made of ⅛in thick obeche wood with legs of 5mm square beading. It is painted with button polish in pine colour.

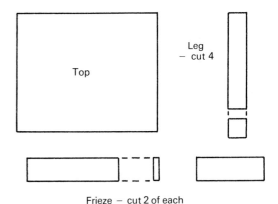

Frieze − cut 2 of each

130 Scale pattern for the bedside table

Draw the pattern pieces onto the wood and cut them with a razor-toothed saw, ensuring that the four table legs are exactly the same length with perfectly square ends. Glue the four frieze pieces in place between the legs, so that the frieze is slightly recessed. Glue the assembled legs to the underside of the top, so that it overhangs slightly at each side. Sand the table with fine abrasive paper. Paint the table with one coat of button polish, sand gently with very fine abrasive paper, and wax polish.

Wardrobes and dressing table (Figs 131 and 132) This unit is made of ⅛in thick obeche wood, stained with button polish to pine colour. The handles are white, glass-headed dressmaker's pins with the shanks cut short.

Draw the pattern pieces onto the wood, ensuring that the measurements and right-angles are correct. Cut the pieces with a razor-toothed saw and sand them with fine abrasive paper.

To assemble the wardrobe, glue one side to the back, then glue the base to the side and back. Glue the shelf in place and then the other side. Make fine holes at the top and bottom edges of the doors to receive the pin hinges and sand the hinged edges slightly rounded so that the doors swing open freely. Make fine holes in the base and the underside of the top to receive the pins. When the pin

131 Scale pattern for the wardrobes

188

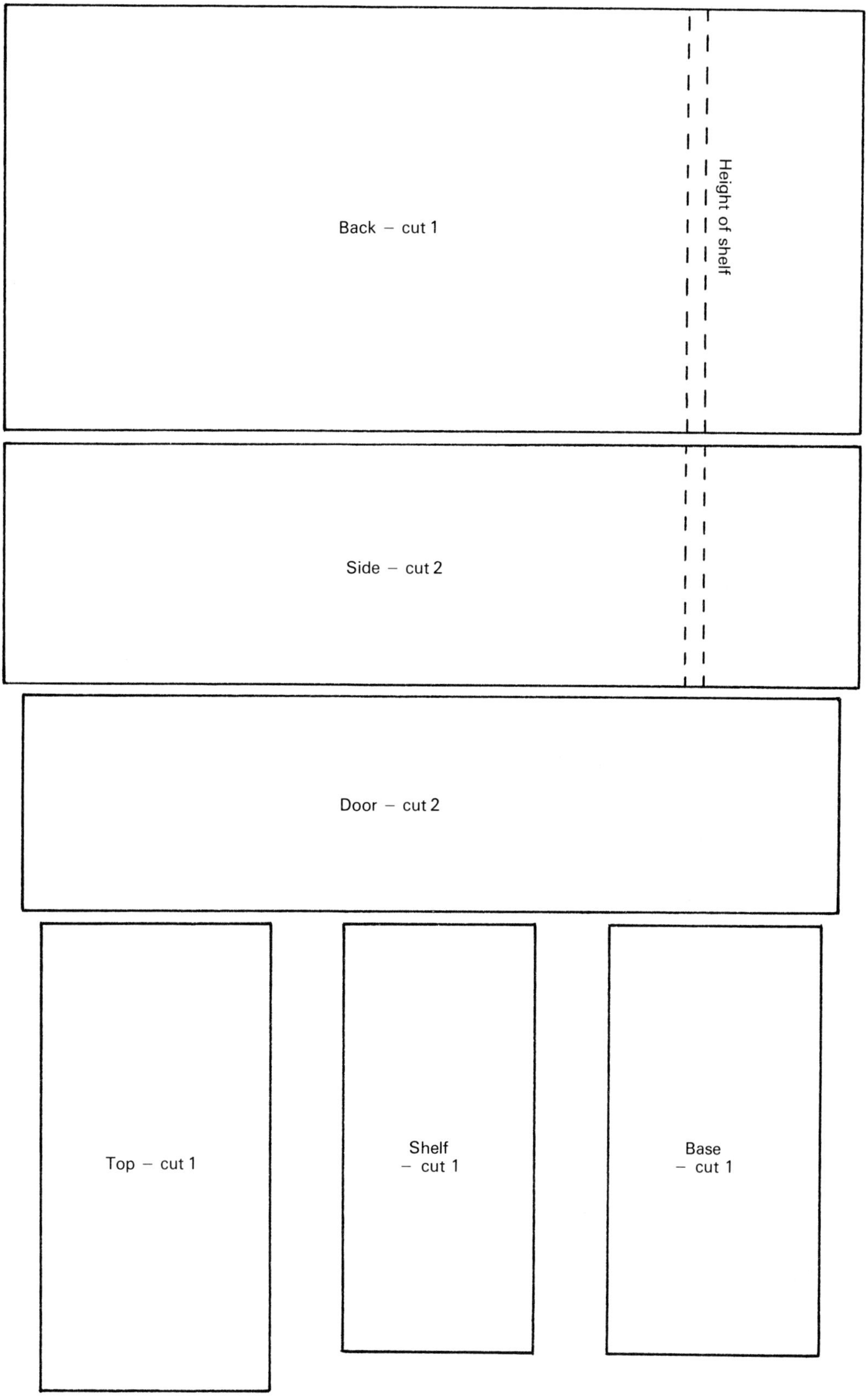

Back – cut 1

Height of shelf

Side – cut 2

Door – cut 2

Top – cut 1

Shelf
– cut 1

Base
– cut 1

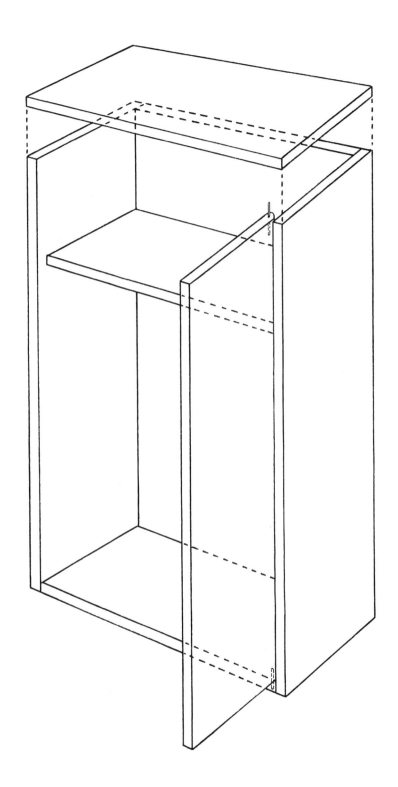

132 Assembling the wardrobe

hinges are properly aligned, glue the top in place. Sand the wardrobe with fine abrasive paper and stain with button polish. Sand again with very fine abrasive paper and wax polish. Mark the positions of the door handles and bore fine holes with a small drill or pin. Cut the shanks short on the dressmaker's pins and glue them into the holes. Make the second wardrobe in the same way.

To assemble the dressing-table (Figs 133 and 134), glue the sides and the back to the base, then glue the top in place. Check that the drawer front fits snugly into the space. Cut the bottom, back and sides from unstained wood, assemble the drawer to fit the space, sand, stain and polish it as for the wardrobe, and fix the drawer handles as before. The mirror is cut by a glass merchant and framed with ¼in wide wood-strip with mitred corners. The mirror and frame are stuck to a backing of thin cardboard. Sand the frame, stain and polish it to match the drawer unit.

The modern wardrobe and dressing-table unit from the parents' bedroom

Glue the dressing table between the wardrobes, 1¾in from the floor, glueing the mirror to the back of the drawer unit. Tape across the back of the mirror onto both wardrobes with masking tape to reinforce the join. The stool in this bedroom is a commercial one, but Chapter 5 gives directions for making one.

The bathroom fittings
The bathroom fittings are from a commercial range of dolls'-house furniture (Lundby). The original backing pieces on the bath, washbasin and loo were removed by soaking the entire unit in hot water to soften the glue and gently prising the backing away. The pieces were then glued to the bathroom walls and floor. The shower-and-tap attachment was glued to the wall at the head of the bath, and the towel rail with its felt towel glued to the side wall at

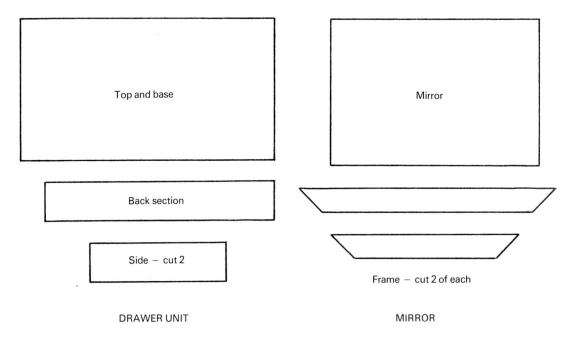

Top and base

Mirror

Back section

Side – cut 2

Frame – cut 2 of each

DRAWER UNIT

MIRROR

133   Scale pattern for the drawer unit and mirror

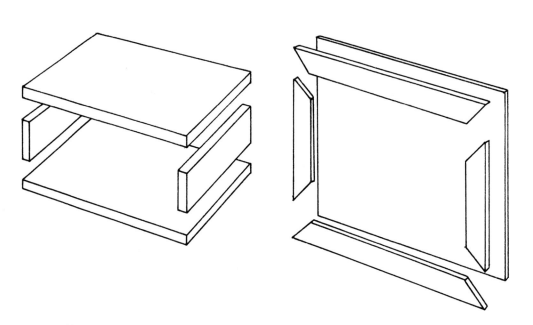

134   Assembling the drawer unit and mirror
frame

the foot of the bath. The bathroom cabinet (also Lundby) was glued to the wall above the washbasin. The scales, bath rack and tooth mugs are commercial (Lundby).

If you prefer to make the bathroom fittings, consult Chapters 4 and 6.

The twins'-bedroom furniture

Desk This desk was made from a cupboard-and-drawer unit — a leftover from the commercial kitchen unit which included the cooker. The top is a piece of wood similar to the drawer and cupboard fronts. The desk is $3\frac{1}{4} \times 1\frac{1}{2} \times 2\frac{3}{4}$in. To make a similar desk, consult Chapter 5. Use $^3/_{32}$in thick obeche wood for the desk, and glass-headed dressmaker's pins, with the shanks cut short, for handles.

Desk chair (*see* Fig 42) See Chapter 5 for general instructions on making chairs. This chair has legs of 4mm square beading, with a $^3/_{32}$in thick obeche-wood seat. The seat is 1in square, the front legs 1in long, the back legs 2in long. The chair has a seat pad covered in cotton.

Chest of drawers (Fig 135) This is made of $^3/_{32}$in thick obeche wood, stained with button polish to pine colour. The handles are brass gimp pins.

Draw the pattern pieces onto the wood, ensuring that the measurements and right-angles are correct. Cut the pieces with a razor-toothed saw and chamfer the side and front edges of the top. Sand all pieces with fine abrasive paper. Glue one side to the back, then

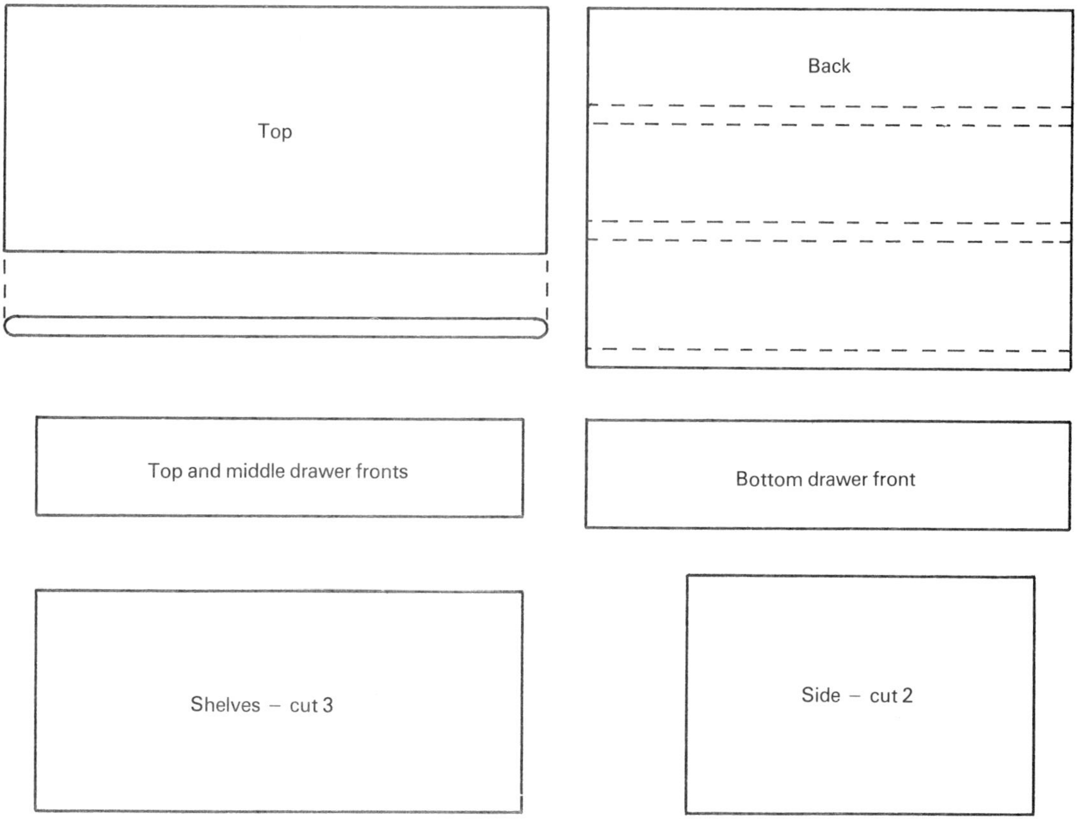

135 Scale pattern for the chest of drawers

glue the shelves and base in place, followed by the other side. Glue the top in place, overhanging slightly at the sides and front.

Check that the drawer fronts fit snugly into the spaces. Cut the bottom, back and side pieces for the drawers from unstained wood and assemble them to fit into the spaces. Sand the shell and drawer fronts with fine abrasive paper and paint on one coat of button polish. Sand gently with very fine abrasive paper and apply several coats of wax polish, well-buffed between coats.

Mark the handle positions on the drawer fronts and drill fine holes. Cut the shanks of the gimp pins and push them into the holes, fixing them with a dab of glue over the pinhole on the inside of the drawer.

Bunk beds (Figs 136 and 137) These are made of ⅛in thick obeche wood with posts of 5mm square beading. The ladder is made of fine wood-strip with toothpick rungs. The beds are stained pine colour with button polish.

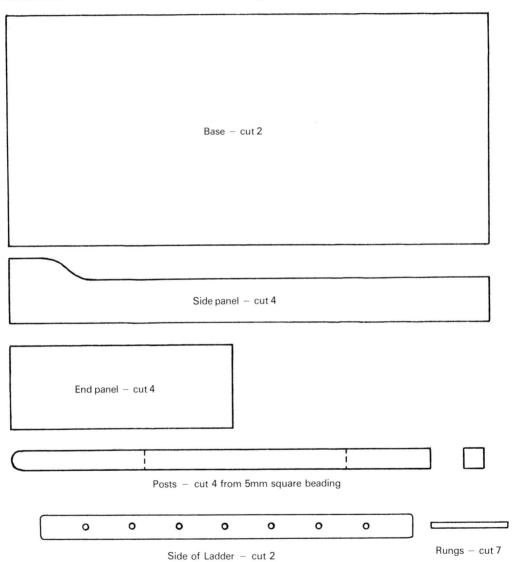

Base – cut 2

Side panel – cut 4

End panel – cut 4

Posts – cut 4 from 5mm square beading

Side of Ladder – cut 2

Rungs – cut 7

136 Scale pattern for the bunk beds and ladder

194

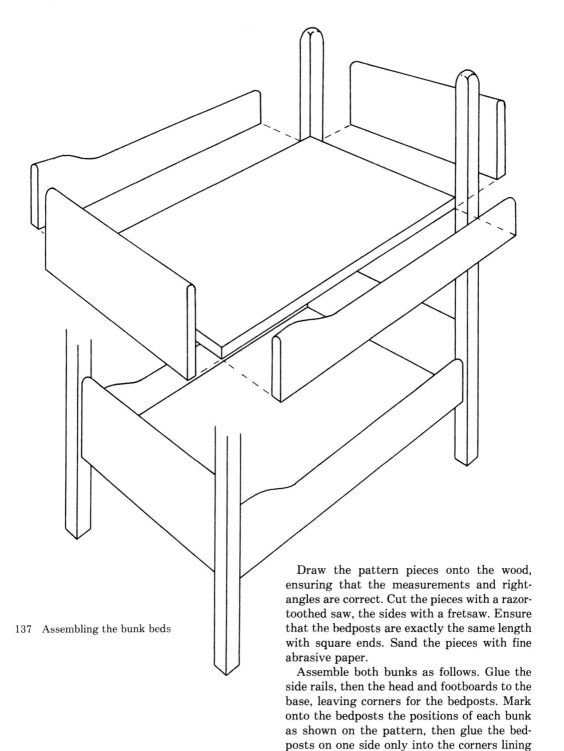

137 Assembling the bunk beds

Draw the pattern pieces onto the wood, ensuring that the measurements and right-angles are correct. Cut the pieces with a razor-toothed saw, the sides with a fretsaw. Ensure that the bedposts are exactly the same length with square ends. Sand the pieces with fine abrasive paper.

Assemble both bunks as follows. Glue the side rails, then the head and footboards to the base, leaving corners for the bedposts. Mark onto the bedposts the positions of each bunk as shown on the pattern, then glue the bed-posts on one side only into the corners lining up the bunks to the marks on the posts. Leave the bunks on their sides as the glue dries, then

The bunk beds from the children's bedroom, complete with matching linen

turn them over and glue the other side's bedposts in place. Leave the bunks on their sides until the glue is dry. Sand with fine abrasive paper, and stain with button polish. We also faced the headboards and footboards with white Fablon to imitate melamine.

To make the ladder, cut two 4in pieces of wood-strip. Mark and drill fine holes in both pieces as shown on the pattern. Glue the ends of the toothpick lengths and push them into the holes. Paint the ladder with button polish to match the bunks, and glue it lightly to the footboards.

Use the bed-base pattern to cut mattresses for the bunks from ½in thick foam, and make cotton covers for the mattresses. Make a sheet and pillow for each bunk — we used a plain-turquoise cotton for the sheets and a turquoise-and-white printed cotton for the pillows and duvet covers. The duvets are cotton bags, 5in square, lightly stuffed with

terylene wadding, and the open ends slip-stitched. Use matching fabric for the curtains and duvet covers.

The kitchen furniture
The kitchen furniture and accessories are from the commercial ranges of dolls'-house furniture. The top of the sink unit (Caroline's Home) was painted with silver enamel paint to represent stainless steel, (it was originally white). The cupboard unit and fridge (Caroline's Home) were taped together at right-angles and covered with a thick-cardboard worktop, which itself was covered with brown Fablon. The washing machine (Caroline's Home) fitted neatly into the space left beside the sink.

The cooker (Lundby) was glued to a backing, with a drawer unit and cupboard. The backing was removed and the rest used to make the desk in the children's bedroom. The cooker (originally orange) was painted with white-gloss enamel and mounted on a block of black-painted wood. The cooker hood was also

The modern armchair and sofa upholstered in fashionable cord material

painted white and stuck to the wall. The wall cupboard (Caroline's Home) which matches the sink and cupboard units, was glued to the side wall above the worktop. A worktop covered with brown Fablon was glued to the top of the washing machine.

The round, white-plastic table and chairs (Caroline's Home) were bought as a set. The patterned transfer which originally covered the table top was removed by soaking in hot water. The ironing-board, clock, pedal-bin, coffee-maker, toaster, saucepans, and wall shelf are all commercial (Lundby). When choosing pieces from the commercial ranges, remember to consider the space available, as in a life-size kitchen.

If you prefer to make rather than buy the kitchen furniture and accessories, consult Chapters 5 and 6. A one-portion jam or butter container painted with silver enamel paint makes an acceptable sink, with a silver-painted obeche-wood draining board. A white-enamel-painted cupboard makes a passable

cooker with black press-studs or washers for rings, glass-headed pins for knobs, and perspex for the oven window.

The lounge/dining room furniture
The lounge/dining room contains a combination of bought and home-made furniture and accessories. The matching wall unit, dining table and chairs (Lundby) are made of wood, stained rosewood. The telephone table (Lundby) is also rosewood colour with paper tiles; the coffee table (Lundby) is similar, but stained pine colour. The television set originally had a picture which we replaced with a piece of plain-grey paper; this and the stereo record-player with hinged perspex lid (both Caroline's Home) are very realistic. The wooden magazine-rack (Lundby), stool (Caroline's Home) and yellow-needlecord swivel chair (Lundby) are commercial pieces.

197

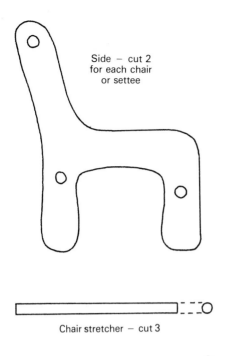

Side — cut 2
for each chair
or settee

Chair stretcher — cut 3

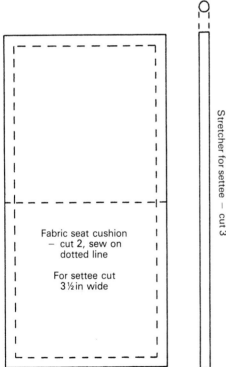

Fabric seat cushion
— cut 2, sew on
dotted line

For settee cut
3½in wide

Stretcher for settee — cut 3

138 Scale pattern for the armchair and sofa

Sofa and chair (Fig 138) The sofa and chair (the style and finish of these pieces was copied from the Habitat catalogue) are made of ⅛in thick obeche wood with stretchers of fine dowelling. They are stained with button polish to pine colour. The cushions are made of rust-coloured needlecord.

The method for both sofa and chair is the same, only the width of the dowelling varies. Draw the pattern pieces onto the wood, ensuring that the grain line is vertical, and cut the dowelling stretchers exactly the same length. Cut the side pieces with a fretsaw, and round the edges by sanding with fine abrasive paper. Drill three holes for the stretchers through each side piece, as shown on the pattern, the same diameter as the dowelling. Assemble the chair frame by glueing one end of the stretchers, pushing them into the holes on one side piece, then likewise with the other ends. When the glue is dry, sand the chair frame with fine abrasive paper and paint on one coat of button polish. Sand gently with very fine abrasive paper and wax polish.

Make one large cushion, lightly stuffed, for each piece; 3¼ × 1½in for the chair, 3¼in square for the sofa. Divide the cushions into 2 or 4 equal sections by stitching across the middle. Fit the cushions to the chair and sofa and secure by oversewing a few stitches at each side around the stretchers.

Record cupboard (Figs 139 and 140) This is made of ³/₃₂in thick obeche wood, stained to pine colour with button polish.

Draw the pattern pieces onto the wood ensuring that the measurements and right-angles are correct. Cut the pieces with a razor-toothed saw and sand with fine abrasive paper. Glue one side to the back, the base into the back and side, and the other side to the back and base. Glue the partition to the back and base, then the top into the sides and back, resting on the glued top edge of the partition. Sand with fine abrasive paper and paint with one coat of button polish. Sand gently with very fine abrasive paper and wax polish.

If you prefer to make all the pieces for the lounge/dining room, instructions and patterns are given in Chapters 5, 8 and 9. A television set can be made from a block of wood, faced with grey paper and framed with a piece of plastic packaging (eg empty razor-blade dispensers). Small blocks of wood, appropriately painted, will make stereo speakers and the record-player could be a block of wood covered with a picture of a deck, with a small plastic lid, hinged with tape.

Accessories
Full details of the home-made accessories are given in Chapter 6.

Rugs The cream fur rug in the parents' bedroom is a rectangle of fur fabric backed with iron-on Vilene. The red rug in the kitchen and the brown-and-green rug in the lounge are both from a commercial dolls'-house range (Caroline's Home). The bath mat is a piece of felt.

Lights The light fittings in the house are all chosen from the commercial dolls'-house ranges. The house is wired for electricity as described in Chapter 3. The wires are taped across the ceilings to emerge from holes drilled through the back wall. There is a ceiling light in each room and on the landing and a lamp on the television in the lounge.

Mirrors and pictures The mirror in the dressing table was cut to the required size at a glass merchant's, as was the mirror in the twins' bedroom which is framed with fine wood-strip stained with button polish. The elaborately framed mirror on the stairs is commercial (Caroline's Home).

The picture above the bed in the parents' bedroom was cut from a magazine and framed with fine wood-strip stained with button polish. The gilt-plastic-framed rose print is commercial. The Mucha poster on the bathroom door was cut from a catalogue, and glued to the door with wallpaper paste. The cork noticeboards in the children's bedroom and the kitchen were cut from a cork floor tile and covered with a selection of tiny pictures from magazines. The football rosette is made from an inch of narrow ribbon gathered tightly along one edge, the calendar is from a catalogue advertisement. The prints in the lounge are all magazine pictures, framed in fine wood-strip stained with button polish. The memory-board in the kitchen was cut

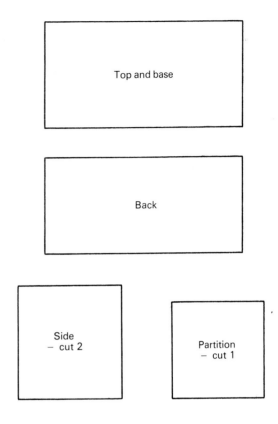

139 Scale pattern for the record cupboard

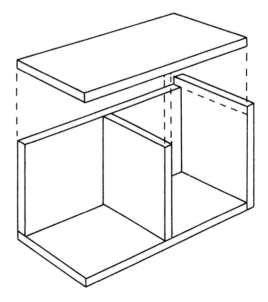

140 Assembling the record cupboard

199

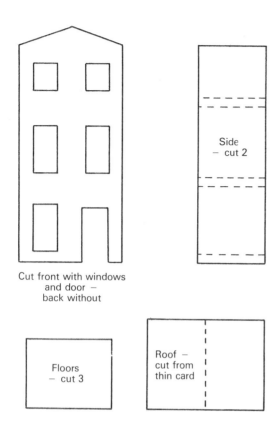

Cut front with windows
and door —
back without

Side
— cut 2

Floors
— cut 3

Roof —
cut from
thin card

141   Scale pattern for the dolls'-house dolls'
house

from a catalogue advertisement and backed
with thin cardboard.

The perfume bottles on the dressing table
are made of glass beads, the velvet flowers are
in a wooden-bead vase. The lace mats are
motifs cut from lace trimming.

The toys in the childrens' bedroom are a
selection of small plastic toys from the toyshop. The dolls' house (Fig 141) is a 2½in high
copy of the Victorian town house. It is made of
^{3}/$_{32}$in obeche wood, and painted with poster
colour. Use the pattern given to cut and
assemble the pieces. The roof is made of firm
cardboard, the front hinged on with a strip of
surgical tape before painting. The truly
intrepid might like to try their hands at
making furniture!

The plants in the house are a selection of
dried flowers and plastic leaves in pots made
of beads and toothpaste caps. The records are
a magazine advertisement, backed with firm
cardboard.

The mother, father and twins are made from
beads and pipecleaners — full instructions can
be found in Chapter 11.

The Garage (Figs 142 and 143)
The garage is made of ¼in thick plywood,
papered to match the house. The roof is
covered with rough, green, sugar paper. The
pin-hinged doors are made of ⅛in thick obeche
wood, and the door frame is of ¼in square
beading.

Draw the pattern pieces onto the wood, cut
them with a saw and sand thoroughly. To
assemble the garage, glue and pin one side to
the base. Glue and pin the back to the side and
base, then the other side in place. Glue and pin
the front piece between the sides, ensuring
that the top edges of the three pieces line up.

Paper the outside of the garage to match the
house, and paint or paper the inside of the
garage to your taste — we used white
emulsion paint. Paper or paint the garage base
to represent stone paving, gravel or concrete.

Glue and pin the garage roof in place. The
back and right-side edges fit flush with the
walls, the front and left-side edges overhang
the walls. Cover the garage roof with sugar
paper, tucking the edges of the paper under
the overhanging sides of the roof.

Cut and paint the three door-frame pieces,
and glue them into the doorway, mitring the
corners. Cut and paint the under-frame strip,
and leave it aside until the doors are complete.
Cut the garage doors with a razor-toothed
saw, sand the hinged sides slightly round to
allow the doors to open freely, and sand the
doors with fine abrasive paper. Paint the
doors on both sides with one or two under-
coats of matt enamel and one coat of gloss
enamel. Drill small holes into the top and
bottom edges of the doors for the pin hinges.
Cut dressmaker's pins and push them into the
holes. Try the doors in place and mark the pin
positions on the base and the under-frame
strip. Drill holes in the base and the under-
frame strip to receive the pins. Fit the pins in
the top of the doors into the holes in the strip,
and glue along the top edge of the strip. Fit
the pins in the bottom of the doors into the
holes in the base and push the under-frame
strip, with the doors, into the doorframe.

Cut, sand and paint pieces of fine wood-strip

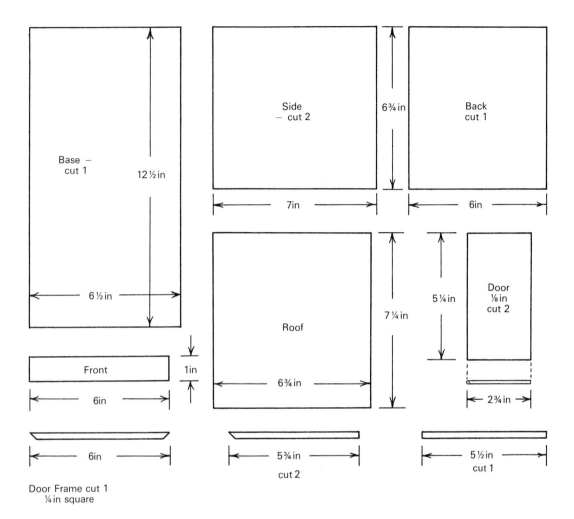

Base –
cut 1

12½in

6½in

Side
– cut 2

6¾in

7in

Back
cut 1

6in

Front

1in

6in

Roof

6¾in

7¼in

5¼in

Door
⅛in
cut 2

2¾in

Door Frame cut 1
¼in square

6in

5¾in
cut 2

5½in
cut 1

and glue them to the front and left walls under the overhanging roof. Cut a tiny wooden block and glue it to the floor inside the doors to prevent them swinging inwards. Cut the shanks off map pins and glue them into fine holes drilled in the doors, to make handles. The right wall of the garage and the right edge of the base are glued to the left side of the house. Align the front edges of the garage base and house — the back of the garage projects beyond the back of the house.

Finishing
We used a length of white, plastic farmyard fencing (from a toy shop) glued to the base, a plastic dustbin (originally a pencil sharpener)

142 Plans for the garage

and two small plastic plants to furnish the yard.

The house signs (Gemini House) are drawn with felt pen onto thin slices of log, cut at an angle, varnished and glued to the wall beside the front and back doors.

Variations
As described, this house is typical of modern estate houses found all over England. However, the basic plan is simple, and the house is large enough to adapt to many different periods (Fig 144).

Using the Tudor cottage as a guide, the

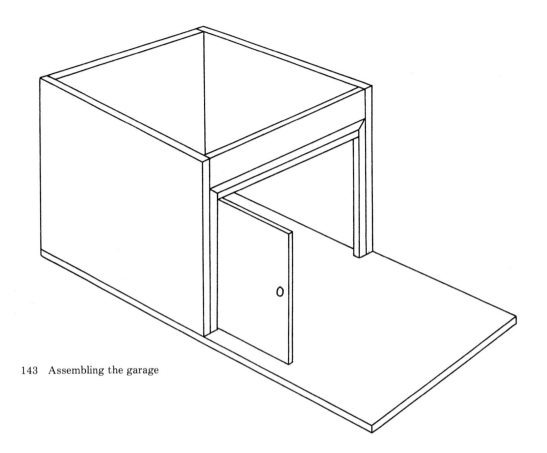

143 Assembling the garage

exterior could be decorated with brick and timber to make a larger Tudor house. The commercial plastic windows could be used, but should be painted black or dark brown, and the doors should be planked. The roof should have dark-red tiles, and, as a Tudor house must have fireplaces, there should be chimneys. The garage could be exchanged for a stable, and the garden area covered with brick or grass paper.

Inside, the house could be partitioned as in the plans, but the open-plan stairs should be replaced by a more substantial staircase. The larger room downstairs would be the hall, the smaller, the kitchen. Upstairs, there would be two bedchambers and a small storeroom. Consult Chapter 9 for decorating and furnishing ideas.

These plans could also be used to make a larger Georgian house. Here again, the red-brick paper and white-plastic commercial windows would be suitable for the exterior,

with grey slates for the roof. The Georgian house also needs chimneys, and might well have a stable with a cobbled or paved yard. The front door should be an imposing panelled one, with a pillared surround and pediment. The interior should be partitioned to make a central hall and staircase, with equal-sized rooms on either side. This would provide a kitchen, parlour and two bedchambers. Consult Chapter 9 for Georgian interiors.

The wide, low proportions of this house make it especially suitable for adaptation to a stone farmhouse. The exterior should be papered with stone paper, or painted to resemble stone using a household-exterior paint containing grit, eg Sandtex. The commercial plastic windows can be used (unless you prefer to make your own) but painted to resemble stone, with characteristic drip-stones, cut from thick cardboard, glued above each window. The front door would be fairly heavy, hung from a wooden or stone door-

144 Variations on the modern house plans

frame, with a dripstone or porch. The chimney stacks might be built of brick at each gable end of the house. The outbuilding might be a large barn, stable or store room, with a larger yard area, perhaps paved or cobbled or laid out as a garden. The roof of such a house might be grey slate, or stone tiles which generally graduated from larger tiles at the eaves to thinner tiles at the ridge.

The farmhouse staircase should be fairly substantial, rising from a large stone-flagged kitchen. The walls would probably be rough-plastered (woodchip paper) and whitewashed (magnolia emulsion). The smaller room down-stairs would be a parlour with a planked floor, the walls whitewashed or covered with a small-print old-fashioned wallpaper. The bedrooms also would have planked floors and whitewashed or papered walls. The ceilings throughout the house might be beamed — in the kitchen with hooks to hang hams, bacon joints and onions, etc. Such houses look best with the heavy, simple pieces which are typical of farmhouses — a large oak dresser with a display of pewter, heavy refectory table, and oak settle by the fire. The beds would have patchwork quilts, there would be home-made braided rugs on the floors, a warming pan on the wall, a spinning wheel in the corner and the master's gun above the mantelshelf.

The proportions, especially the fairly shallow pitch of the roof, make this house suit-able for a Regency house. The walls should be colour-washed to represent stucco. The roof should be grey slates, and the windows fairly large sashes, with small glazing bars dividing each window into six or nine panes. The front door should be panelled, with a semi-circular fanlight above and pilasters at either side. Inside, the house should be partitioned to make a central hall and staircase, with wide, shallow stairs and a simple banister rail and posts.

The kitchen, parlour and two bedrooms would be of equal size, with fireplaces and chimney breasts on the gable walls. The kitchen would have pale, painted walls, and a stone-flagged or tiled floor. Its large fireplace would contain an open coal fire in a basket grate, with an oven to one side and a boiler for water on the other. There might be a stone sink with a pump for water, a heavy dresser for china, a table and a couple of chairs — though Regency kitchens were still fairly primitive. The parlour would be papered in one of the fashionable, light, pretty papers, perhaps striped or flower sprigged. The polished-wood floor would be covered with a carpet, and the curtains of light-printed cotton or chintz would be looped back to allow light into the room. The fireplace surround would be an elegant wooden affair with a gilt-framed over-mantel mirror. The furniture would also be simple and elegant — a Grecian sofa with striped upholstery and bolster cushions, a bookcase, a sideboard, a dining table and chairs and a small work table. The bedrooms would also be papered in light colours to match the curtains. The polished-wood floors would be covered with rugs, and the fireplaces would have basket grates and wooden surrounds. The beds would be elegant four-posters with chintz curtains and the bedroom furnishings could include a dressing table, bow-fronted chest of drawers and a wash-stand.

Accessories might include a pole screen by the parlour fire, a bracket clock on the mantel-shelf and black-paper silhouettes framed with oval mounts.

11 Dolls

Most people feel that a dolls' house is not quite complete until it is inhabited. The variety of dolls'-house occupants is of course enormous, not necessarily confined to dolls. A house might be inhabited by a family of teddy bears or mice, or miniature cats and dogs. More usually, though, the tenants are dolls. They might be beautiful wax or porcelain antiques, gypsy clothes-pegs wrapped in cloth or modern plastic dolls.

This chapter gives instructions and patterns for bead and pipecleaner dolls. We have found that, suitably dressed, these simple dolls look quite at home in any period or modern dolls' house. The materials and method given here are the same for any size doll.

Materials

To make each doll you will need:
one round wooden or plastic bead for the head
darning wool, embroidery silk or animal wool for the hair
three 6in pipecleaners
one pair of white shoelaces
approximately 4in of tubular-gauze finger bandage
a little cotton wool for padding
flesh-coloured paint (poster or enamel)
felt pens to mark the face

Method

To make a 1:16 scale adult doll which will be approximately 4½in tall the bead should be ¾in in diameter. Cut 1in off the pipecleaner which will be used for arms — the other two pipecleaners are used full length.

Fold one full-length pipecleaner in half and push the ends into a 2in length of shoelace. Glue the shoelace-covered pipecleaner firmly into the hole in the bead (Fig 145). Push the shortened pipecleaner into a length of shoelace so that it is completely enclosed. Tuck in the raw ends of shoelace and oversew neatly to form the hands. Stitch the arms to the body ¼in below the head. Push the third pipecleaner into a length of shoelace and oversew the ends as for the arms. Take the looped end of the body and fold it up to just under the arms. Fold the leg length in half and hook it through the body, stitching through legs and body.

Pad the body with cottonwool — the amount determined by whether you want a thin or fat doll. Hold the cottonwool in place by pulling a length of tubular-gauze finger-bandage up over the cottonwool. Stitch the gauze along each shoulder and under the crutch, tucking the raw edges inside, and the doll has ready-made vest and pants. If you want to make a definite waistline, run a gathering thread through the gauze at the waist, pull it up and fasten off the ends. Using flesh-coloured paint, paint the head, neck, hands and any part of the arms or legs which will show when the doll is dressed, and leave the paint to dry thoroughly.

The hair can be made from darning wool or embroidery silk, though the latter usually looks better. For a man's hair, make a parting by backstitching with small, neat stitches through a skein of embroidery silk. Coat the head sparingly with a glue such as UHU and place the hair carefully on the head with the parting where you want it. Ease the strands of silk out so that they cover the head, leaving no bald patches, unless you want them! When the glue is quite dry, trim the hair into shape with small, sharp scissors. Ladies' hair can be made in the same way, whether long or short, loose or tied back. To make a bun, pull the ends of the silk back and tie another strand

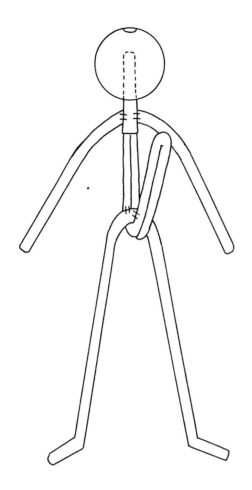

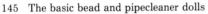

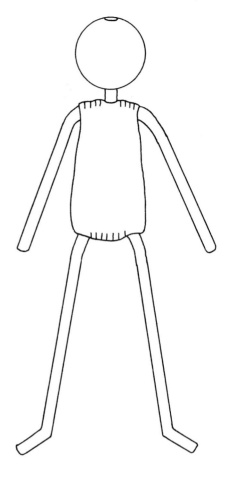

145 The basic bead and pipecleaner dolls

tightly around to form a pony tail. When the glue is completely dry, plait the pony tail, coil it around on top of the head and stick it in place with a little glue.

Animal wool (available from chemist shops) makes convincing white hair for elderly dolls, but is a little difficult to work with. Apply the hair to the head as described and, when the glue is completely dry, spray the wool with hair lacquer to hold it in place. This also applies if you prefer to use the fibre hair sold in art and craft shops.

Draw the features lightly in pencil, and when you are satisfied, colour the eyes, nose and mouth with felt pens. A little pink felt pen, carefully applied, makes rosy cheeks, and a touch of white paint in the corner of each eye gives the face character.

Other sizes
To adapt this method to other sizes, measurements are as follows.
1:16 scale child dolls — use a ½in diameter bead, cut 2in off the arm pipecleaner, 1in off the body length and 1in off the leg length. This will make a doll approximately 3¾in tall.

1:12 scale adult dolls (Fig 146a) — Use a 1in diameter bead and full-length arm, body and leg pipecleaners. Hook only ½in of the body over the leg length. This will make a doll approximately 6in tall.

1:12 scale child dolls Use the measurements given for 1:16 scale adult dolls.

146 How to lengthen the body for 1:12 scale adult dolls, with clothes patterns for the 1:12 scale

206

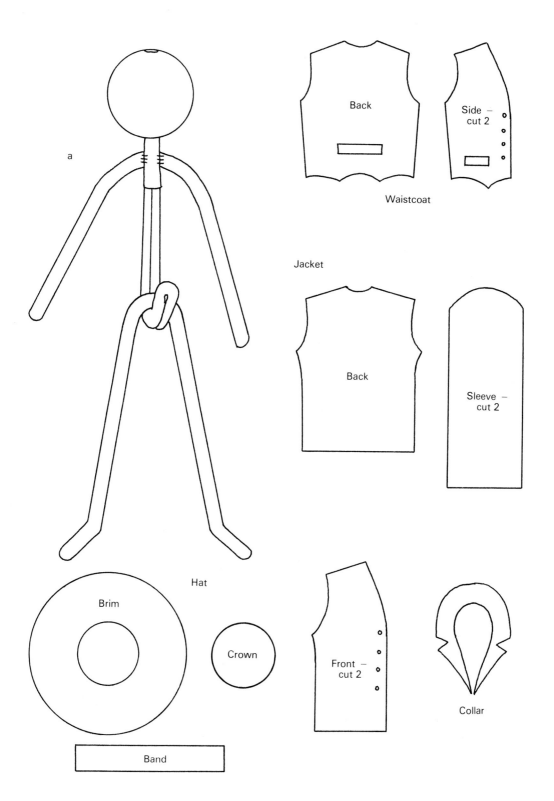

a

Waistcoat

Back

Side –
cut 2

Jacket

Back

Sleeve –
cut 2

Hat

Brim

Crown

Front –
cut 2

Collar

Band

Babies Babies can be made by cutting the top 1½in off a wooden clothes-peg, sanding it smooth and painting it flesh colour. The baby's face is marked in felt pen, with a little wool or silk stuck to the head for hair. When the baby is wrapped in a shawl or placed in a cradle, arms and legs are not needed!

Babies can also be made using beads and pipecleaners. Use a bead a little smaller than ½in. The body pipecleaner should be 1½in long, the arm length 1½in and the leg length 2in. Proceed as before.

Clothes (Figs 146—151)

Full-size patterns are given in 1:12 and 1:16 scales. The lines drawn are the sewing lines, so when using the patterns allow ⅛in extra all-round for seams and hems, except when using felt. Dolls' clothes are fiddly to make, so these are simple garments, though the experienced needleperson may prefer to adapt them.

Materials used for dolls' clothes should be fine and lightweight and should not fray easily. Any design should be tiny and colours should match the period and type of house. Felt is a good choice for trousers, jackets, waistcoats and jumpers as it does not fray and the seams can be oversewn together, making the garment less bulky. Natural cottons are good, especially for blouses, shirts and skirts, as they crease and hang well.

Shirt This is cut in one piece, using the appropriate scale pattern and adding ⅛in seam allowance. Fold the shirt where indicated by dotted lines and, working on the wrong side of the fabric, sew the seams along the underarms and body. Clip the seams slightly at the underarm curve and turn through to the right side. Slip the shirt onto the doll with the opening at the front. Fold the raw edge of the left-front under and slipstitch the left-front over the right-front. If required, French knots can be worked down the front to represent buttons. Run a gathering thread around each sleeve at the cuff, pull up, tucking the raw edges inside, and fasten off. If necessary, run a gathering thread around the neck edge to pull in the neckline. Fold the raw edges of the collar-band to the inside and press the folds, then slipstitch the collar-band to the neck of the shirt, covering the raw edge. A collar can be cut from white felt and stuck in place over the collar-band. A tiny bow tie, made from narrow ribbon, can be stuck or sewn to the shirt under the collar.

Trousers Cut two trouser pieces in felt, using the appropriate scale pattern. Sew the two pieces together at the centre-front and centre-back seams from waist to crutch. Sew the leg seams — up one leg, through the crutch and down the other leg. Turn the trousers through to the right side and slip them onto the doll, tucking the shirt inside. Run a gathering thread around the top of the trousers and pull up to fit the dolls' waist. If required, a belt, cut from a narrow strip of felt can be stuck to the trousers to cover the gathering thread.

Waistcoat Cut one back and two front pieces from felt. Oversew the fronts to the back at the shoulder and side seams. Turn through to the right side and slip the waistcoat onto the doll, over the shirt. Overlap the left-front over the right-front and make three or four French knots to represent buttons. Cut the pocket flap and backstrap, if required, and stick or sew them in place.

Jacket Cut one back, two fronts, two sleeves and one collar from felt. Oversew the fronts to the back at the shoulder seams. Oversew the sleeves into the armholes, stretching the sleeve head gently around the curve. Sew the underarm and body seams in one. Turn the jacket through to the right side and put it onto the doll. Glue the underside of the collar and position it carefully over the neck and front edges of the jacket. Overlap the left-front over the right-front and sew three or four French knots to represent buttons. Cut pocket flaps, if required, and stick them in place.

Hat Cut one crown, one hat-band and one brim from felt. Oversew the hat-band seam, then oversew or blanket stitch the crown to the top edge of the hat-band and the brim to the lower edge. Trim the hat if required. This pattern can be used to make a lady's hat by cutting the brim larger and trimming the finished hat with ribbons, flowers or feathers.

147   Clothes patterns for 1:12 scale dolls

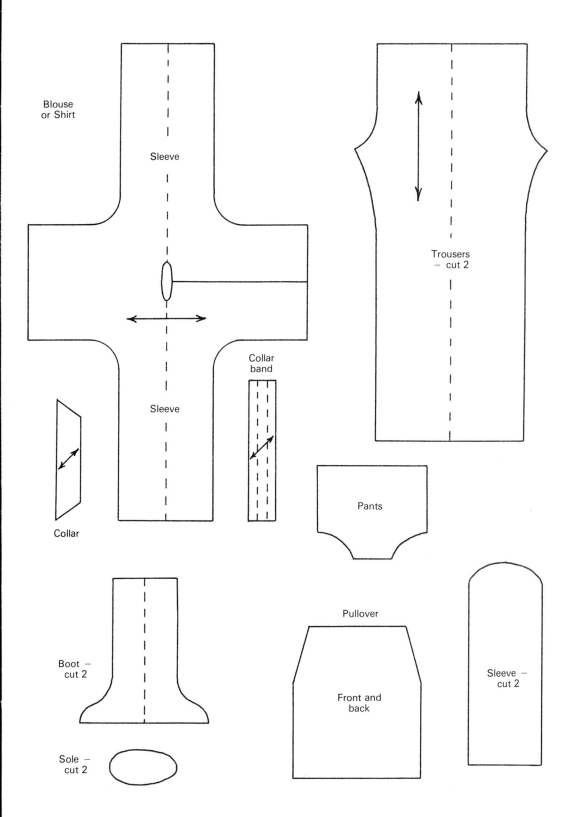

Blouse
or Shirt

Sleeve

Sleeve

Collar

Collar
band

Trousers
– cut 2

Pants

Pullover

Boot –
cut 2

Sole –
cut 2

Front and
back

Sleeve –
cut 2

209

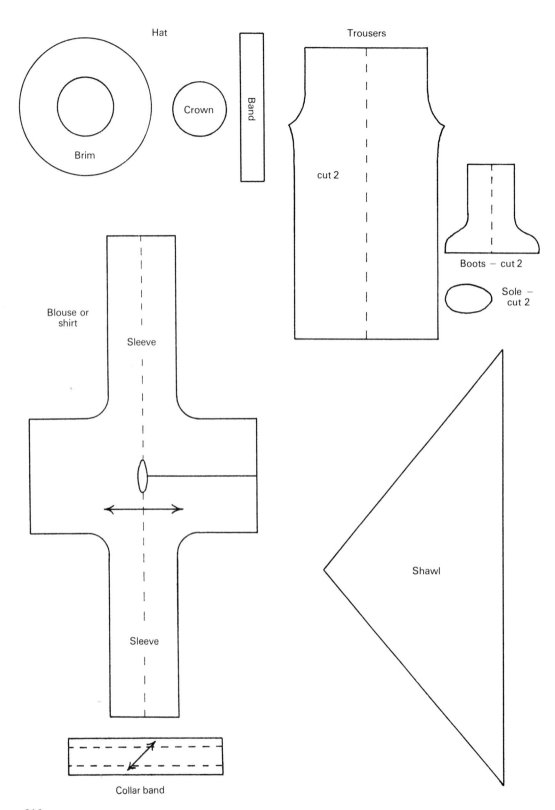

Hat

Crown

Band

Brim

Trousers

cut 2

Boots – cut 2

Sole –
cut 2

Blouse or
shirt

Sleeve

Sleeve

Shawl

Collar band

210

Boots Cut two boots and two soles from felt. Fold the boot along the dotted line indicated in the pattern. Starting at the toe, blanket stitch the edges together, over the foot and up the leg. Slip the boot up the doll's leg and bend the doll's foot sharply forward into the foot of the boot. Holding the doll upside-down, place the sole over the foot and oversew or blanket stitch it to the bottom edge of the boot. If necessary, secure the boot to the leg with a few small stitches.

Blouse The blouse is made from the same pattern as the shirt, but the opening is at the back. The collar-band can be used to neaten the neck edge, with or without the collar; or use a piece of gathered-lace trimming instead. The cuffs could also be trimmed with lace.

Skirt The skirt is a rectangle of fabric, varying in size for different lengths and scales.

In 1:16 scale: for a long skirt, cut a piece 7½ × 3¼in, for a short skirt, 6 × 2in.

In 1:12 scale: for a long skirt, cut a piece 8 × 4¼in, for a short skirt, 6½ × 3in.

Seam the short edges together and make a narrow hem along one long edge. Run a gathering thread along the other long edge and slip the skirt onto the doll, tucking the blouse inside. Pull up the gathering thread to fit the doll's waist, tucking the raw edges inside, and fasten off. Distribute the gathers evenly and slipstitch the top edge of the skirt in place. If you prefer, the gathered skirt could be stitched to a waistband, but, unless you use a very fine fabric, this can be bulky.

Make a dress by using the same fabric for a blouse and skirt, and hiding the waist with narrow ribbon tied in a bow at the back.

Petticoat Medium-weight Vilene makes good petticoats under long skirts, as it is stiff enough to make the doll stand upright. Cut the petticoat ½in shorter and narrower than the skirt, and hem the bottom edge for extra stiffness. Gather the top edge and pull up to fit the dolls' waist. A narrow lace trimming can be sewn to the petticoat hem if it is to be visible.

148 149 150 and 151 Clothes patterns for adult dolls in 1:16 scale and child dolls in 1:12 scale (pages 210—12)

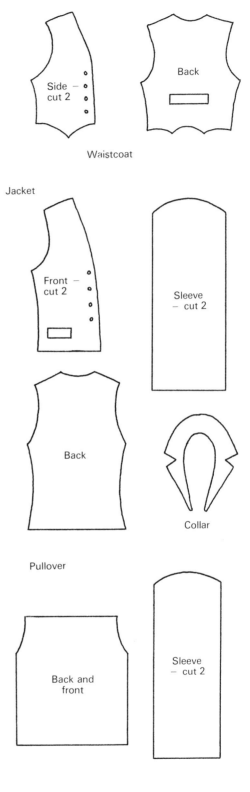

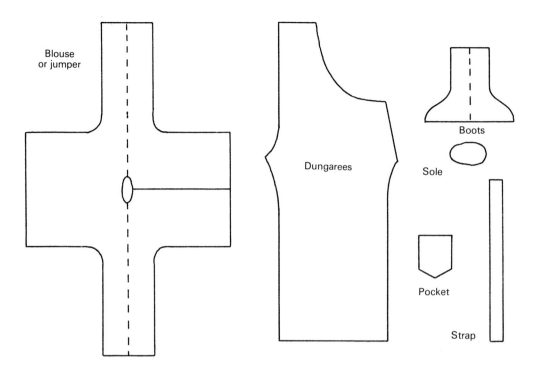

Blouse or jumper

Dungarees

Boots

Sole

Pocket

Strap

Baby's dress

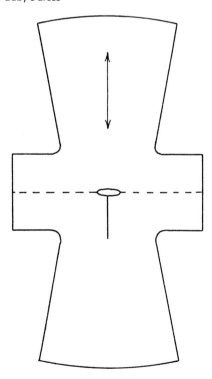

Jumper This can be made from felt, or the top of a sock, using the finished edge of the sock for the hem and cuffs.

Cut a back, front, and two sleeves. Oversew the front to the back at the shoulder seams, ⅛in in from the armhole. Oversew the sleeves into the armholes. Sew the underarm and body seams in one and turn the jumper through to the right side. Ease the jumper over the doll's head, pushing the arms into the sleeves. Oversew the shoulder seams closed from the armhole seam to the neck.

Apron Aprons or pinafores can be made from small rectangles of fabric, lace or broderie anglaise. Hem three edges of the apron, and gather the top edge. Sew the gathered edge to a piece of narrow ribbon for a waistband and use narrow ribbon for shoulder straps.

Stockings and boots Stockings are made by pushing the dolls' legs into shoelaces of the required colour, tucking the raw edges inside and oversewing the shoelace to the top of the leg and toes. This method is useful if you feel that your doll's legs are too thin — another shoe lace fattens them quite considerably.

The ladies and children's boots are made the same way as the men's, in a colour to match the clothes.

Dungarees The children's dungarees are made in felt. Cut the dungaree pieces, two straps and one pocket. Sew the centre-front seam from the bib to the crutch. Sew the centre-back seam from the waist to the crutch. Sew the leg seams up one leg, through the crutch and down the other leg. Turn the dungarees through to the right side and slip them onto the doll, tucking the jumper inside. Stitch the straps, one each side at the top of the bib front, pass them over the shoulders, crossing them at the back, and sew the ends inside the waist at the back. Stick or sew the pocket to the centre of the bib front.

Baby's dress The baby's dress is cut in one piece from white felt, cotton or wide broderie anglaise trimming. Fold the dress along the dotted line indicated on the pattern, and, working on the wrong side of the fabric, stitch the underarm and body seams. Turn a hem at the bottom edge. Clip the seam at the under-arm curve, if necessary, and turn through to the right side. Slip the dress onto the doll with the opening at the back. Slipstitch the back opening closed. Gather the cuffs and pull up, tucking the raw edges inside. Trim the neck-line with a piece of narrow ribbon tied in a bow.

The antique shop
The lady in the antique shop is 1:12 scale. Her hair is auburn embroidery silk, plaited into a bun. She is wearing a cotton dress in a small pink-and-black flower print with a black-felt yoke and cuffs. Her stockings are brown shoe-laces and her boots, black felt. Her brooch is a broken stud ear-ring, stuck to the neckline of her dress.

The Victorian town house
These dolls are 1:16 scale. The master of the house has brown, embroidery silk hair. He is wearing a white-cotton shirt with a black-ribbon bow tie. His jacket and boots are black felt and his trousers are grey felt. His wife has blonde, embroidery silk hair in a bun. She is wearing a stiff, Vilene petticoat trimmed with lace, brown-felt boots and a blouse and skirt of flower-printed cotton in soft browns and greens. Her sash is narrow, brown-satin ribbon. The cook has animal-wool hair in a bun under a lace cap made from a gathered strip of narrow lace edging. She wears a Vilene petti-coat, a blouse and skirt in white-spotted green cotton, a white-cotton pinafore and black-felt boots. The baby has a tuft of embroidery silk for hair, under a cap made of a lace-trimming scrap. He wears a long dress made of white broderie anglaise and a shawl cut from a piece of an old wool vest.

The Tudor cottage
The old couple and their adult daughter are 1:16 scale. The old man has white animal-wool hair. He is wearing a cotton shirt in dark blue with a fine, white stripe, brown-felt trousers and a rust-felt waistcoat. His hat is beige felt and his boots, black felt. His scarf is a scrap of orange felt. His wife, who has animal-wool hair arranged in a bun, wears a brown-cotton skirt over a Vilene petticoat. Her blouse is white lace, her shawl scarlet felt and her boots dark-red felt. Her shopping basket is described in Chapter 6. Their daughter has dark-brown embroidery-silk hair. She wears a blouse, trimmed with narrow lace, and a skirt in blue-and-white printed lawn over a Vilene petticoat. Her sash is blue ribbon and her boots are black felt.

The modern house
This family is also 1:16 scale. The father has brown embroidery-silk hair. He wears a rust-coloured felt jumper, blue-denim trousers and black-felt boots. The mother has blonde embroidery-silk hair plaited into a bun. She wears brown-shoelace stockings and black-felt boots. Her dress is a blouse and skirt in brown, black and cream flower-printed cotton, with a narrow black-ribbon sash. The twins both have long, brown embroidery-silk hair in plaits. They wear yellow-felt jumpers and light-brown felt boots. One twin has red-felt dungarees, the other, blue.

Pets
Dolls'-house pets traditionally come in all shapes and sizes. Cats, dogs, rabbits etc, in china or plastic, can be found in most toy or

gift shops, and many will fit happily into the dolls' house. The plastic cats and dogs can often be improved with careful painting. Felt or fur-fabric animals are sold as key-ring mascots, and porcelain and china miniatures are sold as collector's pieces in china shops. The white-plastic doves sold as wedding-cake decorations will make reasonable budgies, given a coat of paint! Or you might try making a fish tank, using a clear-plastic box for the tank, cutting the fish from orange or gold metallic foil, and adding a little sand and a few plastic water weeds.

Modelling your own animals in Das or clay is quite a challenge, but it can produce some amusing results. Find a picture to use as a model and work the clay into the right shape. When dry, paint the animal with poster colours, using your picture as a guide. The over-large tabby cat in the kitchen of the Victorian house was modelled in Das. The collie dog in the Tudor cottage was made in plaster-of-paris from a mould bought in the local art shop. Neither of these animals is exactly realistic, but they both have a kind of charm!

If your pet requires a basket, consult Chapter 6 and don't forget the blanket and feeding bowl!

12 Renovation

Old dolls' houses are now regarded as antiques, and valued accordingly. A Victorian or Edwardian house in reasonable condition will fetch a high price in an auction or antique shop and is therefore beyond the means of most people. Even the commercial post-war children's dolls' houses like the Triang models are no longer cheap, though obviously not as expensive as the older ones. However, it is still possible to find a dolls' house, in a junk shop or country sale, which the antique dealers have missed, perhaps because it is 'home-made' and of less value than the old commercial houses. It is possible that the old dolls' house of your own childhood is still around, tucked away in some family attic and long forgotten.

Whatever the source of your old dolls' house — auction or attic — it will probably need some restoration work. Over the years, dirt, damp, woodbeetle and central heating can reduce any once-proud mansion to a shabby looking derelict. Unless you are an expert on the restoration of antique furniture, it is possible to do considerable damage by over-enthusiastic renovation. It is therefore wise to give some serious thought to the age, appearance and value of your dolls' house first.

Antique houses

These are Victorian or Edwardian houses (rarely older) perhaps home or carpenter-made, or one of the commercial houses made for children at this time. The house itself might appear crudely made, badly proportioned, even ugly, but if it is in reasonable condition it is potentially valuable and should be treated with respect. Stripping the original paints and papers and removing any fixtures will not only reduce the financial value but would be an act of vandalism similar to sticking Formica on the top of a Regency table! The rule for an antique house should be careful preservation rather than renovation.

Cleaning The first stage is to clean the house, gently but thoroughly. A solution of soap flakes or washing-up liquid in warm water will do the job efficiently, but the old-fashioned cabinet-maker's recipe is a solution of equal parts of linseed oil, vinegar and turpentine with a few drops of methylated spirit. Dust the house with a clean cloth first, then use cottonwool, wrung out in the cleaning solution, to remove dirt from the interior and exterior. This will clean loose dirt from the wood and paintwork but will not affect the patina of old age.

The exterior of the house might be polished wood, in which case a good beeswax polish, well-buffed, will be all that is required. If the exterior is painted, the cleaning may reveal chips and cracks. It is probably best to leave these, but if you feel that you must paint over them, use small tins of enamel paint, mixing carefully to match the colour as closely as possible and apply with an artist's paintbrush.

If the exterior is brick papered, even if the paper is torn, leave it. The modern brick papers are quite different in colour and design from the old ones and stripping off an old paper to replace it with a new one contravenes the first rule of preservation! The exception to this rule is if the paper has obviously been applied later over a house that was originally painted. If this is the case, and you feel that the paper is sufficiently torn to justify removing it, soak it carefully with tepid clean water applied with cottonwool, so that it peels away quite easily. The paintwork underneath can then be cleaned as described.

The interior of the house will probably be papered, quite possibly with several layers of paper. The problem here is in deciding whether to peel away the top layers to reveal the older papers underneath. If the top layer of paper is badly torn and that underneath looks better, soak the wall carefully with tepid clean water applied with cottonwool, and use nothing more drastic than your finger nails to peel it away. Work slowly and carefully, and with luck, removing the torn and dirty top paper might reveal a better one underneath. If there is only one layer of paper on the wall, or you prefer not to excavate, rub gently with a soft pencil rubber or pieces of fresh bread, which will remove most dirt and quite nasty stains. If there are immovable stains or torn patches of paper, these can be concealed by pictures and mirrors or careful placement of furniture. You might feel that the wallpaper in a room is in very bad condition or impossibly ugly and be tempted to replace it with a new one. If this is the case, rather than stripping the old paper, leave it and line the room with thin cardboard, held in place with small pieces of double-sided tape, and carry out the new decorating scheme on the cardboard. This method can be used if you do not feel able to clean or peel the old paper as described, and will protect the paper while allowing you the freedom of decorating the rooms as you please. The dolls'-house floors might be polished wood, painted or papered, and should be treated as the walls.

Repairs Exposed to damp and heat, wood will crack, and joints come apart. Cracks and holes can be filled with plastic wood of the appropriate colour, smoothed with the fingers and then painted if necessary to match the fabric of the house. If the old animal glues used in the joints get damp, they no longer hold. The old glue can be carefully scraped off with a knife blade and a woodwork glue applied to the joint, which will probably need clamping until the glue dries.

Rusty old hinges and locks, if they are still holding firm, can be cleaned with rust remover, metal polish and an old toothbrush. If the hinges have worked loose, they should

be removed, the old holes filled and, if necessary, new hinges, as similar as possible, fitted. It is a good idea to keep the original hinges and anything else you might remove from the house.

Broken pieces of woodwork, turning or carving might be difficult to replace, but if you can find or make replacements, keep a note of the new pieces. The simplest way of recording any replacements and repairs is to take before and after photographs of the interior and exterior, and keep them safely with the pieces you have removed.

The golden rule with an antique dolls' house is to do nothing irrevocable. If you need help, there are good books on antique restoration available from the library, and firms which specialise in repair and renovation of antiques. Your local museum is often a much underrated source of advice and information. They are in the business of preservation and therefore generally sympathetic to anyone with similar aims.

Other old houses
The second category includes all those other old houses which, though not antiques, are still worth preserving. Commercially-made dolls' houses of the early part of this century are rapidly becoming valuable, and, if in good condition, it is probably wise to treat such a house as a potential antique and do nothing drastic. It is a sad fact, though, that the majority of childrens' dolls' houses in this century have been badly treated and are in a poor condition — if they have survived at all! A house in such condition is obviously not worth preserving as previously described, so complete renovation is quite justifiable. However bad the condition, by stripping the house down to its basic parts, repairing and remaking it, almost any house can be saved.

Drastic repairs We were recently given to repair a house in a sad state of dereliction. It was a small Triang house, made in 1928, which had been a toy for many years, then stored in an attic for another twenty. It was crudely made of pine, with a cardboard roof, but even in its battered state it had charm. Woodbeetle had feasted on the base, the hinges were torn out, the windows were missing, the roof was broken and some child with a passion for decorating had plastered hideous 1950s wallpapers all over. All in all, a sad sight!

We began by stripping all the wall and floor papers, sighing over the remaining tiny scraps of original paper. Then we cleaned the house thoroughly inside and out. The base was removed and a new base made of plywood, painted a similar green to the original. The roof, which was torn and broken along the seams, was repaired with many layers of masking tape until it was firm and strong again. All the cracks in the wood were filled with plastic wood and the joints between walls and floors re-glued with woodwork glue. The old broken hinges were removed, the holes filled and new hinges fitted. Broken woodwork around the windows was replaced and the front door was re-hung with new hinges so that it closed properly. The house was now a clean bare shell and we painted it all over with Rentokil fluid to prevent future attacks by woodbeetle. The exterior had originally been cream, so we gave it two coats of cream emulsion paint and papered the roof with green-pantile paper. The interior was decorated with wall and floor papers as similar to the originals as we could find (the parquet floor paper was almost identical). As the house was a commercial one, we used commercial windows, similar to the original ones, though plastic instead of metal. The paintwork was given a fresh coat of ivory gloss, the ceilings ivory emulsion and the front door green gloss. The finishing touch was the flower-garden effect on the front of the house which had originally been crudely painted in oils. As most of this had been rubbed off, we replaced it with flower transfers to resemble a border.

The finished house looked almost new. Very little of the original remained beyond the basic wooden shell, but the owner was delighted and thought it looked much as it had when new. It now has another lease of life with her grandchildren, who, she hopes, will treat it more respectfully than she did.

This kind of drastic restoration is easier, and more fun, than the measures recommended for antique dolls' houses, but it should only be carried out on a house which is obviously quite beyond preservation. It would be tragic to destroy a genuinely beautiful, antique dolls' house simply because it is shabby.

Furnishings

Similar rules apply here. If you are fortunate enough to own an antique house with antique furnishings, aim for preserving rather than re-making. Use small tools such as cotton buds and toothbrushes, and a very gentle touch.

Fabrics Curtains and upholstery tend to deteriorate through dirt and moths rather than fading or hard usage, and generally only need cleaning to look good again. Curtains, bedclothes and other fabric items should be washed in a mild solution of soap flakes in warm water (squeezing gently rather than rubbing) rinsed in clean water, squeezed out and dried flat. If necessary, iron very carefully with a warm iron. Beware with old cottons, especially blue colours, as the dye might not be stable. Unstable colours should not be washed, but you can dry-clean them by spreading the fabric out flat, spraying it with a dry hair-shampoo and brushing gently with an old, clean toothbrush.

Upholstered furniture, carpets and rugs generally need only a good brush with an old toothbrush to remove the dust and dirt, but, if there are grease marks, try dry shampoo or a gentle dabbing with cottonwool wrung out in a mild soap solution.

If the old fabrics are wearing thin or fraying, a piece of lightweight iron-on Vilene, carefully applied to the back will strengthen and help to preserve them.

Wooden furniture Wooden furniture, usually glued together with animal glue, is subject to the same joint trouble as houses. Clean the furniture with the same solutions, using cotton buds to reach the awkward parts, and re-glue the pieces with woodwork glue. Polish the furniture gently with beeswax polish on a soft cloth. Broken chair legs, rails or drawer handles, etc, can be replaced if you can find or make a good match, or the broken piece could be placed in the house with the defective part discreetly hidden.

Metal furniture Many of the older dolls' houses have metal furniture or accessories.

Silver, brass, copper, pewter, Brittania metal or tin can all be cleaned in the same way as life-size items, using the commercial metal-cleaners and polishes. Again, an old toothbrush is useful for cleaning the fiddly bits.

Broken metal furniture is difficult to mend as even super-glue will not join all metals. Soldering is possible on some pieces if the metal is suitable, and fuse-wire can be used to wire a small part such as a chair leg in place. Cleaning these small metal items regularly will prevent future tarnishing, or they can be lacquered with one of the commercial metal lacquers.

Bone and ivory Furniture and ornaments in bone and ivory were once very popular in dolls' houses. To clean them, wipe gently with methylated spirit on cottonwool or a cotton bud. Very yellowed ivory or bone can be bleached with a stiff paste of whiting and hydrogen peroxide. Coat the piece with this paste and leave it outdoors to dry. When dry, remove the paste with a damp cloth and polish with a soft dry cloth. Cracks in bone and ivory can be filled with melted candle wax, rubbed smooth over the crack with a finger.

Glass Glass items, obviously, must be treated very gently — usually washing them in warm water and detergent is sufficient. A few drops of ammonia in the water will remove stubborn marks. Broken glass pieces can be mended with an epoxy resin. Roughen the edges of the glass slightly with glass paper, then join the broken pieces with glue, holding the join with sticky tape until the glue sets.

China Glazed china crockery for dolls' houses was made in quantity during the last century, and surprisingly large amounts have survived. Most pieces need only to be washed in warm water and detergent and dried. Small stains can usually be removed with a little bicarbonate of soda. The coarse china, which is porous and can become badly stained, should be immersed in household bleach for a few hours, then rinsed. Broken pieces can be mended with an epoxy resin or super-glue, taping the join until the glue is set. Gummed brown-paper tape is best for repair work of this type, as it shrinks slightly as it dries, holding the join very tightly.

Oil Paintings If you are lucky enough to have miniature oil paintings in your dolls' house, they might well be dark and dirty. If the painting will come out of its frame easily, remove it, otherwise, clean it in the frame. Either turpentine or white spirit can be used and cotton buds are excellent tools. Work carefully, changing the cotton bud as soon as it gets dirty. When the painting is clean, if it is still murky and brownish, you might wish to remove the old varnish. This is done with a swab of cotton wool, wrung out in acetone (or nail-varnish remover). Have ready another swab, wrung out in turpentine. Wipe quickly and carefully over the picture with the acetone swab and then wipe over again immediately with the turpentine swab. Re-varnish with picture varnish, using an artist's paint brush. When the painting is thoroughly dry, replace it in the frame.

Leather Leather-upholstered furniture will become shabby if it is not cared for, but it can be restored by the following treatment. To clean the piece, make up a mixture of three parts castor oil to two parts surgical spirit and wipe it on with a cottonwool pad or cotton bud, leaving it for twenty-four hours. Then wipe with a piece of cottonwool wrung out in castor oil. If the leather has become hard, rub in a leather cream, then polish with a soft wax polish on a soft cloth, using a coloured polish if necessary. Regular polishing with a soft wax will keep the leather furniture in good condition.

Appendix

Museums

The museums listed here have collections of dolls' houses.

The Rotunda, Grove House, Iffley Turn, Oxford (No children under 16 years are admitted.)

Wallington Hall, Northumberland

The Museum of Childhood, 38 High Street, Edinburgh

The Bethnal Green Museum, Bethnal Green, London

Pollocks Toy Museum, Scala Street, London

The Warwick Doll Museum, Oken's House, Warwick

See also *Museums and Galleries in Great Britain, Discovering Toys and Toy Museums*, Pauline Flick, Shire Publications.

Stockists

The shops listed here specialise in miniature fixtures, fittings and furniture for dolls' houses. Contact directly for details of mail-order services and copies of their catalogues.

The Dolls' House Toys Ltd
29 The Market, Covent Garden, London, WC2 8RE
and
116 Lisson Grove, London NW1
Minutiques Ltd
82B Trafalgar Street, Brighton, Sussex
Polly Flinders
46 London Road, Reigate, Surrey
The Singing Tree
69 New Kings Road, London, SW6
Torbay House Miniatures
The Victorian Arcade, Torwood Street, Torquay, Devon
W. Hobby Ltd
Knights Hill Square, London SE27 0HH

Bibliography

Brunskill, R. W., *Vernacular Architecture*, Batsford (1979)

Greene, Vivien, *English Dolls' Houses*, Bell and Hyman (1979)

——, *Family Dolls' Houses*, Bell and Hyman (1973)

Johnson, Audrey, *How to Make Dolls' Houses*, Bell and Hyman (1977)

McElroy, Joan, *Dolls' House Furniture Book*, Robert Hale (1976)

Stein, Sara, *A Family Dolls' House*, Batsford (1979)

Woodforde, John, *The Truth about Cottages*, Routledge and Kegan Paul (1979)

Yarwood, Doreen, *The English Home*, Batsford (1979)

Magazines

The International Dolls' House News
56 Lincoln Wood, Haywards Heath, Sussex, RH16 1LH

The Home Miniaturist
18 Calvert Road, Dorking, Surrey, RH4 1LB
Both available, quarterly, on subscription. Send SAE to above addresses for details

Index